THE ATHENÆUM PRESS SERIES

THOMAS GRAY.

SELECTIONS

FROM THE POETRY AND PROSE OF

THOMAS GRAY

EDITED

WITH AN INTRODUCTION AND NOTES

BY

WILLIAM LYON PHELPS

A.M. (HARVARD), PH.D. (YALE)

INSTRUCTOR IN ENGLISH LITERATURE AT YALE COLLEGE

GINN & COMPANY

BOSTON · NEW YORK · CHICAGO · LONDON

511.12

Sumner Thomas
S
11-9-44 am
10-18-45 cdm

The Athenæum Press
GINN & COMPANY · PRO-
PRIETORS · BOSTON · U.S.A.

TO THE CLASS OF

1896

YALE COLLEGE

WITH SINCERE AFFECTION

AND RESPECT

PREFACE.

IF there is any excuse needed for another edition of Gray, it may be said that selections from both his poetry and his prose are not commonly found in one volume. Nor, in spite of claims to the contrary, have any of the recent editions faithfully followed the authentic texts. In this volume, no pains have been spared to give as accurate a text as possible ; for the poems numbered in the *Contents* I, II, III, V, VII, IX, XI, XIV, XV, XVI, the text has been taken letter for letter from the *Poems* of 1768, the standard London edition revised and edited by Gray himself, and therefore the authority for everything it contains. The *Long Story* has been taken from the sumptuous *Six Poems* folio of 1753, the only text of that poem edited by its author. The *Ode for Music* has been taken, with the same scrupulous accuracy, from the original quarto of 1769. The *Sonnet* has been copied from the MS. facsimile given by Mr. Gosse in the fourth volume of Gray's *Works* (Macmillan, 1884), which differs in a number of details from the printed copy in the very same edition. The text of the other poems, which are of much less importance, is based on a collation of Mason, Gosse and Bradshaw, although Mason's *Commentary* to the *Alliance*, p. 10, is given *verbatim* as he printed it in 1775. It may be safely said that the text of the poems in this volume is closer to the original editions than anything published since Gray's death. The poems that have been omitted altogether are those parts of his remains that now have little interest, and no permanent value.

The Prose has been taken from Mr. Gosse's four-volume edition of Gray, mentioned above. I greatly regret that the Rev. D. C. Tovey's edition of Gray's *Letters*, already announced by Macmillan, has not yet appeared. Mr. Tovey is so accurate a scholar, and so sensible an editor, that anything he undertakes is sure to be done well.

Gray's own notes to those of his poems published in 1768, have been exactly reproduced (misprints, mistakes and all) in this volume, and will be found, where he himself had them printed, as foot-notes to the text ; but in my notes exact line references have been given for all of Gray's quotations, and the errors or misprints are corrected there.

In most cases indebtedness to previous editors is mentioned wherever it occurs ; but for some commonplace references and references to other passages of Gray it has not been thought necessary in every instance to give the names of editors who have also noted these points. A considerable number of parallel passages will be found in the notes ; this does not imply that the editor is insinuating a lack of originality on Gray's part, nor on the other hand is any attempt made at a pedantic display. In the case of so eclectic a poet, the most striking parallel passages are particularly interesting. Gray himself gives a few parallel passages in his own foot-notes ; but the similarities in these are usually not so noticeable as in those he does not give. Gray's poems reflect his reading ; but to accuse him of plagiarism would be, as Mr. Lowell said, like finding fault with a man for pillaging the dictionary.

The notes on the poems are meant to be sufficiently full for all practical needs and purposes ; those on the prose are very few, and simply explanatory. It did not seem fitting to burden Gray's delightful letters with a mass of annotation.

The poems are printed in the order in which they were written ; this is not only interesting in itself, but throws considerable light on Gray's remarkable change of taste — his transition from Classicism to Romanticism. The selections from the prose also indicate this fact, and a separate section of the *Introduction* is devoted to a discussion of what might be called Gray's poetic evolution. Although to students of the development of literature, this should be the most significant and interesting feature of Gray's work, it is a thing that editors and critics have strangely neglected. The view given in the *Introduction* is founded on patient study and thought. Some parts of it have been reprinted from my chapter on Gray in *The Beginnings of the English Romantic Movement*, Ginn & Co., 1893.

The general editors of the Athenæum Press series have given constant and valuable assistance. Professor Kittredge has not only written an Appendix on Gray's knowledge of Norse, a subject on which Mr. Gosse has strangely blundered, but throughout the Notes, especially those on the Norse poems (of which language the present editor has no knowledge) has steadily furnished me with facts and suggestions. Professor Albert S. Cook and Doctor Hanns Oertel of Yale, have kindly given aid in verifying some references.

W. L. P.

YALE COLLEGE, 22 *February* 1894.

CONTENTS.

———

INTRODUCTION.

		Page
I.	Life	xiii
II.	Gray's Sterility	xvii
III.	Chief Influences that affected Gray's Style	xx
IV.	Gray's Progress toward Romanticism	xxii
V.	Gray's Prose	xxix
VI.	Chronological Table	xxxiv
VII.	Bibliography	xxxv
Appendix — Gray's Knowledge of Norse		xli

POEMS.

I.	Ode on the Spring	1
II.	Ode on a Distant Prospect of Eton College	3
III.	Hymn to Adversity	6
IV.	Sonnet	8
V.	Ode on the Death of a Favourite Cat	9
VI.	The Alliance of Education and Government	10
VII.	Elegy Written in a Country Church-Yard	16
VIII.	A Long Story	21
IX.	The Progress of Poesy	26
X.	Ode on the Pleasure arising from Vicissitude	33
XI.	The Bard	35
XII.	Sketch of his Own Character	43
XIII.	Song	43

PAGE

XIV. THE FATAL SISTERS... 44
XV. THE DESCENT OF ODIN.. 47
XVI. THE TRIUMPHS OF OWEN 51
XVII. THE DEATH OF HOEL.. 52
XVIII. CARADOC 53
XIX. CONAN 54
XX. WILLIAM SHAKESPEARE.. 54
XXI. ODE FOR MUSIC... 55

PROSE.

I. AUTOBIOGRAPHICAL :—

COLLEGE LIFE... 61
MELANCHOLY 62
SKETCH OF HIS OWN CHARACTER 63
MELANCHOLY 64
THE OFFICE OF POET LAUREATE................................. 64
ATTITUDE TOWARD LIFE 66
MELANCHOLY 67
GRAY'S MOTHER 67
CONSOLATION 68
SYMPATHY... 68
THE SHADOW OF DEATH 69
THE ODE ON WALPOLE'S CAT 69
THE ELEGY.. 70
THE ELEGY.. 71
THE ELEGY.. 72
THE PROGRESS OF POESY.. 73
THE "SIX POEMS" OF 1753 73
THE PINDARIC ODES 74
THE PINDARIC ODES 76
HIS OWN AIM IN POETRY.. 77
HIS STERILITY... 78

II. LITERATURE:—

	PAGE
SHAKSPERE, FIELDING, AND POETRY	79
COLLINS AND J. WARTON	81
CONTEMPORARY POETS	82
A BALLAD	83
OSSIAN	84
OSSIAN	85
OSSIAN	86
OSSIAN	88
OSSIAN	89
OSSIAN	89
OSSIAN	90
OSSIAN	90
JEREMY TAYLOR	90
CASTLE OF OTRANTO AND ROUSSEAU	91
DAVID HUME AND SKEPTICISM	92

III. NATURE:—

EARLY APPRECIATION	93
ALPINE SCENERY	94
ALPINE SCENERY	95
ALPINE SCENERY	97
MOUNTAINS	98
JOURNAL IN THE LAKES	99
NOTES ON THE POEMS	127
NOTES ON THE PROSE	177

INTRODUCTION.

I. LIFE.

THOMAS GRAY was born in Cornhill, London, 26 December 1716. His father was Philip Gray, and his mother Dorothy Antrobus Gray. They had twelve children, of whom Thomas was the fifth; all the others died in infancy. Mrs. Gray was compelled to support her son through school and college by her own exertions, as Philip Gray — who was not only brutal but probably crazy — refused to do anything for him. About 1727 Gray went to Eton, and there made the "quadruple alliance" friendship with Horace Walpole, Richard West, and Thomas Ashton. In 1734 he entered Peterhouse, Cambridge, and like so many other eminent men, found the curriculum routine unpalatable. He especially hated mathematics. He made few acquaintances, indulged in no sports, and was probably looked at askance by his fellow-students. He left Cambridge without a degree in 1738. In 1739 he was invited by Horace Walpole to accompany him on a trip over the continent; they went through France and across the Alps to Italy. Here they quarreled and separated in April, 1741, and Gray returned home alone. His father died, 6 November 1741, and Gray lived at Stoke Poges with his mother and her two sisters. The death of his brilliant friend, Richard West, 1 June 1742, profoundly affected Gray; although he seldom spoke of it, he never could allude to it calmly to the day of his death. It was probably the greatest sorrow of his life, though he was most tenderly attached to his mother. In 1742 Gray settled down at Peterhouse, Cambridge, and nibbled at the law. He took his LL.B. in 1743. Greek seems to have been his favorite study, and for six years he gave it intense application. From this time until his death, Cambridge was Gray's home, although he changed from Peterhouse to Pembroke in 1756, and when the British Museum was opened in 1759, he lived at London for two years, in order to enjoy the advantages of the library and manuscripts. Gray had no college standing at Cambridge ; he was not a Fellow, nor had he any official connection with the place until 1768, when he was made Professor of Modern History and Languages. In accordance with the prevailing custom, he delivered no lectures and made no attempt to teach. Gray lived at Cambridge because it was quiet and fairly cheap ; because the libraries were there, and the atmosphere was intellectual ; and because he had a few college friends, though college society in general he despised.

His mother died 11 March 1753, and was buried in the church-yard at Stoke Poges. We cannot quote too often the beautiful inscription Gray placed on her tomb — the "mother of many children, one of whom alone had the misfortune to survive her." Gray's life was lonely. He was never married, and apparently never thought of marrying, unless we magnify his slight and very tame flirtation with Harriet Speed, the heroine of the *Long Story.*

Gray's intimate friends were Horace Walpole (they patched up the Italian quarrel), the Rev. William Mason the poet, the Rev. Norton Nicholls, James Brown the master of Pembroke, Thomas Wharton, and Charles Victor de Bonstetten — a young Swiss gentleman, whom Gray met in 1769, and for whom he had a strange, almost passionate attachment. Bonstetten sat at his feet, and eagerly drank in Gray's words of wisdom and instruction.

Gray never was in good health, and in the spring of 1771 had a dangerous attack of gout in the stomach. He died in his rooms at Pembroke, 30 July 1771, at the age of fifty-four. He was buried at Stoke Poges by his mother's side. In strange accordance with his dislike of publicity, there is no name or inscription on his grave, although a hideous mausoleum, erected in 1799, stands in Stoke Park, close by the church-yard.

With the possible exception of Milton, Gray was the greatest scholar among the English poets. Perhaps it would be better to say that Milton's scholarship was the greatest, and Gray's the best. His knowledge was not of the general information kind; it was indeed remarkably broad, but at the same time extremely accurate. He was an accomplished linguist, a good zoölogist and botanist, thoroughly acquainted with the history of literature, and a careful and enthusiastic student of architecture. He studied nearly everything except mathematics. When Greek was, comparatively speaking, neglected, he worked at it with eagerness, even to the most minute details; the large body of Greek notes he left behind him (*Works*, IV) attests the range and accuracy of his knowledge. He was such a recluse, that it was difficult for even Cambridge students to catch a glimpse of him; he did not dine in the hall, and seldom appeared anywhere except to make a trip to the circulating library. After he became famous, and was acknowledged to be the greatest living poet, people used to watch patiently for his awkward figure to appear. But he gave them no more chances than he could help, as he shrank nervously from popularity. In 1757 he refused the offer of the Laureateship, being too familiar with the history of that office.[1]

In religion Gray was apparently an orthodox Christian, but entirely without missionary zeal. He disliked emotional demonstration, perhaps because his own religious sense was so deep and true. Atheism he hated and despised.

Gray's character had its faults, most of them trivial. He was proud, haughty in a feminine, I had almost said a feline way, and perhaps too contemptuous toward superficiality. He was not agreeable to chance acquaintances, and in differences of opinion was not at all conciliatory; but he had a keen sense of humor, and although never jovial, was often sprightly and playful. His intimate friends loved him, and friends and enemies all respected him. Although he lacked energy, his intellectual and moral purposes were lofty ; he looked on life with serious earnestness, and he was pure in heart. It may be truly said that he was a good man.

The portrait facing the title-page of this volume is taken from the large print in Mason's *Memoirs* of Gray (1775). Of this picture Horace Walpole, writing to Cole, 25 April 1775 (*Letters*, VI, 206), said : " The print, I agree with you, though like, is a very disagreeable likeness, and the worst likeness of him. It gives the primness he had when under constraint ; and there is a blackness in the countenance which was like him only the last time I ever saw him, when I was much struck with it ; and, though I did not apprehend him in danger, it left an impression on me that was uneasy, and almost prophetic of what I heard but too soon after leaving him. Wilson drew the picture under much such impression, and I could not bear it in my room ; Mr. Mason altered it a

[1] See p. 64.

little, but still it is not well, nor gives any idea of the determined virtues of his heart. It just serves to help the reader to an image of the person, whose genius and integrity they must admire, if they are so happy as to have a taste for either."

II. GRAY'S STERILITY.

Very few of the world's great poets have made it easier for the general public to read their "Complete Works" than Gray. The temptation to scribble and to print is one that assails not only the would-be, but the genuine poets. This accounts for the bulky volumes which the student of a later age must buy and con, but which the rank and file of even intelligent readers pass by silently, content to have samples in place of the entire stock. Nor does the student always wish that the master had written more. We wish he had written more in his best vein, but the chances are even that he would not have written in his best vein. There are many of Wordsworth's sonnets which the world has willingly let die ; their titles in the Tables of Contents are merely the headstones of their graves. The *Excursion* — let it be said softly and with a timid glance over the shoulder — is long enough. With a man like Gray — there are not very many men like Gray — the case is different. His sterility is so surprising that it becomes necessary at the outset not only to call attention to it — the price of his "Complete Poetical Works" will do that — but to attempt to explain it. This can be done without resorting to any subtle theories. The view given by Matthew Arnold in his famous essay[1] is entirely without foundation in fact. It is true that there is a curious lack of

[1] Ward's *English Poets*, III, 302.

harmony between Gray's cold, classical style and the Romantic subjects he treated ; this no doubt often made articulation extremely difficult. But Mr. Arnold's theory, that his scantiness of production was caused by his living in the "age of prose and reason" is quite wide of the mark. The reason why Gray wrote so little was not because he was chilled by the public taste of the age ; he would probably have written no more had he lived a hundred years before or since. He was not the man to be depressed by an unfavorable environment ; for his mind was ever open to new influences, and he welcomed with the utmost eagerness all genuine signs of promise. His correspondence shows how closely and intelligently he followed the course of contemporary literature ; he had something to say about every important new book. The causes of his lack of production are simple enough to those who start with no pre-conceived theory, and who prefer a commonplace explanation built on facts to a fanciful one built on phrases. Gray was a scholar, devoted to solitary research, and severely critical ; this kind of temperament is not primarily creative, and does not toss off immortal poems every few weeks. The time that Mason, for example, spent in production, Gray spent in acquisition, and when he did produce, the critical fastidiousness of the scholar appeared in every line. All his verses bear evidence of the most painstaking labor and rigorous self-criticism. Again, during his whole life he was handicapped by wretched health, which, although never souring him, made his temperament melancholy, and acted as a constant check on what creative activity he really possessed. And finally, he abhorred publicity and popularity. No one who reads his correspondence can doubt this fact. He hated to be dragged out from his scholarly seclusion, and evidently preferred complete

obscurity to any noisy public reputation. This reserve
was never affected ; it was uniformly sincere, like everything else in Gray's character. His reticence was indeed
extraordinary, keeping him not only from writing, but
from publishing what he did write. He wrote, in English
and Latin, more than sixty poems, but only twelve
appeared in print during his lifetime ; and his prose is all
posthumous. Gray's own friends would have had no difficulty in explaining his scantiness of production. Horace
Walpole, writing to George Montagu, 3 Sept. 1748,
says : " I agree with you most absolutely in your opinion
about Gray ; he is the worst company in the world. From
a melancholy turn, from living reclusely, and from a little
too much dignity, he never converses easily ; all his words
are measured and chosen, and formed into sentences ;
his writings are admirable ; he himself is not agreeable."
Again, referring to Gray's slowness in composition,
Walpole writes to Montagu, 5 May 1761. He is talking
about Gray's proposed History of Poetry, and he says :
" If he rides Pegasus at his usual foot-pace, [he] will
finish the first page two years hence." In the composition of his poems as well as in his studies, Gray was
thorough ; he disliked all short cuts to knowledge.
Observe his admirable remark on such things : " Mr.
Gray always considered, that the Encyclopædias and
universal Dictionaries of various kinds, with which the
world now abounds so much, afforded a very unfavour-
able symptom of the age in regard to its literature ; as
no real or profound learning can be obtained but at
the fountain-head." [1] The adjective that perhaps best
expresses Gray is *fastidious*. He was as severe on the
children of his own brain as he was on those of others ;
he never let them appear in public until he was sure

[1] Mathias, *Observations*, 1815, p. 50.

everything was exactly as it should be. Even his greatest poem pleases more by its exquisite finish than by its depth of feeling. These three reasons, then, his scholarly temperament, his bad health, and his dignified reserve, account satisfactorily for his lack of fertility. If we wish to know why so deep and strong a nature produced so little poetry, we must look at the man, and not at his contemporaries.

III. CHIEF INFLUENCES THAT AFFECTED GRAY'S STYLE.

Two English poets exerted a powerful impression upon Gray — Dryden and Milton. The former influenced Gray's style in his early Odes; in his later poems Dryden's influence is scarcely discernible, but Gray never ceased to admire Dryden's verse, freely acknowledging how much he had gained from him, and listening impatiently when Dryden was censured. Yet for Dryden's character Gray had nothing but contempt.[1] Spenser was a favorite of Gray's, as he has been with nearly all the poets. Gray usually read Spenser just before composing; but it was Milton whose influence was most powerful and continuous. About 1750 the Miltonic school of poets included the principal English men of verse — Collins, the Wartons, Mason and others; and Gray was no exception.[2] The abundance of Miltonic words and phrases in Gray's poems is everywhere noticeable; and the *Elegy* was simply the culmination of a class of literature which derived its inspiration directly from *Il Penseroso*.

[1] See p. 65.

[2] For an account of the influence of Milton on eighteenth century literature, see the editor's *Beginnings of the English Romantic Movement*, chap. v.

Gray's style was also greatly influenced by his profound knowledge of the classics; among the Greek poets, Pindar perhaps had the most pronounced effect on his style. The polish, finish, and chiseled perfection of Gray's verse was doubtless owing in no small degree to his study and admiration of Greek; even after Gray adopted Romantic themes his style is often strictly Classic. Gray's Latin poems are very little read now-a-days, but they attest his knowledge and interest in Roman literature; and they called out words of praise from that famous Latinist, Dr. Johnson.

The influence of French and Italian poetry — in both these languages he was a good scholar — affected Gray strongly. His admiration for Racine is well known;[1] but among contemporary French authors he was especially influenced by Gresset.[2] Gray called him a "great master,"[3] and quoted some of his verses in a letter to Wharton.[3] His plays seemed to have perfectly charmed Gray, who said, "The *Méchant* is the best comedy I ever read."[4] Moreover, according to Mason, Gresset is responsible for one of Gray's poems; for the *Épître à ma Sœur* inspired him to write his *Ode on the Pleasure Arising from Vicissitude*.[5] It is interesting, in view of the great contrast between the men, to recall the fact that when in Paris in 1739, Gray dined with the Abbé Prévost, the author of that masterpiece of passion, *Manon Lescaut*. Of the French people and French habits of thought Gray had no very high opinion, although his dislike of Voltaire and Rousseau was doubtless largely due to religious prejudice.

[1] *Works*, II, 167, 232.
[2] Jean Baptiste Louis Gresset (1709–1777).
[3] *Works*, II, 182. [4] *Works*, II, 186.
[5] See notes on that poem.

The Romantic element in Ariosto must have influenced Gray; and from Tasso and Dante he made
translations.[1] In his own poetry Gray curiously unites
the mixture of the Classic and Romantic elements so
noticeable in Tasso. Gray had a profound admiration
for Dante, and the chance quotation of a passage from
the Italian poet was the beginning of his friendship with
Norton Nicholls.[2] Nicholls said that Gray looked up to
the best Italian poets "as his great progenitors, and to
Dante as the father of all."[2]

IV. GRAY'S PROGRESS TOWARD ROMANTICISM.

The most significant thing in the study of Gray's
poetry is his steady progress in the Romantic direction.
Beginning as a classicist and disciple of Dryden, he
ended in thorough-going Romanticism.[3] His early poems
contain nothing Romantic; his *Elegy* has something
of the Romantic mood, but shows many conventional
touches; in the Pindaric Odes the Romantic feeling
asserts itself boldly; and he ends in enthusiastic study of
Norse and Celtic poetry and mythology. Such a steady
growth in the mind of the greatest poet of the time shows
not only what he learned from the age, but what he
taught it. Gray is a much more important factor in the
Romantic movement than seems to be commonly supposed. This will appear from a brief examination of his
poetry.

While at Florence in the summer of 1740, he began to

[1] *Works*, I, 148, 157.

[2] Nicholls's *Reminiscences*, p. 44.

[3] He never despised Dryden, however, though he went far beyond
him. 2 Oct. 1765, he wrote to Beattie, "Remember Dryden, and be
blind to all his faults." *Works*, III, 221.

write an epic poem in Latin, *De Principiis Cogitandi*. Only two fragments were written,[1] but they made a piece of considerable length. This was an attempt to put into poetic form the philosophy of Locke. It shows how little he at that time understood his own future. The Gray of 1760 could no more have done a thing of this sort, than he could have written the *Essay on Man*. In these early years he was completely a Classicist. In 1748, when he was largely under Dryden's influence, he began a didactic poem in the heroic couplet, *On the Alliance of Education and Government*. It is significant that he never finished either of these poems. Mathias says: "When Mr. Nicholls once asked Mr. Gray, why he never finished that incomparable Fragment on 'The Alliance between good Government and good Education, in order to produce the happiness of mankind,' he said, *he could not;* and then explained himself in words of this kind, or to this effect: 'I have been used to write chiefly lyrick poetry, in which, the poems being short, I have accustomed myself to polish every part of them with care; and as this has become a habit, I can scarcely write in any other manner: the labour of this in a *long* poem would hardly be tolerable.'"[2] Gray must have perceived early in this task that the game was not worth the candle.

In 1742 Gray wrote three Odes: *On the Spring*, *On a Distant Prospect of Eton College*, and *To Adversity*. These well-known pieces contain little intimation of his later work. They have nothing of the spirit of Romanticism, and might have been written by any Augustan of sufficient talent. The moralizing is wholly conventional, and the abundance of personified abstractions was in the

[1] The second in 1742.

[2] *Observations*, 1815, p. 52. This passage in itself goes a long way toward explaining Gray's sterility.

height of fashion.[1]   The poems thus far mentioned represent Gray's first period.   He was a disciple of Dryden, and a great admirer of Pope, for writing to Walpole in 1746, he calls Pope "the finest writer, one of them, we ever had.".[2]

Gray's second period is represented by the *Elegy*, which he probably began in 1742 and finished in June 1750.[3] He was in no haste to print it ; the manuscript circulated among his friends, and was first printed anonymously, with a preface by Horace Walpole, 16 February 1751.   How long Gray meant to keep the *Elegy* from the public is uncertain ; circumstances compelled its publication.   On 10 February 1751, the editor of the *Magazine of Magazines* requested permission to print it.   This alarmed Gray ; he flatly refused the editor's request, and wrote instantly to Walpole, asking him to get Dodsley to print it as soon as possible.[4]

The *Elegy* is not a Romantic poem ; its moralizing is conventional, and pleased eighteenth century readers for that very reason.   Scores of poems were written at that time in which the strength of thought was neither above

[1] For remarks on the fashion of Abstractions, see Phelps's *Beginnings of the English Romantic Movement*, especially p. 88. Gray did not always admire these personifications, when others used them.   In a letter to Mason, 19 December 1756 (*Works*, II, 304), in criticising *Caractacus*, he says, "I had rather some of these personages, 'Resignation, Peace, Revenge, Slaughter, Ambition,' were stript of their allegorical garb.   A little simplicity here in the expression would better prepare the high and fantastic strain."

[2] *Works*, II, 130.

[3] Gray's interesting letter to Walpole about the *Elegy*, 12 June 1750, may be found on p. 70.   He says: "You will, I hope, look upon it in the light of a thing with an end to it ; a merit that most of my writings have wanted."   He evidently felt the fragmentary nature of his previous work.

[4] This letter may be found on p. 71.

nor below that of the *Elegy*, and these poems have nearly all perished. What has kept Gray's contribution to the Churchyard school alive and popular through all changes in taste, is its absolute perfection of language. There are few poems in English literature that express the sentiment of the author with such felicity and beauty. This insures its immortality; and it is this fact that deservedly gives it the first place in Gray's literary productions.

But although the *Elegy* is not strictly Romantic, it is different from Gray's earlier work. It is Romantic in its *mood*, and stands as a transition between his period of Classicism and his more highly imaginative poetry. It was the culmination of the *Il Penseroso* school, and that school was in several ways intimately connected with the growth of the Romantic movement. There is one highly significant fact about the composition of the *Elegy*, which shows with perfect distinctness that its author was passing through a period of transition. One of its most famous stanzas Gray originally wrote as follows : —

> " Some Village Cato   with dauntless Breast
>   The little Tyrant of his Fields withstood ;
> Some mute inglorious Tully here may rest ;
>   Some Cæsar, guiltless of his Country's Blood."

The fact that Gray should originally have put down the Latin names, and afterwards inserted in their place the three names Hampden, Milton, Cromwell — taken from comparatively recent English history — is something certainly worth attention. It marks the transition from Classicism to Nationalism. In this stanza he shook off the shackles of pseudo-classicism ; he made up his mind that English historical examples were equal in dignity to those taken from Latin literature. It was a long step forward, and although perhaps a small thing in itself, is an index to a profound change going on in Gray's mind.[1]

Gray's next work shows him well on the way toward Romanticism. In 1754 he wrote *The Progress of Poesy*, and in the same year began *The Bard*, which he finished in 1757. Both these Pindaric Odes were first printed in 1757, on Horace Walpole's press at Strawberry Hill—the first and the best things ever published there. These two odes, especially the latter, are the most imaginative poetry Gray ever produced, and were distinctly in advance of the age. They were above the popular conception of poetry, and their obscurity was increased by their allusiveness. The public did not take to them kindly; many people regarded them as we see Browning and Wagner regarded to-day. Their obscurity was ridiculed, and they were freely parodied.[2] Gray was a little hurt by all this,

---

[1] This point is fully and suggestively treated in the *Saturday Review* for 19 June 1875. Sir William Fraser, in his *Hic et Ubique*, 1893, p. 268, says that Gray wrote one stanza beginning as follows:

"Some village Lais, with all conquering charms."

If this be true, the composition and final blotting of such a stanza are also significant of the transition. With regard to this point, we find in *The Bibliographer*, V, 61 (1884) E. Solly saying that so far as he can find out, this stanza was first published in "Willis's *Current Notes*, July, 1854" with the note that it occurred in some MSS. of Gray. Solly (who has obviously hunted high and low: cf. his observations in *Notes and Queries*, 5th Series, V, 398, summing up a discussion which resulted from Dr. Doran's editorial publication of this stanza as "in the 1st ed." of *Elegy* in *N. & Q.* 5th Ser., III, 100) refuses to accept the stanza as genuine. The full stanza is as follows:

"Some rural Lais, with all-conquering charms,
    Perhaps now moulders in this grassy bourne!
Some Helen, vain to set the fields in arms,
    Some Emma dead, of gentle love forlorn."

[2] See pages 87, 89.

but he had foreseen their probable reception. He had written to Walpole, "I don't know but I may send him [Dodsley] very soon . . . an ode to his own tooth, a high Pindaric upon stilts, which one must be a better scholar than he is to understand a line of, and the very best scholars will understand but a little matter here and there." [1]

In the Pindaric Odes, Gray ceased to follow the age; he struck out ahead of it, and helped to mould its literary taste. From this time people began to regard him as a Romanticist, and to look for wild and extravagant productions from his pen. When the *Castle of Otranto* appeared in 1764, Gray was by many believed to be the author. The *Odes* became much more popular after Gray's death — a sign of growth in public taste. This made Dr. Johnson angry, and had much to do with his satirical treatment of the *Odes* in his wretched *Life of Gray.* He did not like to think that Gray had really taught the people anything, and so he declared that the admiration for Gray was all hypocrisy, just as many honest people to-day make fun of those who admire Wagner's music. Johnson said that in Gray's *Odes* "many were content to be shewn beauties which they could not see"; and the Doctor was thinking of the *Odes* when the following interesting conversation with Boswell took place: "He attacked Gray, calling him 'a dull fellow.' BOSWELL. 'I understand he was reserved, and might appear dull in company; but surely he was not dull in poetry.' JOHNSON. 'Sir, he was dull in company, dull in his closet, dull everywhere. He was dull in a new way, and that made many people think him GREAT. He was a mechanical poet.' He then repeated some ludicrous lines, which

---

[1] *Works*, II, 218.

have escaped my memory, and said, 'Is not that GREAT, like his *Odes?*'"[1]

We now enter upon the third and last period of Gray's literary production. In 1755 Paul Henri Mallet's *Introduction à l'Histoire de Dannemarc* appeared. This had a powerful effect on Gray, and aroused his interest in Northern mythology, which he studied with the utmost enthusiasm. In 1761, Gray wrote *The Fatal Sisters*, and *The Descent of Odin*. Here we find him writing on strictly Romantic themes. Evan Evans's book on Welsh poetry[2] (1764) containing specimens from ancient Welsh bards, inspired Gray again, and he wrote *The Triumphs of Owen*, together with two other shorter pieces.

The *Fatal Sisters*, *Odin*, and *Owen* were published in 1768, in the edition of his writings revised by himself. In 1760, when the Ossianic *Fragments* appeared, Gray was wonderfully aroused. His friends knew he would be excited, for Walpole, writing to Dalrymple, 4 April 1760, said : "You originally pointed him out as a likely person to be charmed with the old Irish poetry you sent me." Gray's letters on Ossian may be found among the selections from his prose in this book; also his interesting remark on the ballad *Child Maurice*, which he greatly enjoyed.

As he advanced in life, Gray's ideas of poetry grew free in theory as well as in practice. His *Observations on English Metre*, written probably in 1760–61, and published in 1814, contains much interesting matter. Gray had planned to write a History of English Poetry, but

---

[1] Boswell's *Johnson*, ed. Hill, II, 374.

[2] *Some Specimens of the Poetry of the Antient Welsh Bards. Translated into English, with Explanatory Notes on the Historical Passages, and a short account of Men and Places mentioned by the Bards, in order to give the Curious some Idea of the Taste and Sentiments of our Ancestors, and their manner of Writing.*

when he heard that Thomas Warton was engaged in that work, he gave up the idea, and handed over his general scheme to Warton. If Gray had completed a history of this kind, it would certainly have been more accurate than Warton's, and would probably have done as much service to Romanticism. A few words may be quoted from the *Observations*, to show how far Gray had advanced in his ideas since 1740. Speaking of Milton, he says: "The more we attend to the composition of Milton's harmony, the more we shall be sensible how he loved to vary his pauses, his measures and his feet, which gives that enchanting air of freedom and wildness to his versification, unconfined by any rules but those which his own feeling and the nature of his subject demands." [1]

V. GRAY'S PROSE.

"I do not pretend to write prose," Gray once remarked; [2] but nevertheless he wrote it admirably. Although Gray often imitated Milton in his poetry, he never attempted to do so in his prose, which Milton wrote, to use his own words, with his left hand. The eighteenth century was the golden age of letter writing; cheap postage had not then done its fatal work on epistolary style. In the letters of Gray we see perhaps the best representatives of the best period; he does not suffer even in comparison with the most famous of all English letter-writers, Horace Walpole. Walpole is more brilliant, but he is also more artificial; and he too evidently was writing for the benefit of posterity. Gray's style has nearly all the charm of Walpole's, and it is simplicity itself. One would imagine that his reserved tempera-

[1] *Works*, I, 332   [2] See p. 77.

ment might make his letters cold, stiff, formal, and
therefore profitless reading; on the contrary, they exhibit
the perfection of ease and grace. Walpole said, "Gray
never wrote anything easily but things of humour.
Humour was his natural and original turn."[1] To those
who know Gray only through the *Elegy*, this remark
seems scarcely true; but it is eminently true of Gray
when writing to his friends. His familiar ways with
Mason, whom he called "Skroddles," his playful tone
with Nicholls, and his mild satires on literary ignorance
and political selfishness, all tend to prove the truth of
Walpole's statement. Nor can any one read Gray's
letters without admiring the man; he is so sensible and
so genuine. His own troubles are mentioned with
reserve, as is fitting; and his sympathy for the sorrows
of others is as full of depth as it is free from gush. His
remarks on men of letters and on current events are
sprightly and often keen; but above all, his prose
epistles are interesting and valuable for the evidence
they show of unfeigned and discriminating appreciation
of nature. In this respect, they are deeply interesting
to the student of Romanticism. He was one of the first
men in Europe who had any real appreciation of wild
and romantic scenery. It has now become so fashionable
to be fond of mountains, and lakes, and picturesque
landscapes, that it seems difficult to believe that all this
is a modern taste. To-day the average summer traveler
speaks enthusiastically of precipices, mountain cascades
and shaded glens, and even to some extent interprets
them by the imagination; but the average eighteenth
century sojourner neither could nor would do anything
of the sort. This appreciation of the picturesque in
external nature has a close kinship with the Romantic

[1] *Letters*, VI, 206.

movement in literature ; for the same emotions are at the foundation of both.

The Classicists had no more love for wild nature than they had for Gothic architecture or Romantic poetry. Let us take Addison as a conspicuous example. "In one of his letters, dated December, 1701, he wrote that he had reached Geneva after 'a very troublesome journey over the Alps. My head is still giddy with mountains and precipices ; and you can't imagine how much I am pleased with the sight of a plain !' This little phrase is a good illustration of the contempt for mountains, of the way they were regarded as wild, barbaric, useless excrescences. . . . The love of mountains is something really of modern, very modern, growth, the first traces of which we shall come across towards the middle of the last century. Before that time we find mountains spoken of in terms of the severest reprobation."[1]

Mountains and wild scenery were considered as objects not of beauty or grandeur, but of horror. But in Gray's letters we hear the modern tone. In this respect he was even more in advance of his contemporaries than in his Romantic poetry. From first to last he was always a lover of wild nature ; and, as this taste was so unfashionable, we may be sure of his sincerity. Toward the close of his life, this feeling in Gray becomes more and more noticeable. His *Journal in the Lakes*[2] is a marvel when we consider its date, for it is written in the true spirit of Wordsworth. But his *early* letters and journals show that he knew how to appreciate romantic scenery. Take two extracts from his *Journal in France* (1739). These words are interest-

[1] T. S. Perry's *English Literature in the Eighteenth Century*, p. 145.

[2] See p. 99.

ing simply as showing what attracted Gray's attention :
" Beautiful way, commonly on the side of a hill, cover'd
with woods, the river Marne winding in the vale below,
and Côteaux, cover'd with vines, riseing gently on the
other side ; fine prospect of the town of Joinville, with
the castle on the top of the mountain, overlooking it. . . .
Ruins of an old castle on the brow of a mountain, whose
sides are cover'd with woods."[1]   Again, describing the
journey to Geneva : " The road runs over a Mountain,
which gives you the first tast of the Alps, in it's magnificent rudeness, and steep precipices ; set out from
Echelles on horseback, to see the Grand Chartreuse, the
way to it up a vast mountain, in many places the road
not 2 yards broad ; on one side the rock hanging over
you, & on the other side a monstrous precipice.   In the
bottom runs a torrent . . . that works its way among
the rocks with a mighty noise, and frequent Falls.   You
here meet with all the beauties so savage and horrid a
place can present you with ; Rocks of various and
uncouth figures, cascades pouring down from an immense
height out of hanging Groves of Pine-Trees, & the
solemn Sound of the Stream, that roars below, all concur
to form one of the most poetical scenes imaginable."[2]

All this is remarkable language for the year 1739.
Probably very few private journals of the eighteenth
century can show anything similar to it ; for Gray's feelings were, at that time, almost exclusively his own.   His
letters, both at that time, and later, on Alpine scenery,
may be read in part in this edition.   All his most important remarks on nature have been included.

By far the most significant of them is the *Journal in the
Lakes*, written in 1769, and published in 1775.   This docu-
ment is of great value, as throwing light on the purely

[1] *Works*, I, 240.   [2] *Works*, I, 244.

imaginative side of Gray's nature. He took this Lake trip alone, and wrote the *Journal* simply to amuse his friend, Dr. Wharton. Here we have a very different view of nature from that given by Dyer, Thomson and even by the Wartons. This remarkable Journal is written in the true Wordsworthian spirit. Gray not only observes but spiritually interprets nature. The *Journal in the Lakes* is one of the most significant pieces of eighteenth century prose.

Mitford said: "No man was a greater admirer of nature than Mr. Gray, nor admired it with better taste." Perhaps Walpole had partly in mind Gray's superior appreciation of Alpine scenery when he wrote, in 1775: "We rode over the Alps in the same chaise, but Pegasus drew on his side, and a cart-horse on mine."[1] There is something noble and truly beautiful in the way in which Walpole always insisted on his own inferiority to Gray. His attitude in this was never cringing; it was a pure tribute of admiration, and that, too, from a sensitive man who had been repeatedly snubbed by the very object of his praise.

It is interesting to notice the strange and strong contrast between the shy, reserved temperament of Gray, and the pronounced radicalism of his literary tastes. Had he been a demonstrative and gushing person like Mason, his utterances about mountains and Ossianic poetry would not seem so singular; but that this secluded scholar, who spent most of his hours over his books in Cambridge and the manuscripts in the British Museum, and who was always slow to speak, should have quietly cultivated tastes so distinctly Romantic — this is a noteworthy fact. It seems to show that the one-man power counts for something in literary developments. Gray

---

[1] Letter to Cole, 10 December 1775.

influenced the age more than the age influenced him; he led rather than followed. In addition to all the various forces silently working in the Romantic movement, we must add the direct influence of the courage and genius of Gray.

VI. CHRONOLOGICAL TABLE.

1716. Birth, 26 December, Cornhill, London.

1734. Enters Peterhouse, Cambridge.

1738. Leaves Cambridge.

1739. Travels on the Continent with Horace Walpole.

1741. Returns home, 1 September.

1741. Death of Gray's father, 6 November.

1742. Death of Richard West, 1 June.

1742. Writes *Ode on the Spring, Eton Ode, Hymn to Adversity, Sonnet,* and (probably) begins the *Elegy.*

1742. Settles down at Peterhouse, Cambridge.

1743. Takes the degree of LL.B at Cambridge.

1747. Writes *Ode on the Death of a Favourite Cat.*

1748. Writes the *Alliance of Education and Government.*

1750. Completes the *Elegy,* and writes *A Long Story.*

1751. *Elegy* published.

1753. Publication of *Six Poems.*

1753. Death of Gray's mother, 11 March.

1754. Writes *Progress of Poesy,* and begins the *Bard.*

1756. Removes from Peterhouse to Pembroke Hall.

1757. Publication of *Pindaric Odes.*

1761. Writes the Norse Poems.

1764. Writes the Welsh Poems.

1768. Standard edition of his *Poems* published in London and Glasgow.

1768. Made Professor of Modern History and Languages at Cambridge.

1769. Writes *Ode for Music,* which is published the same year.

1769. Writes *Journal in the Lakes.*

1771. Death of Gray, 30 July.

VII. BIBLIOGRAPHY.

[The Bibliography up to 1771 is made as complete as possible; after that date, only the more important editions are included.]

An Ode on a Distant Prospect of Eton College. (Anonymous.) London, 1747. Folio.

Odes on Eton, on the Spring, and on the Death of a Favourite Cat. (Anonymous.) In Dodsley's Collection of Poems. Vol. II. London, 1748.

An Elegy Wrote in a Country Church Yard. London, 1751. (Anonymous.)

> This has an Advertisement by H. Walpole; the poem went through four editions in two months, and by 1759 had gone through eleven regular editions.

Designs by Mr. R. Bentley, for Six Poems by Mr. T. Gray. (Vignette.) London, 1753. Folio.

> This beautiful volume contains six full-page prints, and a considerable number of smaller ones in the shape of front and tail pieces, and initial letters. The poems are set up in very large type, and are printed on only one side of the leaves. At the end of the volume are brief explanations of the prints. The poems included are *Spring, Cat, Eton, Long Story, Adversity, Elegy.*

Odes by Mr. Gray. ΦΩΝΑΝΤΑ ΣΥΝΕΤΟΙΣΙ — PINDAR, Olymp. II. (Vignette.) Printed at Strawberry-Hill, For R. and J. Dodsley in Pall-Mall. 1757.

> This is a thin quarto, and the first edition of the two famous Pindaric Odes, which are here called simply *Ode I* and *Ode II.*

Designs by Mr. R. Bentley, for Six Poems by Mr. T. Gray. London, 1765. Folio.

Poems by Mr. Gray. London, 1768.

> This is the standard edition of Gray's poems, a small volume of 120 pages. It contains ten pieces, as follows: *Spring, Cat, Eton, Adversity, Progress of Poesy, Bard, Fatal Sisters, Odin, Owen, Elegy.*

Poems by Mr. Gray. A New Edition. London, 1768.

> This is a reprint of the preceding, with the same paging; but the type is smaller.

Poems by Mr. Gray.   Glasgow, 1768.   Quarto.

> This is a beautiful volume, in large type, and was printed by the
> Foulis Brothers from Gray's own MS. He gave them permission to
> print, to get what profit they could, and he himself sent them the MS.,
> which was the same as that sent to Dodsley at the same time.

Poems by Mr. Gray.   Dublin, 1768.

> This is a small volume, but contains, besides the ten poems in the
> three preceding editions, the *Long Story*, two Latin translations of the
> *Elegy* — *Carmen Elegiacum* and *Elegia* — also parodies on the *Eton
> Ode*, the *Elegy*, and the *Bard*.

A   Select   Collection   of   Poems,   from   the   most   approved   Authors.   Edinburgh.   Printed by A. Donaldson, 1768.   2 vols.

> In these volumes are included *Eton* (I, 128), *Spring* (I, 131), *Cat*
> (I, 133), *Elegy* (I, 220), *Adversity* (I, 225), *Progress of Poesy* (II, 196),
> and *Bard* (II, 201).

Ode Performed in the Senate-House at Cambridge, July 1, 1769, at the Installation of his Grace Augustus-Henry Fitzroy, Duke of Grafton, Chancellor of the University. Set to Music by Dr. Randal, Professor of Music. (Anonymous.)   Cambridge, 1769.   Quarto.

> This is a thin quarto of eight pages, printed in large type.

Poems.   London, 1770.   8vo.

Elegy.   London, 1771.

Poems.   Glasgow, 1773.   18mo.

Poems, etc.   In British Poets (vol. 42).   London, 1773.   8vo.

Elegy.   New Edition.   London, 1775.   8vo.

The Poems of Mr. Gray.   To which are prefixed Memoirs of his Life and Writings, by W. Mason, M.A.   York, 1775.   Quarto.

> This thick quarto is the original standard Life of Gray. Mason
> simply arranged Gray's letters in chronological order, connecting them
> by comments of his own. He also printed among the letters a number
> of Gray's posthumous pieces.

The Poems, etc., by W. Mason, M.A.   The Second Edition. London, 1775.   Quarto.

> This is the same as the preceding.

Poems by Mr. Gray.   Dublin, 1775.   12mo.

> Very nearly the same as the Dublin edition of 1768.

Poems.   [With plates.]   London and Edinburgh, 1776.

The Poems, etc., by W. Mason, M.A.   2 vols.   Dublin, 1776.

> This contains the *Memoirs* also.

The Poems, etc., by W. Mason, M.A.   4 vols.   York, 1778.

> This contains the *Memoirs* also, but in this case the *Poems* come in the first volume, and the *Memoirs* in the other three.

The Poems of Mr. Gray.   With Notes by Gilbert Wakefield, B.A.   London, 1786.   8vo.

> The copious notes in this volume, with the abundance of parallel passages, have been a storehouse for Mitford and subsequent editors.

Designs by Mr. R. Bentley, for Six Poems by Mr. T. Gray. 1789.   Folio.

The Works, etc., by W. Mason, with extracts from the MSS., by T. J. Mathias.   2 vols.   London, 1814.   Quarto.

> Mathias here printed for the first time Gray's observations on English Metre, the Notes on Aristophanes and Plato, and other prose fragments.

Poems, with Life, Notes, and an Essay on his Poetry, by the Rev. J. Mitford.   London, 1814.

> The Rev. John Mitford's name is now inseparably associated with that of Gray.   He was the first man to edit the text with accuracy, and for many years he produced edition after edition, constantly adding new and important matter.   All subsequent editors have drawn largely from Mitford.

Observations on the Writings and on the Character of Mr. Gray.   By T. J. Mathias.   London, 1815.

> This is a reprint in a small volume of the "postscript" to Mathias's edition of Gray's Complete Works in 1814.

Poetical Works, with Life, etc.   Edited by J. Mitford.   "Aldine Poets."   London, 1830.

The Works of Thomas Gray.   Edited by J. Mitford.   4 vols. London (Pickering), 1836.

The Correspondence of Thomas Gray and the Rev. Norton Nicholls.   With Other Pieces Hitherto Unpublished. Edited by the Rev. John Mitford.   London (Pickering), 1843.

This small volume was published as Vol. V to the preceding edition.

Poetical Works.   Eton, 1845.

Mitford wrote a new Life of Gray for this edition.

The Poetical Works of Thomas Gray.   "Aldine."   Edited by J. Mitford.   London (Pickering), 1853.

The Correspondence of Thomas Gray and William Mason, To which are added some Letters addressed by Gray to the Rev. James Brown, D.D.   With Notes and Illustrations, by the Rev. John Mitford.   London, 1853.   8vo.

Poetical Works, with Life, etc.   Edited by J. Mitford. "Aldine."   London, 1866.

The Elegy, and Pindaric Odes.   In Longer English Poems, edited by the Rev. J. W. Hales.   London, 1872.

Select Poems, etc.   Edited by W. J. Rolfe.   New York, 1876. Revised edition, 1886.

The Works of Thomas Gray.   Edited by Edmund Gosse. 4 vols.   London, 1884.

This is now the standard edition of Gray, as it contains more matter than any other.   The letters are all arranged in a chronological order, and several texts of the *Elegy* are given, besides a number of bibliographical notes.   In spite of the claims of this edition, however, the text is not perfectly accurate.

Poetical Works.   Edited by John Bradshaw.   New "Aldine." London, 1891.

Selections from the Poetry and Prose.   Edited by Wm. Lyon Phelps.   Boston, 1894.

Writings About Gray.

[Only those are included that are believed to be most useful.]

Life of Gray. By Dr. Johnson, in his Lives of the Poets. London, 1779–1781.

> This has the well-deserved reputation of being the worst "Life" in the series of which it formed a part; but it is interesting on historical and critical grounds.

An Inquiry into some Passages in Dr. Johnson's Lives, etc. By the Rev. R. Potter. London, 1783.

> Potter, who was an enthusiastic admirer of Gray, and of Romantic poetry in general, sharply attacked Johnson for his strictures on Gray's Pindaric Odes.

Gray. An Essay by Matthew Arnold, prefixed to the selections from Gray in Ward's English Poets. London, 1880.

> For remarks on Arnold's view of Gray's sterility, see *Introduction* to the present edition, part ii.

Life of Gray. By Edmund Gosse. In "English Men of Letters" series. London, 1882. A new edition in 1889.

> This is now the standard "Life," but it is so inaccurate as to be untrustworthy in matters of detail.

Gray. By Leslie Stephen. Article in the Dictionary of National Biography, 1890.

Gray and his Friends. Letters and Relics in great part hitherto unpublished. By Duncan C. Tovey. Cambridge, 1890.

> This book, besides containing an excellent general Introduction on Gray, consists of a number of letters and journals, printed with great accuracy. The book is really a memorial to Richard West.

Gray. An Essay by James Russell Lowell, in Latest Literary Essays. Boston, 1892.

> This essay was first published in the New Princeton Review, 1886; it is one of the most brilliant and charming pieces Mr. Lowell ever composed.

APPENDIX.

GRAY'S KNOWLEDGE OF OLD NORSE.

THE most emphatic assertion of Gray's knowledge of the Old Norse language is made by Mr. Gosse (*Life of Gray*, pp. 160 ff.), who declares that, "whereas there is no absolute proof that Gray was a Welsh scholar," *The Fatal Sisters* and *The Descent of Odin* "were translated direct from the Icelandic."

"It may well inspire us with admiration of the poet's intellectual energy," continues this critic, "to find that he had mastered a language [1] which was hardly known, at that time, by any one in Europe, except a few learned Icelanders, whose native tongue made it easy for them to understand Norrœna. Gray must have puzzled it out for himself, probably with the help of the *Index Linguae Scytho-Scandicae* of Verelius. At that time what he rightly calls the Norse tongue was looked upon as a sort of mystery; it was called 'Runick,' and its roots were supposed to be derived from the Hebrew. *The Fatal Sisters* is a lay of the eleventh century, the text of which Gray found in one of the compilations of Torfœus [read *Torfæus*] (Thormod Torveson), a great collector of ancient Icelandic vellums at the close of the seventeenth century.

". . . *The Descent of Odin* is a finer poem, better paraphrased. Gray found the original in a book by Bartolinus [read *Bartholinus*], one of the five great physicians of that name who flourished in Denmark during the seventeenth century. The poem itself is the *Vegtamskvida*, one of the most powerful and mysterious of those ancient lays which form the earliest collection we possess of Scandinavian poetry. It is probable that Gray never saw the tolerably complete but very inaccurate edition of *Sœmundar* [read *Sæmundar*] *Edda* which existed in his time, nor knew the wonderful history of this collection, which was discovered in Iceland, in 1643, by Brynjólfr

---

[1] Mr. Leslie Stephen, in his life of Gray in the *Dict. of Nat. Biogr.*, refers to Mr. Gosse as authority for the statement that Gray learned Icelandic.

Sveinnson, Bishop of Skálaholt. The text which Gray found in Bartolinus, however, was sufficiently true to enable him to make a better translation of the *Vegtamskvida* than any which has been attempted since, and to make us deeply regret that he did not 'imitate' more of these noble Eddaic chants. He even attempts a philological ingenuity, for, finding that Odin, to conceal his true nature from the Völva, calls himself Vegtam, Gray translates this strange word 'traveller,' evidently tracing it to *veg*, a way. He omits the first stave, which recounts how the Æsir sat in council to deliberate on the dreams of Balder, and he also omits four spurious stanzas, in this showing a critical tact little short of miraculous, considering the condition of scholarship at that time."

This evidence looks convincing, but unfortunately it has no basis of fact. The number of mistakes in the few sentences just quoted is surprising. What is meant by "the tolerably complete but very inaccurate edition of *Sæmundar Edda* which existed in [Gray's] time," it is hard to divine. There was no edition at all of the so-called *Sæmund's Edda* (*i.e.*, *The Poetic Edda*) extant in Gray's time, for none had been published. Gray died in 1771, and the first edition of this *Edda* (the great Copenhagen edition) began to be published in 1787, and was not completed till 1828. Meantime Rask and Afzelius had published a complete edition in one small volume in 1818. Of the more than thirty pieces which compose the *Poetic Edda* only three (*Vǫluspá*, *Hávamál*,[1] and *Vegtamskviða*) had been printed before Gray's death. The only edition of the

---

[1] The *Vǫluspá* and the *Hávamál* had been edited by Resenius (1665) in a volume which was usually bound up with his edition of the *Prose Edda*. The poems were accompanied by a Latin translation by Stefán Óláfsson. The stanzas of the *Hávamál* concerning runes were printed by Resenius as a separate poem, and this division accounts for Mallet's words "le petit poème intitulé *le chapitre runique*, ou *la magie d'Odin*" (*Introd. à l'Hist. de Dannemarc*, 2d ed., II, 285; *Northern Antiquities*, 1770, II, 216). When Mallet first published his second volume (1756), he did not even know whether any part of the *Poetic Edda* was in existence except *Vǫluspá*, *Hávamál* and this so-called *Runic Chapter*, and this uncertainty was shared by the English translator in 1770 (*Northern Antiquities*, II, 201); but before he published his third edition (1787), Mallet had learned better (II, 264 ff.). The *Hávamál* was re-edited by Göransson in 1750. A pretty complete list of the contents of the *Poetic Edda* is given in Peringskjöld's catalogue of Copenhagen MSS. appended to Wanley's *Catalogus* (1705), p. 310. Wanley's *Catalogus* (which Gray knew) forms, with Hickes's *Thesaurus*, the *Antiqua Literatura Septentrionalis*.

Vegtamskviða (the original of *The Descent of Odin*) was that in Bartholin's book.[1] We are forced to conjecture that Mr. Gosse has for the moment confused the *Poetic Edda* with the *Prose Edda* of Snorri, which was edited by Resenius in 1665, and by Göransson in 1746.[2]

All this, to be sure, though it may shake one's confidence in Mr. Gosse's accuracy, does not affect the validity of his arguments from Gray's "philological ingenuity" in translating *Vegtamr* by *Traveller* and from the omission of the four spurious stanzas. But these arguments themselves rest on other misapprehensions. As to the four spurious stanzas, they are omitted by Gray simply because he was unaware of their existence. They do not stand in the Arna-Magnæan MS. or in Bartholin's text, and were not printed at all until 1787, when the Copenhagen editors inserted them in the text from late paper manuscripts.[3] The rendering of *Vegtamr* by *Traveller* would doubtless be significant but for a fact which Mr. Gosse neglects to mention, though it is of the first importance in settling the main question: Bartholin appended to each stanza of the original a literal translation into Latin, and that translation, which renders *Vegtamr* by *Viator*, relieved Gray of the necessity of "attempting a philological ingenuity" in interpreting this strange word.

The fact that Bartholin's texts of the two poems which Gray translated[4] are, like all his other Norse quotations, accompanied by

---

1 The *Vegtamskviða* is not contained in the manuscript discovered by Bishop Brynjólfr Sveinsson, probably in 1643, — the so-called *Codex Regius*. It is preserved (except for some paper copies of no consequence) only in the Arna-Magnæan MS. 748, which contains, to be sure, merely a somewhat different redaction of what is essentially the same collection. The poem was doubtless made known to Bartholin by Arni Magnússon himself.

2 Göransson's Latin version of the first tract in the *Prose Edda* (*The Deception of Gylfi*) was reprinted in *Northern Antiquities*, 1770, II, 273–352.

3 See Bugge, *Norrœn Fornkvæði*, pp. 138–140. Mason reprinted Bartholin's Latin translation in his note at the end of *The Descent of Odin*. Mitford's remark that "the first five stanzas of this Ode are omitted" by Gray is repeated by Dr. Bradshaw without investigation: the fact is that Gray omittèd but one stanza (the first, also omitted by Bartholin) of the genuine text, the other four are those four spurious strophes that misled Mr. Gosse. Ten other spurious lines, which *are* in Bartholin, are accepted by Gray.

4 The *Fatal Sisters* is extracted by Gray from Torfæus, but Torfæus refers to Bartholin, from whom he repeats both the original and the Latin version. Gray too adds a reference to Bartholin. In his preface Bartholin acknowledges his indebtedness to the famous Icelander Arni Magnússon with

literal Latin renderings, has, as has just been suggested, an important
bearing on the general question of Gray's knowledge of the Old
Norse tongue. By the use of these literal renderings, Gray could
have written both *The Fatal Sisters* and *The Descent of Odin* without
reading a word in the original language. What we know of his
scholarly habits and of his insatiate love of investigation makes it
incredible, however, that he should have contented himself with so
humble a process. It is more probable that he carefully compared
the Latin text with the Old Norse and by this means made out
something of the originals. In this he would be assisted by the
striking similarity of many of the Scandinavian words to their
English cognates. Since he is likely to have done this with many
other interesting texts in Bartholin and elsewhere, he may perhaps
have arrived at a halting knowledge of the language : that he ever
" mastered " it, there is at any rate no evidence in his two " Norse
odes."

The notes and introductions which Gray wrote for these Norse
odes seem at first sight to supply some of the evidence which is
lacking in the odes themselves. But an examination of this apparatus
reduces this testimony also to a minimum. Of all the comments
which Gray wrote on *The Descent of Odin*, including the long
note on the seeresses,[1] the material is furnished *in Latin* by
Bartholin and some of it was also accessible to all Europe in Mallet.
The *Preface* to *The Fatal Sisters* is from Torfæus[2] (*Orcades*, i, 10,
pp. 33 ff.) and the other notes are, as before, due to Bartholin. Of
only two bits of information is this not true : the translation of

regard to the Latin versions of the Norse poems that he quotes (" ex ver-
sione, quæ accuratæ docti Islandi Arnæ Magnæi industriæ complementum
suum debet ").

[1] Not printed by Gray, but added by Mason from Gray's papers (see p. 169,
below).

[2] Gray's date for the Battle of Clontarf, — " Christmas day " (*Preface* to
The Fatal Sisters), — is a mere slip. Torfæus (*Orcades*, i, 10, p. 35) clearly
puts the battle on Good Friday : " Die Veneris, qvi, in diem memoriæ pas-
sionis Servatoris, Σωτηρία dictum," etc. Gray's note on the conversion of
the Orcadians is also derived in the main from Torfæus, who (*Orcades*, i, 10,
p. 33) gives an account of the heroic measures adopted in 995 by King Olave
Tryggvason to secure the baptism of Earl Sigurd. All the knowledge which
he shows of the " history of Olaus Tryggueson " in the same note, he could
easily have collected from the *Orcades* and from Torfæus's *Historiæ Rerum
Norvegicarum* (1711 ff., see vi, 7 ff., II, 246 ff.), supplemented perhaps by
Bartholin or by Peringskjöld's Latin version of the *Heimskringla* (1697).

fiolkuñnug (read *fjǫlkunnig*) by *multi-scia* and of *vísinda-kona* by *oraculorum mulier* in the long note inserted by Mason from Gray's papers (see *Descent of Odin*, v. 51, p. 170, below) is not based on anything in Bartholin and seems to betray a knowledge of the component parts of those words. But we cannot build much on this. *Fjǫl-* is a very common prefix and Gray may have found it explained in various places. In the Glossary to Verelius's edition of the *Hervarar Saga* (Upsala, 1672), for example, *all-fiolkunnugur* (put under *f*) is glossed by *multiscius*. In the same Glossary *vísinda menn* is explained by *oraculorum interpretes:* this would furnish Gray with the meaning of *vísinda-*, and *kona* is a very common word, the meaning of which he would infallibly discover by the process of comparison suggested above. We have no real evidence that Gray knew this work of Verelius, but the presumption is perhaps that way. It was certainly known to Warton [1] and Percy,[2] and there was a copy in the Bodleian Library.[3]

Important direct evidence of Gray's interest in Scandinavian study is contained in his well-known letter to Mason, Jan. 13, 1758 (*Works*, II, 350 ff.). In this he insists on the distinction between Celtic and Northern antiquities and expresses himself as follows about Odin: "Woden .himself is supposed not to have been older than Julius Cæsar; but let him have lived when he pleases, it is certain that neither he nor his Valhalla were heard of till many ages after. This is the doctrine of the Scalds, not of the Bards; these are the songs of Hengist and Horsa, a modern new-fangled belief in comparison with that which you ought to possess." [4] "In short," he remarks in

[1] *History of English Poetry*, ed. Hazlitt, I, 120.

[2] See *Five Pieces of Runic Poetry*, 1763, p. 4.

[3] *Catalogus Librorum Septentrionalium* appended to Jónsson (Runolphus Jonas), *Grammaticæ Islandicæ Rudimenta*, Oxford, 1688, p. 179. Of course, as Mr. Gosse suggests, Gray may have used the *Index Linguæ veteris Scytho-Scandicæ sive Gothicæ* of Verelius (Upsala, 1691).

[4] *I.e.*, the Druidical belief, which Mason needed for his *Caractacus*. In his play, Mason makes the chorus of Druids present a sword to the hero:

"Caractacus!
Behold this sword: The sword of old Belinus,
Stain'd with the blood of giants, and its name Trifingus."
(*Poems*, 1764, p. 257.)

In a note (p. 316) he says: "TRIFINGUS. The name of the inchanted sword in the Hervarer Saga." The reader will recognize the famous *Tyrfing*.

the same letter (II, 352), "I am pleased with the Gothic Elysium. Do you think I am ignorant about either that, or the *hell* before, or the *twilight?* I have been there, and have seen it all in Mallet's *Introduction to the History of Denmark* (it is in French), and many other places." The first volume of Mallet's *Introduction* had appeared in 1755, the second (containing a translation of much of the *Prose Edda*) in 1756. If Gray's attention, like that of Europe in general, was first called to the Norse mythology by this work, it is interesting to observe that he had so far extended his reading by the beginning of 1758 as to have seen the chief doctrines of the Odinic system "in many other places." The letter gives us no inkling as to what these places were, but it does inform us what one of them was not: Gray expressly disclaims having read "Keysler," *i.e.*, the *Antiquitates Selectae Septentrionales et Celticae* of Johann Georg Keysler, Hannover, 1720.[1]

In 1761 Gray translated *The Fatal Sisters* and *The Descent of Odin*, and these show that he had been reading the treatise of Thomas Bartholin *De Causis contemnendæ Mortis* (Copenhagen, 1689) with much attention and that he had at any rate consulted the *Orcades* of Torfæus (1697).[2] If, as there seems little reason for doubting, the *Observations on the Pseudo-Rhythmus* (*Works*, I, 361 ff.), intended like the Norse Odes as material for the projected *History of English Poetry*, were written at about the same time,[3] we may

---

[1] Mr. Gosse's suggestion (Gray's *Works*, II, 351) that the "Keysler" mentioned by Gray "was probably the second English edition, of 1757, of Johann Georg Keysler's *Travels through Germany, Hungary, Bohemia, Switzerland, Italy, and Lorrain*" was made in momentary forgetfulness of Mason's letter of Jan. 5, 1758 (*Correspondence of Gray and Mason*, ed. Mitford, p. 120), to which this of Gray's was a reply: Mason mentions the title of the book, and in his reply to Gray (Jan. 16, 1758; *id.*, p. 130), he returns to the subject and gives an extract from Keysler. The work was in its day well-known among antiquaries and is still worth consulting.

[2] Torfæus (Þormóðr Torfason), b. 1636, d. 1719, was a learned Icelander and one of the founders of the science of Northern Antiquities. His most important works (chiefly historical) were written while he was the King of Denmark's historiographer royal for Norway. His *History of the Orkneys* (*Historia Orcadum*, Copenhagen, 1867), is the work here referred to.

[3] The essay contains a note as to *Death and Life* and *Scottish Field*, two poems in the Percy MS.: "I read them in a MS. collection belonging to the Rev. Mr. Thomas Piercy in 1761" (*Works*, I, 371); but this note proves little. In a letter to Montagu, May 5, 1761 (*Letters*, ed. Cunningham, III, 399), Walpole writes: "Gray and Mason were with me, and we listened to

add Sir William Temple's essay *Of Poetry*,[1] the *Literatura Runica* of
Ole Worm (Olaus Wormius), the great Danish antiquary (Copenhagen, 1636; 2d ed., 1651), and the *Linguarum Vett. Septentrionalium Thesaurus* of the celebrated Dr. George Hickes (Oxford, 1705).
Gray's references to the *Thesaurus* in this essay show that he had
used the work with diligence, and in such a use of it he must have
paid some attention to the Old Norse Grammar which it contains.[2]
To Worm he refers for a remark about the Old Norse stanza known
as *dróttkvætt* and for a passage from the tenth-century rhyming scaldic poem the *Ransom of Egill*.[3] The latter reference is particularly
interesting. Gray quotes six lines of the poem in the original (*Works*,
I, 862, n. 2). His quotation is from Worm, but he has transliterated
Worm's Runic characters into Roman letters. This he could of
course easily do without a knowledge of Icelandic by using the tables
of Runic equivalents given in Worm and in Hickes. Worm's book
furnishes a Latin version of the *Ransom*, but no transliteration.[4]

It is far from improbable that Gray knew all these books before
1758. Worm and Hickes were regarded as indispensable to any

the nightingales till one o'clock in the morning. Gray has translated two
noble incantations from the Lord knows who, a Danish Gray, who lived the
Lord knows when. They are to be enchased in a history of English bards,
which Mason and he are writing; but of which the former has not written a
word yet, and of which the latter, if he rides Pegasus at his usual foot-pace,
will finish the first page two years hence." Mr. Gosse (*Life of Gray*, p. 164)
erroneously remarks that Walpole "did not see these poems till they were
printed" in 1768.

[1] From which comes the remark referred to by Gray at beginning of the
essay (*Works of Temple*, ed. of 1770, III, 413). Temple's essay *Of Heroic
Virtue*, the companion-piece to that *Of Poetry*, was also, no doubt, familiar to
Gray, though he does not mention it anywhere: it contains much about Odin.
Mason, whose "no-reading" seems to have been a jest with Gray (*Correspondence of Gray and Mason*, ed. Mitford, p. 130) discovered these two
essays for himself (*id.*, p. 131).

[2] The *Grammaticæ Islandicæ Rudimenta* of Rúnólfr Jónsson (Runolphus
Jonas). Gray does not mention this particular treatise. Of the other contents of the *Thesaurus* he refers expressly in this essay to Hickes's *Institutiones Grammaticæ Anglo-Saxonicæ et Mæso-Gothicæ* and *Institutiones
Grammaticæ Franco-Theotiscæ*. He also refers to Wanley's *Catalogue*.

[3] The *Hǫfuðlausn* of Egill Skalla-Grímsson (Wisén, *Carmina Norrœna*,
I, 20 ff.; Vigfússon, *Corpus Poeticum Boreale*, I, 267 ff.). There is a transliteration as well as a translation in Percy's *Five Pieces of Runic Poetry*, 1763,
pp. 49 ff., 92 ff.

[4] *Literatura Runica*, 2d ed., pp. 207 ff.

serious investigator of English antiquities — a subject in which Gray
was deeply interested. The minute nature of his historical studies
is well indicated by a single note to *The Bard* (v. 11), in which he
quotes Higden's *Polychronicon* and Matthew of Westminster on a
point of Welsh topography (see below, p. 36). It is possible, then,
that he first consulted Worm and Hickes [1] as a student of English
history, and that he was familiar with them when he wrote to Mason
in 1758. If so, we have at once some of the "many other places"
in which Gray had seen the "Gothic Elysium" and other particulars
of the Odinic system.[2]

Another book in Gray's time regarded as of capital importance to the
student of English history, and, therefore, not likely to have been neglected by him, is Robert Sheringham's *De Anglorum Gentis Origine
Disceptatio* (Cambridge, 1670),[3] in which there are a sufficient number
of extracts from the *Prose Edda* (with Latin translations) to inform
the inquirer as to "hell" and "Elysium." Sheringham also dis-
cusses the wanderings and the powers of Odin in an elaborate way.
If to these works Gray had, before 1758, added Bartholin, he was
within bounds in his phrase "and in many other places."

Hickes's *Thesaurus*, whenever Gray studied it, offered him the
original text and an English prose version of a magnificent Old
Norse poem, *The Waking of Angantyr* (from the *Hervarar Saga*).
This translation by Hickes has never received from students of
Romanticism the attention which it deserves. Buried in the great

[1] See note 3 below.

[2] The "Elysium" is mentioned by Torfæus, *Hist. Rerum Noveg.*, iii, 18,
I, 186.

[3] The regard in which Worm, Hickes and Sheringham were held by English antiquaries is shown, not only by the frequency with which they are cited
by eighteenth-century historians, but by an interesting piece of direct testimony: Sir Joseph Ayloffe in answering the inquiries of a correspondent " as
to what are the most proper books to be read by a young student in our antiquities" includes in his list Sheringham, the *Thesaurus*, Worm's *Monu-
menta Danica* "and his other pieces" (see his letter, Dec. 28, 1769, in
Nichols, *Literary Anecdotes*, VIII, 486). Sir William Temple's *Excerpta ex
Edda* and *Excerpta ex Snorrone* in his essay *Of Heroic Virtue* (*Works*, ed.
1770, III, 354) may have been selected from passages quoted by Sheringham,
pp. 234 ff. It will be remembered that *Wormius* was adopted by Pope as a
name for the typical mousing antiquary (*Dunciad*, iii, 188 ; cf. Pope's dis-
claiming note). Blair in his *Critical Dissertation on the Poems of Ossian*,
1763, p. 4, *n.*, refers to Worm and gives the Latin version of the Ragnar
Loðbrók ode.

Thesaurus, it would not have merited much at their hands but for two facts : (1) it was extracted therefrom and printed (along with the Icelandic), with the typographical arrangement of verse, in the *Miscellany Poems* "published by Mr. Dryden," 1716, VI, 387–91, the translator's name not being given ; (2) it was adopted (with due credit) by Percy for his *Runic Poetry*. Whether or not, then, Gray knew Verelius's edition of the *Hervarar Saga*, he had opportunities enough to become acquainted with the gem of the work — this splendid poem. It is curious that Warton seems to say that Gray himself translated *The Waking of Angantyr* — an almost incredible blunder.[1] One collection with which Warton seems to have had some familiarity would have been a joy to Gray: E. J. Björner's *Nordiska Kämpa-Dater* (Stockholm, 1737), a folio containing, in parallel columns, a Latin and a Swedish translation of the Sagas of Hrolf Kraki, Friðþjóf, Ragnar, the Volsungs, and other important texts.

The work to which Gray was chiefly indebted for whatever scholarly knowledge of Scandinavian matters he possessed was undoubtedly the *Antiquitatum Danicarum de Causis contemptæ Mortis a Danis adhuc Gentilibus Libri Tres* (Copenhagen, 1689). The author, Thomas Bartholin the younger (1659–1690), professor at Copenhagen, is justly celebrated as one of the founders of the science of Northern antiquities. His book is very learned, and, for a seventeenth-century polymath, surprisingly methodical. His object is to explain the almost proverbial contempt for death on the part of the heathen Norsemen. First undertaking to prove the fact of this sentiment, he proceeds to trace its causes, quoting copiously from Old Norse texts, many of them unprinted, in prose and verse, — among them not less than eighteen articles of the *Poetic Edda*. In the course of his argument he has occasion to discuss, with much fullness, the ancient Scandinavian beliefs as to the Fates, runes, magic, prophecy, Hel, Valhalla, etc. The whole forms a quarto of more than 700 pages, which is still read with interest by scholars. Gray could have got hold of no better book for his purpose ; and he evidently

---

[1] " This piece [*sc.* the Anglo-Saxon *Battle of Brunanburh*], and many other Saxon odes and songs now extant, are written in a metre resembling that of the scaldic dialogue at the tomb of Angantyr, which has been beautifully translated into English, in the true spirit of the original, and in a genuine strain of poetry, by Gray." *History of English Poetry*, ed. Hazlitt, I, 124. Blair, *Critical Dissertation*, 1763, p. 6, refers to the fact that Hickes's version was published in the *Miscellany Poems*.

studied it with great care, as is shown by his observations that accompany the Norse Odes and by some other facts to which attention is called in the Notes on these poems in the present edition (see below, pp. 164–170). It should not be forgotten, however, that Bartholin, like Worm and Torfæus, never thinks of quoting a particle of Old Norse without appending a literal Latin translation, so that whatever information his book contained was within the reach of every educated man in Europe, whether a student of Norse or not. A close student of his book, however, would inevitably pick up a knowledge of the meanings of some words and phrases and even acquire a sort of ability to read the passages quoted. This is probably the kind of knowledge possessed by Gray. No doubt he had read over the originals of *The Fatal Sisters* and *The Descent of Odin* till he was able, after a fashion, to translate them without looking at his "crib"; but that he ever "mastered the language," as Mr. Gosse thinks, — that he ever was able to translate a poem of which he had never seen a translation, — there is, as we have seen, not a particle of evidence.[1]

G. L. K.

[1] Two linguistic errors of a somewhat elementary character remain as indications of the limits of Gray's knowledge of Old Norse. In the little excursus on seeresses extracted by Mason from the poet's papers and printed as a note to *The Descent of Odin*, v. 51 (see below, p. 170), Gray follows Bartholin (p. 688) in using the dative *sogu* (*i.e.*, *sǫgu*) : "is described at large in Eirik's Rauda Sogu." Bartholin uses this form because the construction of the Latin sentence demands it; in writing English, however, there was no such compulsion, and Gray, if he had been sure of his ground, would doubtless have written *Saga*. In the same note Gray says that the seeresses "were called *Fiolkyngi*," following a bad reading in Bartholin's quotation from *Eiríks Saga Rauða* (p. 689). *Fjǫlkyngi* is an abstract noun meaning *sorcery*, as Gray might have learned, if he had been a close student of the language, from the brief *Dictionarium Islandicum* in Hickes's *Thesaurus* (III, 77) : "fiolkinge, *artes magicæ*," or from a passage of Snorri quoted, in translation, by Sheringham (p. 243).

POEMS.

I.

ODE ON THE SPRING.

Lo! where the rosy-bosom'd Hours,
   Fair VENUS' train appear,
Disclose the long-expecting flowers,
   And wake the purple year!
The Attic warbler pours her throat,   5
Responsive to the cuckow's note,
   The untaught harmony of spring:
While whisp'ring pleasure as they fly,
Cool Zephyrs thro' the clear blue sky
   Their gather'd fragrance fling.   10

Where'er the oak's thick branches stretch
   A broader browner shade;
Where'er the rude and moss-grown beech
   O'er-canopies the glade [1]
Beside some water's rushy brink   15
With me the Muse shall sit, and think
   (At ease reclin'd in rustic state)
How vain the ardour of the Crowd,
How low, how little are the Proud,
   How indigent the Great!   20

Still is the toiling hand of Care:
   The panting herds repose:

[1] —— a bank
O'ercanopied with luscious woodbine.
Shakesp. *Mids. Night's Dream.*

Yet hark, how thro' the peopled air
   The busy murmur glows!
The insect youth are on the wing,   25
Eager to taste the honied spring,
   And float amid the liquid noon:[1]
Some lightly o'er the current skim,
Some shew their gaily-gilded trim
   Quick-glancing to the sun.[2]   30

To Contemplation's sober eye[3]
   Such is the race of Man:
And they that creep, and they that fly,
   Shall end where they began.
Alike the Busy and the Gay   35
But flutter thro' life's little day,
   In fortune's varying colours drest:
Brush'd by the hand of rough Mischance,
Or chill'd by age, their airy dance
   They leave, in dust to rest.   40

Methinks I hear in accents low
   The sportive kind reply:
Poor moralist! and what art thou?
   A solitary fly!
Thy Joys no glittering female meets,   45
No hive hast thou of hoarded sweets,

---

[1] " Nare per æstatem liquidam ——."
                  Virgil. *Georg.* lib. 4.

[2] —— sporting with quick glance
  Shew to the sun their waved coats drop'd with gold.
               Milton's *Paradise Lost*, book 7.

[3] While insects from the threshold preach, etc. — M. Green, in *the Grotto.* Dodsley's *Miscellanies*, Vol. V. p. 161.

No painted plumage to display :
On hasty wings thy youth is flown ;
Thy sun is set, thy spring is gone —
    We frolick, while 'tis May.   50

II.

ODE ON A DISTANT PROSPECT OF ETON COLLEGE.

    Ἄνθρωπος · ἱκανὴ πρόφασις εἰς τὸ δυστυχεῖν.
                      Menander.

YE distant spires, ye antique towers,
    That crown the watry glade,
Where grateful Science still adores
    Her HENRY'S [1] holy Shade ;
And ye, that from the stately brow   5
Of WINDSOR'S heights th' expanse below
    Of grove, of lawn, of mead survey,
Whose turf, whose shade, whose flowers among
Wanders the hoary Thames along
    His silver-winding way.   10

Ah happy hills, ah pleasing shade,
    Ah fields belov'd in vain,
Where once my careless childhood stray'd,
    A stranger yet to pain !
I feel the gales, that from ye blow,   15
A momentary bliss bestow,
    As waving fresh their gladsome wing,
My weary soul they seem to sooth,
And, redolent [2] of joy and youth,
    To breathe a second spring.   20

---

[1] King Henry the Sixth, Founder of the College.
[2] And bees their honey redolent of spring.
        Dryden's *Fable on the Pythag. System.*

Say, Father THAMES, for thou hast seen
    Full many a sprightly race
Disporting on thy margent green
    The paths of pleasure trace,
Who foremost now delight to cleave   25
With pliant arm thy glassy wave?
    The captive linnet which enthrall?
What idle progeny succeed
To chase the rolling circle's speed,
    Or urge the flying ball?   30

While some on earnest business bent
    Their murm'ring labours ply
'Gainst graver hours, that bring constraint
    To sweeten liberty :
Some bold adventurers disdain   35
The limits of their little reign,
    And unknown regions dare descry :
Still as they run they look behind,
They hear a voice in every wind,
    And snatch a fearful joy.   40

Gay hope is theirs by fancy fed,
    Less pleasing when possest ;
The tear forgot as soon as shed,
    The sunshine of the breast :
Theirs buxom health of rosy hue,   45
Wild wit, invention ever-new,
    And lively chear of vigour born ;
The thoughtless day, the easy night,
The spirits pure, the slumbers light,
    That fly th' approach of morn.   50

Alas, regardless of their doom,
   The little victims play!
No sense have they of ills to come,
   Nor care beyond to-day:
Yet see how all around 'em wait   55
The Ministers of human fate,
   And black Misfortune's baleful train!
Ah, shew them where in ambush stand
To seize their prey the murth'rous band!
   Ah, tell them, they are men!   60

These shall the fury Passions tear,
   The vulturs of the mind,
Disdainful Anger, pallid Fear,
   And Shame that sculks behind;
Or pineing Love shall waste their youth,   65
Or Jealousy with rankling tooth,
   That inly gnaws the secret heart,
And Envy wan, and faded Care,
Grim-visag'd comfortless Despair,
   And Sorrow's piercing dart.   70

Ambition this shall tempt to rise,
   Then whirl the wretch from high,
To bitter Scorn a sacrifice,
   And grinning Infamy.
The stings of Falshood those shall try,   75
And hard Unkindness' alter'd eye,
   That mocks the tear it forc'd to flow;
And keen Remorse with blood defil'd,
And moody Madness [1] laughing wild
   Amid severest woe.   80

[1] —— Madness laughing in his ireful mood.
      Dryden's Fable of Palamon and Arcite.

Lo, in the vale of years beneath
    A griesly troop are seen,
The painful family of Death,
    More hideous than their Queen :
This racks the joints, this fires the veins,   85
That every labouring sinew strains,
    Those in the deeper vitals rage :
Lo, Poverty, to fill the band,
That numbs the soul with icy hand,
    And slow-consuming Age.   90

To each his suff'rings : all are men,
    Condemn'd alike to groan,
The tender for another's pain ;
    Th' unfeeling for his own.
Yet ah ! why should they know their fate ?   95
Since sorrow never comes too late,
    And happiness too swiftly flies.
Thought would destroy their paradise.
No more ; where ignorance is bliss,
    'Tis folly to be wise.   100

III.

HYMN TO ADVERSITY.

— Ζῆνα
Τὸν φρονεῖν βροτοὺς ὁδώ-
σαντα, τῶ πάθει μαθὰν
Θέντα κυρίως ἔχειν.
      Æschylus, in Agamemnone.

DAUGHTER of Jove, relentless Power,
Thou Tamer of the human breast,
Whose iron scourge and tort'ring hour,
The Bad affright, afflict the Best !

Bound in thy adamantine chain   5
The Proud are taught to taste of pain,
And purple Tyrants vainly groan
With pangs unfelt before, unpitied and alone.

When first thy Sire to send on earth
Virtue, his darling Child, design'd,   10
To thee he gave the heav'nly Birth,
And bad to form her infant mind.
Stern rugged Nurse ! thy rigid lore
With patience many a year she bore :
What sorrow was, thou bad'st her know,   15
And from her own she learn'd to melt at others' woe.

Scared at thy frown terrific, fly
Self-pleasing Folly's idle brood,
Wild Laughter, Noise, and thoughtless Joy,
And leave us leisure to be good.   20
Light they disperse, and with them go
The summer Friend, the flatt'ring Foe ;
By vain Prosperity received,
To her they vow their truth, and are again believed.

Wisdom in sable garb array'd   25
Immers'd in rapt'rous thought profound,
And Melancholy, silent maid
With leaden eye, that loves the ground,
Still on thy solemn steps attend :
Warm Charity, the gen'ral Friend,   30
With Justice to herself severe,
And Pity dropping soft the sadly-pleasing tear.

Oh, gently on thy Suppliant's head,
Dread Goddess, lay thy chast'ning hand !
Not in thy Gorgon terrors clad,   35
Nor circled with the vengeful Band

(As by the Impious thou art seen)
With thund'ring voice, and threat'ning mien,
With screaming Horror's funeral cry,
Despair, and fell Disease, and ghastly Poverty.   40

Thy form benign, oh Goddess, wear,
Thy milder influence impart,
Thy philosophic Train be there
To soften, not to wound my heart,
The gen'rous spark extinct revive,   45
Teach me to love and to forgive,
Exact my own defects to scan,
What others are, to feel, and know myself a Man.

IV.

SONNET

[ON THE DEATH OF RICHARD WEST.]

In vain to me the smileing Mornings shine,
    And redning Phœbus lifts his golden Fire:
The Birds in vain their amorous Descant joyn;
    Or chearful Fields resume their green Attire:
These Ears, alas! for other Notes repine,   5
    A different Object do these Eyes require.
My lonely Anguish melts no Heart, but mine;
    And in my Breast the imperfect Joys expire.
Yet Morning smiles the busy Race to chear,
    And new-born Pleasure brings to happier Men: 10
The Fields to all their wonted Tribute bear:
    To warm their little Loves the Birds complain:
I fruitless mourn to him, that cannot hear,
    And weep the more, because I weep in vain.

At Stoke, Aug. 1742.

V.

ODE ON THE DEATH OF A FAVOURITE CAT,

DROWNED IN A TUB OF GOLD FISHES.

'TWAS on a lofty vase's side,
Where China's gayest art had dy'd
   The azure flowers, that blow;
Demurest of the tabby kind,
The pensive Selima reclin'd,   5
   Gazed on the lake below.

Her conscious tail her joy declar'd;
The fair round face, the snowy beard,
   The velvet of her paws,
Her coat, that with the tortoise vies,   10
Her ears of jet, and emerald eyes,
   She saw; and purr'd applause.

Still had she gaz'd; but 'midst the tide
Two angel forms were seen to glide,
   The Genii of the stream: 15
Their scaly armour's Tyrian hue
Thro' richest purple to the view
   Betray'd a golden gleam.

The hapless Nymph with wonder saw:
A whisker first and then a claw,   20
   With many an ardent wish,
She stretch'd in vain to reach the prize.
What female heart can gold despise?
   What Cat's averse to fish?

Presumptuous Maid! with looks intent   25
Again she stretch'd, again she bent,
   Nor knew the gulf between.

(Malignant Fate sat by, and smil'd)
The slipp'ry verge her feet beguil'd,
   She tumbled headlong in.   30

Eight times emerging from the flood
She mew'd to ev'ry watry God,
   Some speedy aid to send.
No Dolphin came, no Nereid stirr'd :
Nor cruel *Tom*, nor *Susan* heard.   35
   A Fav'rite has no friend !

From hence, ye Beauties, undeceiv'd,
Know, one false step is ne'er retriev'd,
   And be with caution bold.
Not all that tempts your wand'ring eyes   40
And heedless hearts, is lawful prize ;
   Nor all, that glisters, gold.

VI.

THE ALLIANCE OF EDUCATION AND GOVERNMENT.

A FRAGMENT.

Commentary.[1]

THE Author's subject being (as we have seen) *The
necessary Alliance between a good Form of Government and
a good Mode of Education, in order to produce the Happiness of Mankind,* the Poem opens with two similes ; an
uncommon kind of exordium : but which I suppose the 5
Poet intentionally chose, to intimate the analogical method
he meant to pursue in his subsequent reasonings. 1st,

[1] "On carefully reviewing the scattered papers in prose which he
writ, as hints for his own use in the prosecution of this work, I think
it best to form part of them into a kind of commentary." — *Mason.*

He asserts that men without education are like sickly
plants in a cold or barren soil, (line 1 to 5, and 8 to 12 ;)
and, 2dly, he compares them, when unblest with a just 10
and well regulated government, to plants that will not
blossom or bear fruit in an unkindly and inclement air
(l. 5 to 9, and l. 13 to 22). Having thus laid down
the two propositions he means to prove, he begins by
examining into the characteristics which (taking a general 15
view of mankind) all men have in common one with
another (l. 22 to 39) ; they covet pleasure and avoid pain
(l. 31) ; they feel gratitude for benefits (l. 34) ; they desire
to avenge wrongs, which they effect either by force or
cunning (l. 35) ; they are linked to each other by their 20
common feelings, and participate in sorrow and in joy (l.
36, 37). If then all the human species agree in so many
moral particulars, whence arises the diversity of national
characters ? This question the Poet puts at l. 38, and
dilates upon to l. 64. Why, says he, have some nations 25
shewn a propensity to commerce and industry ; others to
war and rapine ; others to ease and pleasure ? (l. 42 to
46) Why have the Northern people overspread, in all
ages, and prevailed over the Southern ? (l. 46 to 58) Why
has Asia been, time out of mind, the seat of despotism, 30
and Europe that of freedom ? (l. 59 to 64). Are we from
these instances to imagine men necessarily enslaved to
the inconveniences of the climate where they were born ?
(l. 64 to 72) Or are we not rather to suppose there is a
natural strength in the human mind, that is able to van- 35
quish and break through them ? (l. 72 to 84) It is con-
fest, however, that men receive an early tincture from the
situation they are placed in, and the climate which produces them (l. 84 to 88). Thus the inhabitants of the
mountains, inured to labour and patience, are naturally 40
trained to war (l. 88 to 96) ; while those of the plain

are more open to any attack, and softened by ease and
plenty (l. 96 to 99). Again, the Ægyptians, from the
nature of their situation, might be the inventors of home-
navigation, from a necessity of keeping up an intercourse 45
between their towns during the inundation of the Nile
(l. 99 to . . .). These persons would naturally have the
first turn to commerce, who inhabited a barren coast like
the Tyrians, and were persecuted by some neighbouring
tyrant ; or were drove to take refuge on some shoals, like 50
the Venetian and Hollander ; their discovery of some
rich island, in the infancy of the world, described. The
Tartar hardened to war by his rigorous climate and
pastoral life, and by his disputes for water and herbage
in a country without land-marks, as also by skirmishes 55
between his rival clans, was consequently fitted to
conquer his rich Southern neighbours, whom ease and
luxury had enervated : Yet this is no proof that liberty
and valour may not exist in Southern climes, since the
Syrians and Carthaginians gave noble instances of both ; 60
and the Arabians carried their conquests as far as the
Tartars. Rome also (for many centuries) repulsed those
very nations, which, when she grew weak, at length
demolished her extensive Empire. * * *

ESSAY I.

. . . Πόταγ', ὦ 'γαθε ; τὰν γὰρ ἀοιδὰν
Οὔτι πω εἰς Ἀΐδαν γε τὸν ἐκλελάθοντα φυλαξεῖς.
Theocritus, Id. I. 63.

As sickly Plants betray a niggard earth,
Whose barren bosom starves her gen'rous birth,
Nor genial warmth, nor genial juice retains
Their roots to feed, and fill their verdant veins :

And as in climes, where Winter holds his reign, 5
The soil, tho' fertile, will not teem in vain,
Forbids her gems to swell, her shades to rise,
Nor trusts her blossoms to the churlish skies :
So draw Mankind in vain the vital airs,
Unform'd, unfriended, by those kindly cares, 10
That health and vigour to the soul impart,
Spread the young thought, and warm the opening heart :
So fond Instruction on the growing powers
Of Nature idly lavishes her stores,
If equal Justice with unclouded face 15
Smile not indulgent on the rising race,
And scatter with a free, tho' frugal hand
Light golden showers of plenty o'er the land :
But Tyranny has fix'd her empire there
To check their tender hopes with chilling fear, 20
And blast the blooming promise of the year.
    This spacious animated scene survey
From where the rolling Orb, that gives the day,
His sable sons with nearer course surrounds
To either pole, and life's remotest bounds. 25
How rude soe'er th' exteriour form we find,
Howe'er opinion tinge the varied mind,
Alike, to all the kind, impartial Heav'n
The sparks of truth and happiness has giv'n :
With sense to feel, with memory to retain, . 30
They follow pleasure, and they fly from pain ;
Their judgment mends the plan their fancy draws,
Th' event presages, and explores the cause.
The soft returns of gratitude they know,
By fraud elude, by force repell the foe, 35
While mutual wishes, mutual woes endear
The social smile, and sympathetic tear.

Say, then, thro' ages by what fate confin'd
To different climes seem different souls assign'd?
How measur'd laws and philosophic ease   40
Fix, and improve the polish'd arts of peace ;
There industry and gain their vigils keep,
Command the winds, and tame th' unwilling deep.
Here force and hardy deeds of blood prevail ;
There languid Pleasure sighs in every gale.   45
Oft o'er the trembling nations from afar
Has Scythia breath'd the living cloud of war ;
And, where the deluge burst, with sweepy sway
Their arms, their kings, their gods were roll'd away.
As oft have issued, host impelling host,   50
The blue-eyed myriads from the Baltick coast.
The prostrate South to the Destroyer yields
Her boasted titles, and her golden fields :
With grim delight the Brood of winter view
A brighter day, and Heav'ns of azure hue,   55
Scent the new fragrance of the breathing rose,
And quaff the pendent vintage as it grows.
Proud of the yoke, and pliant to the rod,
Why yet does Asia dread a monarch's nod,
While European freedom still withstands   60
Th' encroaching tide, that drowns her lessening lands ;
And sees far off with an indignant groan
Her native plains, and Empires once her own.
Can opener skies and suns of fiercer flame
O'erpower the fire, that animates our frame ;   65
As lamps, that shed at eve a chearful ray,
Fade and expire beneath the eye of day?
Need we the influence of the Northern star
To string our nerves and steel our hearts to war?
And, where the face of nature laughs around,   70
Must sick'ning virtue fly the tainted ground?

Unmanly thought! what seasons can controul,
What fancied zone can circumscribe the soul,
Who, conscious of the source from whence she springs,
By reason's light, on resolution's wings,   75
Spite of her frail companion, dauntless goes
O'er Libya's deserts and thro' Zembla's snows?
She bids each slumb'ring energy awake,
Another touch, another temper take,
Suspends th' inferior laws, that rule our clay: 80
The stubborn elements confess her sway;
Their little wants, their low desires, refine,
And raise the mortal to a height divine.

  Not but the human fabric from the birth
Imbibes a flavour of its parent earth.   85
As various tracts enforce a various toil,
The manners speak the idiom of their soil.
An iron-race the mountain-cliffs maintain,
Foes to the gentler genius of the plain:
For where unwearied sinews must be found   90
With side-long plough to quell the flinty ground,
To turn the torrent's swift-descending flood,
To brave the savage rushing from the wood,
What wonder, if to patient valour train'd
They guard with spirit, what by strength they gain'd?   95
And while their rocky ramparts round they see,
The rough abode of want and liberty,
(As lawless force from confidence will grow)
Insult the plenty of the vales below?
What wonder, in the sultry climes, that spread   100
Where Nile redundant o'er his summer-bed
From his broad bosom life and verdure flings,
And broods o'er Ægypt with his wat'ry wings,
If with advent'rous oar and ready sail
The dusky people drive before the gale;   105

Or on frail floats to distant cities ride,
That rise and glitter o'er the ambient tide.

*   *   *

"I find also among these papers a single couplet much to
beautiful to be lost, though the place where he meant to introduce
it cannot be ascertained." — *Mason*.

When Love could teach a monarch to be wise,
And Gospel-light first dawn'd from BULLEN's Eyes.

VII.

ELEGY

WRITTEN IN A COUNTRY CHURCH-YARD.

THE Curfew tolls [1] the knell of parting day,
     The lowing herd wind slowly o'er the lea,
The plowman homeward plods his weary way,
     And leaves the world to darkness and to me.

Now fades the glimmering landscape on the sight,   5
     And all the air a solemn stillness holds,
Save where the beetle wheels his droning flight,
     And drowsy tinklings lull the distant folds;

Save that from yonder ivy-mantled tow'r
     The mopeing owl does to the moon complain   10
Of such, as wand'ring near her secret bow'r,
     Molest her ancient solitary reign.

---

[1] ———— squilla di lontano,
Che paia 'l giorno pianger, che si muore.
           Dante. *Purgat. l.* 8.

Beneath those rugged elms, that yew-tree's shade,
    Where heaves the turf in many a mould'ring heap,
Each in his narrow cell for ever laid,   15
    The rude Forefathers of the hamlet sleep.

The breezy call of incense-breathing Morn,
    The swallow twitt'ring from the straw-built shed,
The cock's shrill clarion, or the echoing horn,
    No more shall rouse them from their lowly bed.   20

For them no more the blazing hearth shall burn,
    Or busy housewife ply her evening care :
No children run to lisp their sire's return,
    Or climb his knees the envied kiss to share.

Oft did the harvest to their sickle yield,   25
    Their furrow oft the stubborn glebe has broke ;
How jocund did they drive their team afield !
    How bow'd the woods beneath their sturdy stroke !

Let not Ambition mock their useful toil,
    Their homely joys, and destiny obscure ;   30
Nor Grandeur hear with a disdainful smile,
    The short and simple annals of the poor.

The boast of heraldry, the pomp of pow'r,
    And all that beauty, all that wealth e'er gave,
Awaits alike th' inevitable hour.   35
    The paths of glory lead but to the grave.

Nor you, ye Proud, impute to These the fault,
    If Mem'ry o'er their Tomb no Trophies raise,
Where thro' the long-drawn isle and fretted vault
    The pealing anthem swells the note of praise.   40

Can storied urn or animated bust
　Back to its mansion call the fleeting breath?
Can Honour's voice provoke the silent dust,
　Or Flatt'ry sooth the dull cold ear of Death?

Perhaps in this neglected spot is laid   45
　Some heart once pregnant with celestial fire;
Hands, that the rod of empire might have sway'd,
　Or wak'd to extasy the living lyre.

But Knowledge to their eyes her ample page
　Rich with the spoils of time did ne'er unroll;   50
Chill Penury repress'd their noble rage,
　And froze the genial current of the soul.

Full many a gem of purest ray serene,
　The dark unfathom'd caves of ocean bear :
Full many a flower is born to blush unseen,   55
　And waste its sweetness on the desert air.

Some village-Hampden, that with dauntless breast
　The little Tyrant of his fields withstood;
Some mute inglorious Milton here may rest,
　Some Cromwell guiltless of his country's blood.   60

Th' applause of list'ning senates to command,
　The threats of pain and ruin to despise,
To scatter plenty o'er a smiling land,
　And read their hist'ry in a nation's eyes,

Their lot forbad : nor circumscrib'd alone   65
　Their growing virtues, but their crimes confin'd;
Forbad to wade through slaughter to a throne,
　And shut the gates of mercy on mankind,

The struggling pangs of conscious truth to hide,
    To quench the blushes of ingenuous shame,   70
Or heap the shrine of Luxury and Pride
    With incense kindled at the Muse's flame.

Far from the madding crowd's ignoble strife,
    Their sober wishes never learn'd to stray ;
Along the cool sequester'd vale of life   75
    They kept the noiseless tenor of their way.

Yet ev'n these bones from insult to protect
    Some frail memorial still erected nigh,
With uncouth rhimes and shapeless sculpture deck'd,
    Implores the passing tribute of a sigh.   80

Their name, their years, spelt by th' unletter'd muse,
    The place of fame and elegy supply :
And many a holy text around she strews,
    That teach the rustic moralist to die.

For who to dumb Forgetfulness a prey,   85
    This pleasing anxious being e'er resign'd,
Left the warm precincts of the chearful day,
    Nor cast one longing ling'ring look behind ?

On some fond breast the parting soul relies,
    Some pious drops the closing eye requires ;   90
Ev'n from the tomb the voice of Nature cries,
    Ev'n in our Ashes live their wonted Fires.[1]

> [1] Ch' i veggio nel pensier, dolce mio fuoco,
>   Fredda una lingua, & due begli occhi chiusi
>   Rimaner doppo noi pien di faville.
>   *Petrarch. Son.* 169.

For thee, who mindful of th' unhonour'd Dead
    Dost in these lines their artless tale relate ;
If chance, by lonely contemplation led,   95
    Some kindred Spirit shall inquire thy fate,

Haply some hoary-headed Swain may say,
    ' Oft have we seen him at the peep of dawn
' Brushing with hasty steps the dews away
    ' To meet the sun upon the upland lawn.   100

' There at the foot of yonder nodding beech
    ' That wreathes its old fantastic roots so high,
' His listless length at noontide would he stretch,
    ' And pore upon the brook that babbles by.

Hard by yon wood, now smiling as in scorn,   105
    ' Mutt'ring his wayward fancies he would rove,
' Now drooping, woeful wan, like one forlorn,
    ' Or craz'd with care, or cross'd in hopeless love.

' One morn I miss'd him on the custom'd hill,
    ' Along the heath and near his fav'rite tree ;   110
' Another came ; nor yet beside the rill,
    ' Nor up the lawn, nor at the wood was he ;

' The next with dirges due in sad array
    ' Slow thro' the church-way path we saw him born.
' Approach and read (for thou can'st read) the lay, 115
    ' Grav'd on the stone beneath yon aged thorn.'

THE EPITAPH.

HERE rests his head upon the lap of Earth
    A Youth to Fortune and to Fame unknown.
Fair Science frown'd not on his humble birth,
    And Melancholy mark'd him for her own.   120

Large was his bounty, and his soul sincere,
   Heav'n did a recompence as largely send:
He gave to Mis'ry all he had, a tear,
   He gain'd from Heav'n ('twas all he wish'd) a friend.

No farther seek his merits to disclose,   125
   Or draw his frailties from their dread abode,
(There they alike in trembling hope repose,)[1]
   The bosom of his Father and his God.

VIII.

A LONG STORY.

In Britain's Isle, no matter where,
   An ancient pile of building stands :
The Huntingdons and Hattons there
   Employ'd the power of Fairy hands

To raise the cieling's fretted height,   5
   Each pannel in achievements cloathing,
Rich windows that exclude the light,
   And passages, that lead to nothing.

Full oft within the spatious walls,
   When he had fifty winters o'er him,   10
My grave [2] Lord-Keeper led the Brawls :
   The Seal, and Maces, danc'd before him.

His bushy beard, and shoe-strings green,
   His high-crown'd hat, and sattin-doublet,
Mov'd the stout heart of England's Queen,   15
   Tho' Pope and Spaniard could not trouble it.

[1] ——— paventosa speme.
Petrarch. Son. 114.
[2] Hatton, prefer'd by Queen Elizabeth for his graceful Person and fine Dancing.

What, in the very first beginning !
    Shame of the versifying tribe !
Your Hist'ry whither are you spinning?
    Can you do nothing but describe?   20

A House there is, (and that's enough)
    From whence one fatal morning issues
A brace of Warriors, not in buff,
    But rustling in their silks and tissues.

The first came cap-a-pee from France,   25
    Her conqu'ring destiny fulfilling,
Whom meaner Beauties eye askance,
    And vainly ape her art of killing.

The other Amazon kind Heaven
    Had arm'd with spirit, wit, and satire :   30
But COBHAM had the polish given,
    And tip'd her arrows with good-nature.

To celebrate her eyes, her air ——
    Coarse panegyricks would but teaze her.
Melissa is her Nom de Guerre.   35
    Alas, who would not wish to please her !

With bonnet blue and capucine,
    And aprons long they hid their armour,
And veil'd their weapons bright and keen
    In pity to the country-farmer.   40

Fame in the shape of Mr. P——t
    (By this time all the Parish know it)
Had told, that thereabouts there lurk'd
    A wicked Imp they call a Poet,

Who prowl'd the country far and near,   45
    Bewitch'd the children of the peasants,
Dried up the cows, and lam'd the deer,
    And suck'd the eggs, and kill'd the pheasants.

My Lady heard their joint petition,
    Swore by her coronet and ermine,   50
She'd issue out her high commission
    To rid the manour of such vermin.

The Heroines undertook the task,
    Thro' lanes unknown, o'er stiles they ventur'd,
Rap'd at the door, nor stay'd to ask,   55
    But bounce into the parlour enter'd.

The trembling family they daunt,
    They flirt, they sing, they laugh, they tattle,
Rummage his Mother, pinch his Aunt,
    And up stairs in a whirlwind rattle.   60

Each hole and cupboard they explore,
    Each creek and cranny of his chamber,
Run hurry-skurry round the floor,
    And o'er the bed and tester clamber,

Into the Drawers and China pry,   65
    Papers and books, a huge Imbroglio !
Under a tea-cup he might lie,
    Or creased, like dogs-ears, in a folio.

On the first marching of the troops
    The Muses, hopeless of his pardon,   70
Convey'd him underneath their hoops
    To a small closet in the garden.

So Rumor says.   (Who will, believe.)
   But that they left the door a-jarr,
Where, safe and laughing in his sleeve,   75
   He heard the distant din of war.

Short was his joy.   He little knew,
   The power of Magick was no fable.
Out of the window, whisk, they flew,
   But left a spell upon the table.   80

The words too eager to unriddle
   The Poet felt a strange disorder :
Transparent birdlime form'd the middle,
   And chains invisible the border.

So cunning was the Apparatus,   85
   The powerful pothooks did so move him,
That, will he, nill he, to the Great-house
   He went, as if the Devil drove him.

Yet on his way (no sign of grace,
   For folks in fear are apt to pray)   90
To Phœbus he prefer'd his case,
   And beg'd his aid that dreadful day.

The Godhead would have back'd his quarrel,
   But with a blush on recollection
Own'd, that his quiver and his laurel   95
   'Gainst four such eyes were no protection.

The Court was sate, the Culprit there,
   Forth from their gloomy mansions creeping
The Lady *Janes* and *Joans* repair,
   And from the gallery stand peeping :   100

Such as in silence of the night
    Come (sweep) along some winding entry
(*Styack*[1] has often seen the sight)
    Or at the chappel-door stand sentry ;

In peaked hoods and mantles tarnish'd,   105
    Sour visages, enough to scare ye,
High Dames of honour once, that garnish'd
    The drawing-room of fierce Queen Mary !

The Peeress comes.   The Audience stare,
    And doff their hats with due submission ;   110
She curtsies, as she takes her chair,
    To all the People of condition.

The Bard with many an artful fib,
    Had in imagination fenc'd him,
Disproved the arguments of *Squib*,[2]   115
    And all that *Groom*[3] could urge against him.

But soon his rhetorick forsook him,
    When he the solemn hall had seen ;
A sudden fit of ague shook him,
    He stood as mute as poor *Macleane*.[4]   120

Yet something he was heard to mutter,
    ' How in the park beneath an old-tree
'(Without design to hurt the butter,
    ' Or any malice to the poultry,)

' He once or twice had pen'd a sonnet ;   125
    ' Yet hoped, that he might save his bacon :
' Numbers would give their oaths upon it,
    ' He ne'er was for a conj'rer taken.

[1] The House-Keeper.
[2] Groom of the Chambers.
[3] The Steward.
[4] A famous Highwayman hang'd the week before.

The ghostly Prudes with hagged face
    Already had condemn'd the sinner.   130
My Lady rose, and with a grace ——
    She smiled, and bid him come to dinner.

' Jesu-Maria ! Madam Bridget,
  ' Why, what can the Vicountess mean ?
(Cried the square Hoods in woful fidget)   135
  ' The times are alter'd quite and clean !

' Decorum's turn'd to mere civility ;
  ' Her air and all her manners shew it.
' Commend me to her affability !
  ' Speak to a Commoner and Poet !   140

[*Here* 500 *Stanzas are lost.*]

And so God save our noble King,
    And guard us from long-winded Lubbers,
That to eternity would sing,
    And keep my Lady from her Rubbers.

IX.

THE PROGRESS OF POESY.

A PINDARIC ODE.

Φωνᾶντα συνετοῖσιν · ἐς
Δὲ τὸ πᾶν ἑρμηνέων χατίζει.
                Pindar, Olymp. II.

ADVERTISEMENT.

  When the Author first published this and the following Ode, he
was advised, even by his Friends, to subjoin some few explanatory
Notes; but had too much respect for the understanding of his
Readers to take that liberty.

I. 1.

Awake, Æolian lyre, awake,[1]
And give to rapture all thy trembling strings.
From Helicon's harmonious springs
A thousand rills their mazy progress take:
The laughing flowers, that round them blow,   5
Drink life and fragrance as they flow.
Now the rich stream of music winds along
Deep, majestic, smooth, and strong,
Thro' verdant vales, and Ceres' golden reign:
Now rowling down the steep amain,   10
Headlong, impetuous, see it pour:
The rocks, and nodding groves rebellow to the roar.

I. 2.

Oh! Sovereign of the willing soul,[2]
Parent of sweet and solemn-breathing airs,
Enchanting shell! the sullen Cares,   15
And frantic Passions hear thy soft controul.
On Thracia's hills the Lord of War,
Has curb'd the fury of his car,

[1] Awake, my glory: awake, lute and harp.
                 David's Psalms.

Pindar styles his own poetry, with its musical accompanyments, Αἰολη`ὶς μολπὴ, Αἰόλιδες χορδαὶ, Αἰολίδων πνοαὶ αὐλῶν, Æolian song, Æolian strings, the breath of the Æolian flute.

The subject and simile, as usual with Pindar, are united. The various sources of poetry, which gives life and lustre to all it touches, are here described; its quiet majestic progress enriching every subject (otherwise dry and barren) with a pomp of diction and luxuriant harmony of numbers; and its more rapid and irresistible course, when swoln and hurried away by the conflict of tumultuous passions.

[2] Power of harmony to calm the turbulent sallies of the soul. The thoughts are borrowed from the first Pythian of Pindar.

And drop'd his thirsty lance at thy command.
Perching on the scept'red hand [1]   20
Of Jove, thy magic lulls the feather'd king
With ruffled plumes, and flagging wing :
Quench'd in dark clouds of slumber lie
The terror of his beak, and light'nings of his eye.

I. 3.

Thee the voice, the dance, obey,[2]   25
Temper'd to thy warbled lay.
O'er Idalia's velvet-green
The rosy-crowned Loves are seen
On Cytherea's day
With antic Sports, and blue-eyed Pleasures,   30
Frisking light in frolic measures ;
Now pursuing, now retreating,
Now in circling troops they meet :
To brisk notes in cadence beating
Glance their many-twinkling feet.[3]   35
Slow melting strains their Queen's approach declare :
    Where'er she turns the Graces homage pay.
With arms sublime, that float upon the air,
    In gliding state she wins her easy way :
O'er her warm cheek, and rising bosom, move   40
The bloom of young Desire, and purple light of
        Love.[4]

[1] This is a weak imitation of some incomparable lines in the same
Ode.

[2] Power of harmony to produce all the graces of motion in the
body.

[3] Μαρμαρυγὰς θηεῖτο ποδῶν · θαύμαζε δὲ θυμῷ.

Homer.   *Od.* Θ.

[4] Λάμπει δ' ἐπὶ πορφυρέῃσι
Παρείῃσι φῶς ἔρωτος.

Phrynichus, apud Athenæum.

II. 1.

Man's feeble race what Ills await,[1]
Labour, and Penury, the racks of Pain,
Disease, and Sorrow's weeping train,
And Death, sad refuge from the storms of Fate !   45
The fond complaint, my Song, disprove,
And justify the laws of Jove.
Say, has he giv'n in vain the heav'nly Muse?
Night, and all her sickly dews,
Her Spectres wan, and Birds of boding cry,   50
He gives to range the dreary sky :
Till down the eastern cliffs afar [2]
Hyperion's march they spy, and glitt'ring shafts of
      war.

II. 2.

In [3] climes beyond the solar [4] road,
Where shaggy forms o'er ice-built mountains roam,   55
The Muse has broke the twilight-gloom
To chear the shiv'ring Native's dull abode.

[1] To compensate the real and imaginary ills of life, the Muse was given to Mankind by the same Providence that sends the Day by its chearful presence to dispel the gloom and terrors of the Night.

[2] Or seen the Morning's well-appointed Star
Come marching up the eastern hills afar.

Cowley.

[3] Extensive influence of poetic Genius over the remotest and most uncivilized nations : its connection with liberty, and the virtues that naturally attend on it.   (See the Erse, Norwegian, and Welch Fragments, the Lapland and American songs.)

[4] "Extra anni solisque vias."

Virgil.

"Tutta lontana dal camin del sole."

Petrarch, Canzon 2.

And oft, beneath the od'rous shade
Of Chili's boundless forests laid,
She deigns to hear the savage Youth repeat   60
In loose numbers wildly sweet
Their feather-cinctured Chiefs, and dusky Loves.
Her track, where'er the Goddess roves,
Glory pursue, and generous Shame,
Th' unconquerable Mind, and Freedom's holy flame. 65

II. 3.

Woods, that wave o'er Delphi's steep,[1]
Isles, that crown th' Ægean deep,
Fields, that cool Ilissus laves,
Or where Mæander's amber waves
In lingering Lab'rinths creep,   70
How do your tuneful Echo's languish,
Mute, but to the voice of Anguish?
Where each old poetic Mountain
Inspiration breath'd around:
Ev'ry shade and hallow'd Fountain   75
Murmur'd deep a solemn sound:
Till the sad Nine in Greece's evil hour
Left their Parnassus for the Latian plains.
Alike they scorn the pomp of tyrant-Power,
And coward Vice, that revels in her chains.   80
When Latium had her lofty spirit lost,
They sought, oh Albion! next thy sea-encircled coast.

[1] Progress of Poetry from Greece to Italy, and from Italy to
England.   Chaucer was not unacquainted with the writings of
Dante or of Petrarch.   The Earl of Surrey and Sir Tho. Wyatt
had travelled in Italy, and formed their taste there; Spenser
imitated the Italian writers; Milton improved on them: but this
School expired soon after the Restoration, and a new one arose on
the French model, which has subsisted ever since.

III. 1.

Far from the sun and summer-gale,
In thy green lap was Nature's [1] Darling laid,
What time, where lucid Avon stray'd,   85
To Him the mighty Mother did unveil
Her aweful face : The dauntless Child
Stretch'd forth his little arms, and smiled.
This pencil take (she said) whose colours clear
Richly paint the vernal year :   90
Thine too these golden keys, immortal Boy !
This can unlock the gates of Joy ;
Of Horrour that, and thrilling Fears,
Or ope the sacred source of sympathetic Tears.

III. 2.

Nor second He,[2] that rode sublime   95
Upon the seraph-wings of Extasy,
The secrets of th' Abyss to spy.
He pass'd the flaming bounds of Place and Time :[3]
The living Throne, the saphire-blaze,[4]
Where Angels tremble, while they gaze,   100
He saw ; but blasted with excess of light,
Closed his eyes in endless night.[5]

[1] Shakespear.
[2] Milton.

[3] "—— flammantia moenia mundi."
Lucretius.

[4] For the spirit of the living creature was in the wheels. — And
above the firmament, that was over their heads, was the likeness of
a throne, as the appearance of a saphire-stone. — This was the
appearance of the glory of the Lord. — *Ezekiel* i. 20, 26, 28.

[5] Ὀφθαλμῶν μὲν ἄμερσε· δίδου δ' ἡδεῖαν ἀοιδήν.
Homer. *Od.*

Behold, where Dryden's less presumptuous car,
Wide o'er the fields of Glory bear
Two Coursers of ethereal race,[1]   105
With necks in thunder cloath'd, and long-resounding
    pace.[2]

III. 3.

Hark, his hands the lyre explore !
Bright-eyed Fancy hovering o'er
Scatters from her pictur'd urn
    Thoughts, that breath, and words, that burn.[3] 110
But ah ! 'tis heard no more [4] ————
Oh ! Lyre divine, what daring Spirit
Wakes thee now? tho' he inherit
Nor the pride, nor ample pinion,
That the Theban Eagle bear [5]   115
Sailing with supreme dominion
Thro' the azure deep of air :

[1] Meant to express the stately march and sounding energy of Dryden's rhimes.

[2] Hast thou cloathed his neck with thunder?

Job.

[3] Words, that weep, and tears, that speak.

Cowley.

[4] We have had in our language no other odes of the sublime kind, than that of Dryden on St. Cecilia's day : for Cowley (who had his merit) yet wanted judgment, style, and harmony, for such a task. That of Pope is not worthy of so great a man. Mr. Mason indeed of late days has touched the true chords, and with a masterly hand, in some of his Choruses, — above all in the last of Caractacus,

Hark ! heard ye not yon footstep dread? etc.

[5] Διὸς πρὸς ὄρνιχα θεῖον. Olymp. 2. Pindar compares himself to that bird, and his enemies to ravens that croak and clamour in vain below, while it pursues its flight, regardless of their noise.

Yet oft before his infant eyes would run
Such forms, as glitter in the Muse's ray
With orient hues, unborrow'd of the Sun :   120
Yet shall he mount, and keep his distant way
Beyond the limits of a vulgar fate,
Beneath the Good how far — but far above the Great.

X.

ODE ON THE PLEASURE ARISING FROM VICISSITUDE.

Now the golden Morn aloft
    Waves her dew-bespangled wing,
With vermeil-cheek and whisper soft
    She woo's the tardy spring ;
Till April starts, and calls around   5
The sleeping fragrance from the ground ;
And lightly o'er the living scene
Scatters his freshest, tenderest green.

New-born flocks, in rustic dance,
    Frisking ply their feeble feet ;   10
Forgetful of their wintry trance,
    The Birds his presence greet ;
But chief, the Sky-lark warbles high
His trembling thrilling ecstasy ;
And, lessening from the dazzled sight,   15
Melts into air and liquid light.

Rise, my soul ! on wings of fire,
    Rise the rapturous choir among ;
Hark ! 'tis Nature strikes the lyre,
    And leads the general song.   20

*   *   *

Yesterday the sullen year
 Saw the snowy whirlwind fly ;
Mute was the musick of the air,
 The Herd stood drooping by ;
Their raptures now that wildly flow,   25
No yesterday, nor morrow know ;
'Tis man alone that Joy descries
With forward and reverted eyes.

Smiles on past Misfortune's brow
 Soft Reflection's hand can trace ;   30
And o'er the cheek of Sorrow throw
 A melancholy grace ;
While Hope prolongs our happier hour,
Or deepest shades, that dimly lower
And blacken round our weary way,   35
Gilds with a gleam of distant day.

Still, where rosy Pleasure leads,
 See a kindred Grief pursue ;
Behind the steps that Misery treads,
 Approaching Comfort view ;   40
The hues of Bliss more brightly glow,
Chastised by sabler tints of woe ;
And blended form, with artful strife,
The strength and harmony of Life.

See the Wretch, that long has tost   45
 On the thorny bed of Pain,
At length repair his vigour lost,
 And breathe and walk again ;
The meanest flowret of the vale,
The simplest note that swells the gale,   50
The common Sun, the air, the skies,
To him are opening Paradise.

Humble Quiet builds her cell,
    Near the source whence Pleasure flows ;
She eyes the clear chrystalline well,   55
    And tastes it as it goes.

       *   *   *

XI.

THE BARD.

A PINDARIC ODE.

ADVERTISEMENT.

The following Ode is founded on a Tradition current in Wales, that EDWARD THE FIRST, when he compleated the conquest of that country, ordered all the Bards, that fell into his hands, to be put to death.

I. I.

  'Ruin seize thee, ruthless King !
'Confusion on thy banners wait,
'Tho' fann'd by Conquest's crimson wing
'They mock the air with idle state.[1]
'Helm, nor Hauberk's [2] twisted mail,   5
'Nor even thy virtues, Tyrant, shall avail
'To save thy secret soul from nightly fears,
'From Cambria's curse, from Cambria's tears !'
Such were the sounds, that o'er the crested [3] pride
    Of the first Edward scatter'd wild dismay,   10

[1] Mocking the air with colours idly spread.
Shakespear's King John.

[2] The Hauberk was a texture of steel ringlets, or rings interwoven, forming a coat of mail, that sate close to the body, and adapted itself to every motion.

[3] The crested adder's pride.
Dryden's Indian Queen.

As down the steep of Snowdon's[1] shaggy side
He wound with toilsome march his long array.
Stout Glo'ster[2] stood aghast in speechless trance :
To arms! cried Mortimer,[3] and couch'd his quiv'ring
    lance.

I. 2.

  On a rock, whose haughty brow   15
Frowns o'er old Conway's foaming flood,
Robed in the sable garb of woe,
With haggard eyes the Poet stood ;
(Loose his beard, and hoary hair[4]
Stream'd, like a meteor, to the troubled air)[5]   20
And with a Master's hand, and Prophet's fire,
Struck the deep sorrows of his lyre.

[1] *Snowdon* was a name given by the Saxons to that mountainous
tract, which the Welch themselves call *Craigian-eryri :* it included
all the highlands of Caernarvonshire and Merionethshire, as far east
as the river Conway.   R. Hygden speaking of the castle of Conway
built by King Edward the first, says, " Ad ortum amnis Conway ad
clivum montis Erery " ; and Matthew of Westminster, (ad ann.
1283), " Apud Aberconway ad pedes montis Snowdoniæ fecit erigi
castrum forte."

[2] Gilbert de Clare, surnamed the Red, Earl of Gloucester and
Hertford, son-in-law to King Edward.

[3] Edmond de Mortimer, Lord of Wigmore.

They both were *Lords-Marchers*, whose lands lay on the borders
of Wales, and probably accompanied the king in this expedition.

[4] The image was taken from a well-known picture of Raphaël,
representing the Supreme Being in the vision of Ezekiel : there are
two of these paintings (both believed original), one at Florence, the
other at Paris.

[5] Shone, like a meteor, streaming to the wind.
                                              Milton's Paradise Lost.

' Hark, how each giant-oak, and desert cave,
' Sighs to the torrent's aweful voice beneath!
' O'er thee, oh King! their hundred arms they wave,   25
' Revenge on thee in hoarser murmurs breath ;
' Vocal no more, since Cambria's fatal day,
' To high-born Hoel's harp, or soft Llewellyn's lay.

I. 3.

' Cold is Cadwallo's tongue,
' That hush'd the stormy main :   30
' Brave Urien sleeps upon his craggy bed :
' Mountains, ye mourn in vain
' Modred, whose magic song
' Made huge Plinlimmon bow his cloud-top'd head.
' On dreary Arvon's shore they lie,[1]   35
' Smear'd with gore, and ghastly pale :
' Far, far aloof th' affrighted ravens sail ;
' The famish'd Eagle[2] screams, and passes by.
' Dear lost companions of my tuneful art,
' Dear, as the light that visits these sad eyes, [3]   40
' Dear, as the ruddy drops that warm my heart,[3]
' Ye died amidst your dying country's cries —
' No more I weep.   They do not sleep.

[1] The shores of Caernarvonshire opposite to the isle of Anglesey.
[2] Cambden and others observe, that eagles used annually to build their aerie among the rocks of Snowdon, which from thence (as some think) were named by the Welch *Craigian-eryri,* or the crags of the eagles.   At this day (I am told) the highest point of Snowdon is called *the eagle's nest.*   That bird is certainly no stranger to this island, as the Scots, and the people of Cumberland, Westmoreland, etc. can testify : it even has built its nest in the Peak of Derbyshire. (See Willoughby's Ornithol. published by Ray.)

[3] As dear to me as are the ruddy drops,
    That visit my sad heart. — *Shakesp. Jul. Cæsar.*

'On yonder cliffs, a griesly band,
'I see them sit, they linger yet,   45
'Avengers of their native land :
'With me in dreadful harmony they join,[1]
'And weave [1] with bloody hands the tissue of thy line.'

II. 1.

  "Weave the warp, and weave the woof,
"The winding-sheet of Edward's race.   50
"Give ample room, and verge enough
"The characters of hell to trace.
"Mark the year, and mark the night,
"When Severn shall re-eccho with affright [2]
"The shrieks of death, thro' Berkley's roofs that ring,   55
"Shrieks of an agonizing King !
"She-Wolf [3] of France, with unrelenting fangs,
"That tear'st the bowels of thy mangled Mate,
"From thee be born, who o'er thy country hangs [4]
"The scourge of Heav'n.   What Terrors round him wait ! 60
"Amazement in his van, with Flight combined,
"And sorrow's faded form, and solitude behind.

II. 2.

   " Mighty Victor, mighty Lord,
"Low on his funeral couch he lies ! [5]
"No pitying heart, no eye, afford   65
"A tear to grace his obsequies.

---

[1] See the Norwegian Ode, that follows.

[2] Edward the Second, cruelly butchered in Berkley-Castle.

[3] Isabel of France, Edward the Second's adulterous Queen.

[4] Triumphs of Edward the Third in France.

[5] Death of that King, abandoned by his Children, and even
robbed in his last moments by his Courtiers and his Mistress.

" Is the sable Warriour [1] fled?
" Thy son is gone.   He rests among the Dead.
" The Swarm, that in thy noon-tide beam were born?
" Gone to salute the rising Morn.   70
" Fair laughs [2] the Morn, and soft the Zephyr blows,
" While proudly riding o'er the azure realm'
" In gallant trim the gilded Vessel goes ;
" Youth on the prow, and Pleasure at the helm ;
" Regardless of the sweeping Whirlwind's sway,   75
" That, hush'd in grim repose, expects his evening-prey.

II. 3.

  " Fill high the sparkling bowl, [3]
" The rich repast prepare,
" Reft of a crown, he yet may share the feast :
" Close by the regal chair   80
" Fell Thirst and Famine scowl
" A baleful smile upon their baffled Guest.
" Heard ye the din of battle [4] bray,
" Lance to lance, and horse to horse ?
" Long Years of havock urge their destined course,   85
" And thro' the kindred squadrons mow their way.
" Ye Towers of Julius, [5] London's lasting shame,
" With many a foul and midnight murther fed,

[1] Edward, the Black Prince, dead some time before his Father.

[2] Magnificence of Richard the Second's reign.   See Froissard, and other contemporary Writers.

[3] Richard the Second, (as we are told by Archbishop Scroop and the confederate Lords in their manifesto, by Thomas of Walsingham, and all the older Writers,) was starved to death.   The story of his assassination by Sir Piers of Exon, is of much later date.

[4] Ruinous civil wars of York and Lancaster.

[5] Henry the Sixth, George Duke of Clarence, Edward the Fifth, Richard Duke of York, etc. believed to be murthered secretly in the Tower of London.   The oldest part of that structure is vulgarly attributed to Julius Cæsar.

"Revere his Consort's[1] faith, his Father's[2] fame,
"And spare the meek Usurper's[3] holy head.   90
"Above, below, the rose[4] of snow,
"Twined with her blushing foe, we spread:
"The bristled Boar[5] in infant-gore
"Wallows beneath the thorny shade.
"Now, Brothers, bending o'er th' accursed loom   95
"Stamp we our vengeance deep, and ratify his doom.

III. 1.

"Edward, lo! to sudden fate
"(Weave we the woof. The thread is spun)
"Half of thy heart we consecrate.[6]
"(The web is wove. The work is done.)"   100
'Stay, oh stay! nor thus forlorn
'Leave me unbless'd, unpitied, here to mourn:
'In yon bright track, that fires the western skies,
'They melt, they vanish from my eyes.
'But oh! what solemn scenes on Snowdon's height 105
'Descending slow their glitt'ring skirts unroll?

[1] Margaret of Anjou, a woman of heroic spirit, who struggled hard to save her Husband and her Crown.

[2] Henry the Fifth.

[3] Henry the Sixth very near being canonized. The line of Lancaster had no right of inheritance to the Crown.

[4] The white and red roses, devices of York and Lancaster.

[5] The silver Boar was the badge of Richard the Third; whence he was usually known in his own time by the name of *the Boar*.

[6] Eleanor of Castile died a few years after the conquest of Wales. The heroic proof she gave of her affection for her Lord is well known. The monuments of his regret, and sorrow for the loss of her, are still to be seen at Northampton, Geddington, Waltham, and other places.

'Visions of glory, spare my aching sight,
'Ye unborn Ages, crowd not on my soul !
'No more our long-lost Arthur[1] we bewail.
'All-hail, ye genuine Kings,[2] Britannia's Issue, hail ! 110

III. 2.

 'Girt with many a Baron bold
'Sublime their starry fronts they rear ;
'And gorgeous Dames, and Statesmen old
'In bearded majesty, appear.
'In the midst a Form divine !   115
'Her eye proclaims her of the Briton-Line ;
'Her lyon-port,[3] her awe-commanding face,
'Attemper'd sweet to virgin-grace.
'What strings symphonious tremble in the air,
'What strains of vocal transport round her play !   120
'Hear from the grave, great Taliessin,[4] hear ;
'They breathe a soul to animate thy clay.
'Bright Rapture calls, and soaring, as she sings,
'Waves in the eye of Heav'n her many-colour'd wings.

[1] It was the common belief of the Welch nation, that King Arthur was still alive in Fairy-Land, and should return again to reign over Britain.

[2] Both Merlin and Taliessin had prophesied, that the Welch should regain their sovereignty over this island ; which seemed to be accomplished in the House of Tudor.

[3] Speed relating an audience given by Queen Elizabeth to Paul Dzialinski, Ambassadour of Poland, says, " And thus she, lion-like rising, daunted the malapert Orator no less with her stately port and majestical deporture, than with the tartnesse of her princelie checkes."

[4] Taliessin, Chief of the Bards, flourished in the VIth century. His works are still preserved, and his memory held in high veneration among his Countrymen.

III. 3.

'The verse adorn again   125
'Fierce War, and faithful Love,[1]
'And Truth severe, by fairy Fiction drest.
'In buskin'd[2] measures move
'Pale Grief, and pleasing Pain,
'With Horrour, Tyrant of the throbbing breast.   130
'A Voice,[3] as of the Cherub-Choir,
'Gales from blooming Eden bear ;
'And distant warblings lessen on my ear,[4]
'That lost in long futurity expire.
'Fond impious Man, think'st thou, yon sanguine cloud, 135
'Rais'd by thy breath, has quench'd the Orb of day?
'To-morrow he repairs the golden flood,
'And warms the nations with redoubled ray.
'Enough for me : With joy I see
'The different doom our Fates assign.   140
'Be thine Despair, and scept'red Care,
'To triumph, and to die, are mine.'
He spoke, and headlong from the mountain's height
Deep in the roaring tide he plung'd to endless night.

[1] Fierce wars and faithful loves shall moralize my song.   *Spenser's Proëme to the Fairy Queen.*
[2] Shakespear.
[3] Milton.
[4] The succession of Poets after Milton's time.

XII.

SKETCH OF HIS OWN CHARACTER.

WRITTEN IN 1761, AND FOUND IN ONE OF HIS POCKET-BOOKS.

Too poor for a bribe, and too proud to importune ;
He had not the method of making a fortune ;
Could love, and could hate, so was thought somewhat
    odd ;
No very great wit, he believ'd in a God.   5
A Post or a Pension he did not desire,
But left Church and State to Charles Townshend and
    Squire.

XIII.

SONG.

THYRSIS, when we parted, swore
   Ere the spring he would return —
Ah ! what means yon violet flower !
   And the buds that deck the thorn !
'Twas the Lark that upward sprung !   5
'Twas the Nightingale that sung !

Idle notes ! untimely green !
   Why this unavailing haste ?
Western gales and skies serene
   Speak not always winter past.   10
Cease, my doubts, my fears to move,
Spare the honour of my love.

XIV.

THE FATAL SISTERS.

AN ODE, (FROM THE NORSE-TONGUE,)

IN THE ORCADES of THORMODUS TORFÆUS; HAFNIÆ, 1697,
Folio: and also in BARTHOLINUS.

VITT ER ORPIT FYRIR VALFALLI, &C

ADVERTISEMENT.

The Author once had thoughts (in concert with a Friend) of giving
the History of English Poetry : In the Introduction to it he meant
to have produced some specimens of the Style that reigned in
ancient times among the neighbouring nations, or those who had
subdued the greater part of this Island, and were our Progenitors :
the following three Imitations made a part of them. He has long
since drop'd his design, especially after he had heard, that it was
already in the hands of a Person well qualified to do it justice, both
by his taste, and his researches into antiquity.

PREFACE.

In the Eleventh Century *Sigurd*, Earl of the Orkney-Islands, went
with a fleet of ships and a considerable body of troops into Ireland,
to the assistance of *Sictryg with the silken beard*, who was then
making war on his father-in-law *Brian*, King of Dublin : the Earl
and all his forces were cut to pieces, and *Sictryg* was in danger of a
total defeat ; but the enemy had a greater loss by the death of
Brian, their King, who fell in action. On Christmas-day, (the day of
the battle), a Native of *Caithness* in Scotland saw at a distance a
number of persons on horseback riding full speed towards a hill,
and seeming to enter into it. Curiosity led him to follow them,
till looking through an opening in the rocks he saw twelve gigantic
figures resembling women : they were all employed about a loom;
and as they wove, they sung the following dreadful Song; which
when they had finished, they tore the web into twelve pieces, and
(each taking her portion) galloped Six to the North and as many
to the South.

Now the storm begins to lower,
(Haste, the loom of Hell prepare,)
Iron-sleet of arrowy shower [1]
Hurtles in the darken'd air. [2]

Glitt'ring lances are the loom,   5
Where the dusky warp we strain,
Weaving many a Soldier's doom,
Orkney's woe, and *Randver's* bane.

See the griesly texture grow,
('Tis of human entrails made,)   10
And the weights, that play below,
Each a gasping Warriour's head.

Shafts for shuttles, dipt in gore,
Shoot the trembling cords along.
Sword, that once a Monarch bore,   15
Keep the tissue close and strong.

Mista black, terrific Maid,
Sangrida, and *Hilda* see,
Join the wayward work to aid :
'Tis the woof of victory.   20

NOTE. — The *Valkyriur* were female Divinities, Servants of *Odin*
(or *Woden*) in the Gothic mythology. Their name signifies *Chusers
of the slain.* They were mounted on swift horses, with drawn
swords in their hands ; and in the throng of battle selected such as
were destined to slaughter, and conducted them to *Valkalla*, the
hall of *Odin*, or paradise of the Brave ; where they attended the
banquet, and served the departed Heroes with horns of mead and
ale.

[1] How quick they wheel'd ; and flying, behind them shot
Sharp sleet of arrowy shower ——
Milton's Par. Regained.

[2] The noise of battle hurtled in the air.
Shakesp. Jul. Cæsar.

Ere the ruddy sun be set,
Pikes must shiver, javelins sing,
Blade with clattering buckler meet,
Hauberk crash, and helmet ring.

(Weave the crimson web of war)   25
Let us go, and let us fly,
Where our Friends the conflict share,
Where they triumph, where they die.

As the paths of fate we tread,
Wading thro' th' ensanguin'd field :   30
Gondula, and *Geira*, spread
O'er the youthful King your shield.

We the reins to slaughter give,
Ours to kill, and ours to spare :
Spite of danger he shall live.   35
(Weave the crimson web of war.)

They, whom once the desart-beach
Pent within its bleak domain,
Soon their ample sway shall stretch
O'er the plenty of the plain.   40

Low the dauntless Earl is laid,
Gor'd with many a gaping wound :
Fate demands a nobler head ;
Soon a King shall bite the ground.

Long his loss shall Eirin weep,   45
Ne'er again his likeness see ;
Long her strains in sorrow steep,
Strains of Immortality !

Horror covers all the heath,
Clouds of carnage blot the sun.   50
Sisters, weave the web of death ;
Sisters, cease, the work is done.

Hail the task, and hail the hands !
Songs of joy and triumph sing !
Joy to the victorious bands ;   55
Triumph to the younger King.

Mortal, thou that hear'st the tale,
Learn the tenour of our song.
Scotland, thro' each winding vale
Far and wide the notes prolong.   60

Sisters, hence with spurs of speed :
Each her thundering faulchion wield ;
Each bestride her sable steed.
Hurry, hurry to the field.

XV.

THE DESCENT OF ODIN.

AN ODE, (FROM THE NORSE-TONGUE,)

IN BARTHOLINUS, de causis contemnendæ mortis ; HAFNIÆ, 1689,
Quarto.

UPREIS ODINN ALLDA GAUTR, &C.

UPROSE the King of Men with speed,
And saddled strait his coal-black steed ;
Down the yawning steep he rode,
That leads to HELA'S [1] drear abode.

[1] *Niflheimr*, the hell of the Gothic nations, consisted of nine
worlds, to which were devoted all such as died of sickness, old-age,
or by any other means than in battle : Over it presided HELA, the
Goddess of Death.

Him the Dog of Darkness spied,   5
His shaggy throat he open'd wide,
While from his jaws, with carnage fill'd,
Foam and human gore distill'd :
Hoarse he bays with hideous din,
Eyes that glow, and fangs, that grin ;   10
And long pursues, with fruitless yell,
The Father of the powerful spell.
Onward still his way he takes,
(The groaning earth beneath him shakes,)
Till full before his fearless eyes   15
The portals nine of hell arise.

   Right against the eastern gate,
By the moss-grown pile he sate ;
Where long of yore to sleep was laid
The dust of the prophetic Maid.   20
Facing to the northern clime,
Thrice he traced the runic rhyme ;
Thrice pronounc'd, in accents dread,
The thrilling verse that wakes the Dead ;
Till from out the hollow ground   25
Slowly breath'd a sullen sound.

   PR. What call unknown, what charms presume
To break the quiet of the tomb ?
Who thus afflicts my troubled sprite,
And drags me from the realms of night ?   30
Long on these mould'ring bones have beat
The winter's snow, the summer's heat,
The drenching dews, the driving rain !
Let me, let me sleep again.
Who is he, with voice unblest,   35
That calls me from the bed of rest ?

O. A Traveller, to thee unknown,
Is he that calls, a Warriour's Son.
Thou the deeds of light shalt know ;
Tell me what is done below,   40
For whom yon glitt'ring board is spread,
Drest for whom yon golden bed.

Pr. Mantling in the goblet see
The pure bev'rage of the bee,
O'er it hangs the shield of gold ;   45
'Tis the drink of *Balder* bold :
Balder's head to death is giv'n.
Pain can reach the Sons of Heav'n !
Unwilling I my lips unclose :
Leave me, leave me to repose.   50

O. Once again my call obey.
Prophetess, arise, and say,
What dangers *Odin's* Child await,
Who the Author of his fate.

Pr. In *Hoder's* hand the Heroe's doom :   55
His Brother sends him to the tomb.
Now my weary lips I close :
Leave me, leave me to repose.

O. Prophetess, my spell obey,
Once again arise, and say,   60
Who th' Avenger of his guilt,
By whom shall *Hoder's* blood be spilt.

Pr. In the caverns of the west,
By *Odin's* fierce embrace comprest,
A wond'rous Boy shall *Rinda* bear,   65
Who ne'er shall comb his raven-hair,

Nor wash his visage in the stream,
Nor see the sun's departing beam ;
Till he on *Hoder's* corse shall smile
Flaming on the fun'ral pile.   70
Now my weary lips I close :
Leave me, leave me to repose.

   O. Yet a while my call obey.
Prophetess, awake, and say,
What Virgins these, in speechless woe,   75
That bend to earth their solemn brow,
That their flaxen tresses tear,
And snowy veils, that float in air.
Tell me, whence their sorrows rose :
Then I leave thee to repose.   80

   Pr. Ha ! no Traveller art thou,
King of Men, I know thee now,
Mightiest of a mighty line ———

   O. No boding Maid of skill divine
Art thou, nor Prophetess of good ;   85
But Mother of the giant-brood !

   Pr. Hie thee hence, and boast at home,
That never shall Enquirer come
To break my iron-sleep again ;
Till *Lok* [1] has burst his tenfold chain.   90
Never, till substantial Night
Has reassum'd her ancient right ;
Till wrap'd in flames, in ruin hurl'd,
Sinks the fabric of the world.

---

[1] *Lok* is the evil Being, who continues in chains till the *Twilight of the Gods* approaches, when he shall break his bonds ; the human race, the stars, and sun, shall disappear ; the earth sink in the seas, and fire consume the skies : even Odin himself and his kindred-deities shall perish. For a farther explanation of this mythology, see Mallet's Introduction to the History of Denmark, 1755, Quarto.

XVI.

THE TRIUMPHS OF OWEN.

A FRAGMENT.

FROM MR. EVANS'S Specimens of the Welch Poetry; LONDON,
1764, Quarto.

ADVERTISEMENT.

OWEN succeeded his Father GRIFFIN in the Principality of
North-Wales, A.D. 1120. This battle was fought near forty Years
afterwards.

> OWEN'S praise demands my song,
> OWEN swift, and OWEN strong;
> Fairest flower of Roderic's stem,
> Gwyneth's[1] shield, and Britain's gem.
> He nor heaps his brooded stores,   5
> Nor on all profusely pours;
> Lord of every regal art,
> Liberal hand, and open heart.
>
>   Big with hosts of mighty name,
> Squadrons three against him came;   10
> This the force of Eirin hiding,
> Side by side as proudly riding,
> On her shadow long and gay
> Lochlin[2] plows the watry way;
> There the Norman sails afar   15
> Catch the winds, and join the war:
> Black and huge along they sweep,
> Burthens of the angry deep.

[1] North-Wales.   [2] Denmark.

 Dauntless on his native sands
The Dragon-Son of Mona stands ;[1]   20
In glitt'ring arms and glory drest,
High he rears his ruby crest.
There the thund'ring strokes begin,
There the press, and there the din ;
Talymalfra's rocky shore   25
Echoing to the battle's roar.
Where his glowing eye-balls turn,
Thousand Banners round him burn.
Where he points his purple spear,
Hasty, hasty Rout is there,   30
Marking with indignant eye
Fear to stop, and shame to fly.
There Confusion, Terror's child,
Conflict fierce, and Ruin wild,
Agony, that pants for breath,   35
Despair and honourable Death.

   * * *

XVII.

THE DEATH OF HOEL.

AN ODE, SELECTED FROM THE GODODIN.

HAD I but the torrent's might,
With headlong rage and wild affright
Upon Deïra's squadrons hurl'd,
To rush, and sweep them from the world !

 [1] The red Dragon is the device of Cadwallader, which all his
descendants bore on their banners.

Too, too secure in youthful pride,   5
By them my friend, my Hoel, died,
Great Cian's son ; of Madoc old
He ask'd no heaps of hoarded gold ;
Alone in nature's wealth array'd,
He ask'd and had the lovely maid.   10

To Cattraeth's vale in glitt'ring row
Thrice two hundred warriors go ;
Every warrior's manly neck
Chains of regal honour deck,
Wreath'd in many a golden link ;   15
From the golden cup they drink
Nectar that the bees produce,
Or the grape's extatic juice.
Flush'd with mirth and hope they burn ;
But none from Cattraeth's vale return,   20
Save Aëron brave, and Conan strong,
(Bursting through the bloody throng)
And I, the meanest of them all,
That live to weep and sing their fall.

XVIII.

CARADOC.

Have ye seen the tusky boar,
Or the bull, with sullen roar,
On surrounding foes advance ?
So Caradoc bore his lance.

XIX.

CONAN.

Conan's name, my lay, rehearse,
Build to him the lofty verse,
Sacred tribute of the bard,
Verse, the hero's sole reward.
As the flame's devouring force ;   5
As the whirlwind in its course ;
As the thunder's fiery stroke,
Glancing on the shiver'd oak ;
Did the sword of Conan mow
The crimson harvest of the foe.   10

XX.

WILLIAM SHAKESPEARE

TO MRS. ANNE, REGULAR SERVANT TO THE REV. MR. PRECENTOR
OF YORK.

A moment's patience, gentle Mistress Anne ;
   (But stint your clack for sweet St. Charitie)
'Tis Willy begs, once a right proper man,
   Though now a book, and interleaved you see.

Much have I borne from canker'd critic's spite,   5
   From fumbling baronets and poets small,
Pert barristers, and parsons nothing bright,
   But what awaits me now is worst of all.

'Tis true, our master's temper natural
   Was fashion'd fair in meek and dove-like guise ; 10
But may not honey's self be turn'd to gall
   By residence, by marriage, and sore eyes?

If then he wreak on me his wicked will,
   Steal to his closet at the hour of prayer;
And (when thou hear'st the organ piping shrill)   15
   Grease his best pen, and all his scribbles, tear.

Better to bottom tarts and cheesecakes nice,
   Better the roast meat from the fire to save,
Better be twisted into caps for spice,
   Than thus be patch'd and cobbled in one's grave.   20

So York shall taste what Clouet never knew,
   So from our works sublimer fumes shall rise;
While Nancy earns the praise to Shakespeare due,
   For glorious puddings and immortal pies.

XXI.

ODE FOR MUSIC.

[PERFORMED AT THE INSTALLATION OF THE CHANCELLOR OF
THE UNIVERSITY OF CAMBRIDGE, 1769.]

AIR.

" HENCE, avaunt, ('tis holy ground)
" Comus, and his midnight-crew,
" And Ignorance with looks profound,
" And dreaming Sloth of pallid hue,
" Mad Sedition's cry profane,   5
" Servitude that hugs her chain,
" Nor in these consecrated bowers
" Let painted Flatt'ry hide her serpent-train in flowers.

CHORUS.

" Nor Envy base, nor creeping Gain
" Dare the Muse's walk to stain,   10
" While bright-eyed Science watches round:
" Hence, away, 'tis holy Ground!

RECITATIVE.

From yonder realms of empyrean day
Bursts on my ear th' indignant lay :
There sit the sainted Sage, the Bard divine,   15
The Few, whom Genius gave to shine
Through every unborn age, and undiscovered clime.
Rapt in celestial transport they,   *(accomp.)*
Yet hither oft a glance from high
They send of tender sympathy   20
To bless the place, where on their opening soul
First the genuine ardor stole.
'Twas *Milton* struck the deep-toned shell,
And, as the choral warblings round him swell,
Meek *Newton's* self bends from his state sublime,   25
And nods his hoary head, and listens to the rhyme.

AIR.

" Ye brown o'er-arching Groves,
" That Contemplation loves,
" Where willowy *Camus* lingers with delight !
" Oft at the blush of dawn   30
" I trod your level lawn,
" Oft woo'd the gleam of *Cynthia* silver-bright
" In cloisters dim, far from the haunts of Folly,
" With Freedom by my Side, and soft-ey'd Melancholy.

RECITATIVE.

But hark ! the portals sound, and pacing forth   35
With solemn steps and slow
High Potentates and Dames of royal birth
And mitred Fathers in long order go :
Great *Edward* with the lillies on his brow

From haughty *Gallia* torn,   40
And sad *Chatillon*, on her bridal morn
That wept her bleeding Love, and princely *Clare*,
And *Anjou's* Heroïne, and the paler Rose,
The rival of her crown, and of her woes,
And either *Henry* there,   45
The murther'd Saint, and the majestic Lord,
That broke the bonds of *Rome*.
(Their tears, their little triumphs o'er,   (*accomp.*)
Their human passions now no more,
Save Charity, that glows beyond the tomb)   50
All that on *Granta's* fruitful plain
Rich streams of regal bounty pour'd,
And bad these aweful fanes and turrets rise,
To hail their *Fitzroy's* festal morning come;
And thus they speak in soft accord   55
The liquid language of thc skies.

QUARTETTO.

" What is Grandeur, what is Power?
" Heavier toil, superior pain.
" What the bright reward we gain?
" The grateful mem'ry of the Good.   60
" Sweet is the breath of vernal shower,
" The bee's collected treasures sweet,
" Sweet music's melting fall, but sweeter yet
" The still small voice of Gratitude.

RECITATIVE.

Foremost and leaning from her golden cloud   65
The venerable *Marg'ret* see!
" Welcome, my noble Son, (she cries aloud)
" To this, thy kindred train, and me:

" Pleas'd in thy lineaments we trace
" A *Tudor's* fire, a *Beaufort's* grace.   70

AIR.

" Thy liberal heart, thy judging eye,
" The flower unheeded shall descry,
" And bid it round heaven's altars shed
" The fragrance of it's blushing head :
" Shall raise from earth the latent gem   75
" To glitter on the diadem.

RECITATIVE.

" Lo, *Granta* waits to lead her blooming band,
" Not obvious, not obtrusive, She
" No vulgar praise, no venal incense flings ;
" Nor dares with courtly tongue refin'd   80
" Profane thy inborn royalty of mind :
" She reveres herself and thee.
" With modest pride to grace thy youthful brow
" The laureate wreath, that *Cecil* wore, she brings,
" And to thy just, thy gentle hand   85
" Submits the Fasces of her sway,
" While Spirits blest above and Men below
" Join with glad voice the loud symphonious lay.

GRAND CHORUS.

" Thro' the wild waves as they roar
" With watchful eye and dauntless mien   90
" Thy steady course of honor keep,
" Nor fear the rocks, nor seek the shore :
" The Star of *Brunswick* smiles serene,
" And gilds the horrors of the deep.

PROSE.

[The selections from Gray's prose are divided into three parts; first, those that are Autobiographical, — throwing light on his own character, or referring to his poems; second, those of a Literary nature, — containing allusions to contemporary writings; third, those expressing appreciation of Nature. The titles have been supplied.]

AUTOBIOGRAPHICAL.

COLLEGE LIFE.

TO RICHARD WEST.

You must know that I do not take degrees, and, after this term, shall have nothing more of college impertinences to undergo, which I trust will be some pleasure to you, as it is a great one to me. I have endured lectures daily and hourly since I came last, supported by the hopes of being shortly at full liberty to give myself up to my friends and classical companions, who, poor souls! though I see them fallen into great contempt with most people here, yet I cannot help sticking to them, and out of a spirit of obstinacy (I think) love them the better for it; and indeed, what can I do else? Must I plunge into metaphysics? Alas, I cannot see in the dark; nature has not furnished me with the optics of a cat. Must I pore upon mathematics? Alas, I cannot see in too much light; I am no eagle. It is very possible that two and two make four, but I would not give four farthings to demonstrate this ever so clearly; and if these be the profits of life, give me the amusements of it. The people I behold all around me, it seems, know all this and more, and yet I do not know one of them who inspires me with any ambition of being like him. Surely it was of this place, now Cambridge, but formerly known by the name of Babylon, that the prophet spoke when he said, "The wild beasts of the desert shall dwell there, and their houses shall be full of doleful creatures, and owls shall build there, and satyrs shall dance there; their forts and

towers shall be a den forever, a joy of wild asses; there shall the great owl make her nest, and lay and hatch and gather under her shadow; it shall be a court of dragons;
30 the screech owl also shall rest there, and find for herself a place of rest." You see here is a pretty collection of desolate animals, which is verified in this town to a tittle, and perhaps it may also allude to your habitation, for you know all types may be taken by abundance of
35 handles; however, I defy your owls to match mine.

If the default of your spirits and nerves be nothing but the effect of the hyp, I have no more to say. We all must submit to that wayward queen; I too in no small degree own her sway,

40   I feel her influence while I speak her power.

But if it be a real distemper, pray take more care of your health,[1] if not for your own at least for our sakes, and do not be so soon weary of this little world : I do not know what refined friendships you may have contracted in the
45 other, but pray do not be in a hurry to see your acquaintance above; among your terrestrial familiars, however, though I say it, that should not say it, there positively is not one that has a greater esteem for you than yours most sincerely, etc.

PETERHOUSE, *December, 1736.*

MELANCHOLY.

TO RICHARD WEST.

August 22, 1737.

*   *   *   *   *   *   *   *   *

Low spirits are my true and faithful companions; they get up with me, go to bed with me, make journeys and

----

[1] West was a consumptive.

returns as I do ; nay, and pay visits, and will even affect to be jocose, and force a feeble laugh with me ; but most commonly we sit alone together, and are the prettiest 5 insipid company in the world. * * *

SKETCH OF HIS OWN CHARACTER.

TO RICHARD WEST.

FLORENCE, *April 21, 1741.*

I KNOW not what degree of satisfaction it will give you to be told that we shall set out from hence the 24th of this month, and not stop above a fortnight at any place in our way.   This I feel, that you are the principal pleasure I have to hope for in my own country.   Try at 5 least to make me imagine myself not indifferent to you ; for I must own I have the vanity of desiring to be esteemed by somebody, and would choose that somebody should be one whom I esteem as much as I do you.   As I am recommending myself to your love, methinks I ought 10 to send you my picture (for I am no more what I was, some circumstances excepted, which I hope I need not particularize to you) ; you must add then, to your former idea, two years of age, a reasonable quantity of dulness, a great deal of silence, and something that rather 15 resembles, than is, thinking ; a confused notion of many strange and fine things that have swum before my eyes for some time, a want of love for general society, indeed an inability to it.   On the good side you may add a sensibility for what others feel, and indulgence for their 20 faults and weaknesses, a love of truth, and detestation of everything else.   Then you are to deduct a little impertinence, a little laughter, a great deal of pride, and some spirits.   These are all the alterations I know of, you

25 perhaps may find more. Think not that I have been obliged for this reformation of manners to reason or reflection, but to a severer school-mistress, Experience. One has little merit in learning her lessons, for one cannot well help it ; but they are more useful than others, 30 and imprint themselves in the very heart. * * *

MELANCHOLY.

TO RICHARD WEST.

LONDON, *May 27, 1742.*

MINE, you are to know, is a white Melancholy, or rather Leucocholy for the most part ; which, though it seldom laughs or dances, nor ever amounts to what one calls Joy or Pleasure, yet is a good easy sort of a state, 5 and *ça ne laisse que de s'amuser.* The only fault of its insipidity ; which is apt now and then to give a sort of *Ennui,* which makes one form certain little wishes that signify nothing. But there is another sort, black indeed, which I have now and then felt, that has somewhat in it 10 like Tertullian's rule of faith, *Credo quia impossibile est;* for it believes, nay, is sure of everything that is unlikely, so it be but frightful ; and on the other hand excludes and shuts its eyes to the most possible hopes, and everything that is pleasurable ; from this the Lord deliver us ! 15 for none but he and sunshiny weather can do it. * * *

THE OFFICE OF POET–LAUREATE.

TO THE REV. WILLIAM MASON.

December 19, 1757.

DEAR MASON — Though I very well know the bland emollient saponaceous qualities both of sack and silver, yet if any great man would say to me, " I make you rat-catcher to his Majesty, with a salary of £300 a year and two butts of the best Malaga ; and though it has been usual to catch a mouse or two, for form's sake, in public once a year, yet to you, sir, we shall not stand upon these things," I cannot say I should jump at it ; nay, if they would drop the very name of the office, and call me Sinecure to the King's Majesty, I should still feel a little awkward, and think everybody I saw smelt a rat about me ; but I do not pretend to blame any one else that has not the same sensations ; for my part I would rather be serjeant trumpeter or pinmaker to the palace.   Neverthe-less I interest myself a little in the history of it, and rather wish somebody may accept it that will retrieve the credit of the thing, if it be retrievable, or ever had any credit.   Rowe was, I think, the last man of character that had it.   As to Settle, whom you mention, he belonged to my lord mayor not to the king.   Eusden was a person of great hopes in his youth, though at last he turned out a drunken parson.   Dryden was as disgraceful to the office, from his character, as the poorest scribbler could have been from his verses.   The office itself has always humbled the professor hitherto (even in an age when kings were somebody), if he were a poor writer by mak-ing him more conspicuous, and if he were a good one by setting him at war with the little fry of his own pro-fession, for there are poets little enough to envy even a poet-laureat.

I am obliged to you for your news ; pray send me some more, and better of the sort.   I can tell you nothing in return ; so your generosity will be the greater ; — only Dick is going to give up his rooms, and live at Ashwell. Mr. Treasurer sets Sir M. Lamb at nought, and says he has sent him reasons half a sheet at a time ; and Mr.

Brown attests his veracity as an eye-witness. I have had
nine pages of criticism on the "Bard" sent me in an
anonymous letter, directed to the Reverend Mr. G. at
40 Strawberry Hill; and if I have a mind to hear as much
more on the other Ode, I am told where I may direct.
He seems a good sensible man, and I dare say a clergyman. He is very frank, and indeed much ruder than he
means to be. Adieu, dear Mason, and believe me that I
45 am too.

ATTITUDE TOWARD LIFE.

TO THE REV. WILLIAM MASON.

January 3, 1758.

DEAR MASON — A life spent out of the world has its
hours of despondence, its inconveniences, its sufferings,
as numerous and as real (though not quite of the same
sort) as a life spent in the midst of it. The power we
5 have, when we will exert it, over our own minds, joined
to a little strength and consolation, nay, a little pride we
catch from those that seem to love us, is our only support
in either of these conditions. I am sensible I cannot
return to you so much of this assistance as I have
10 received from you. I can only tell you that one who has
far more reason than you (I hope) will ever have to look
on life with something worse than indifference, is yet
no enemy to it, and can look backward on many bitter
moments partly with satisfaction, and partly with patience,
15 and forward too, on a scene not very promising, with
some hope and some expectations of a better day.

* * * * * * * * *

MELANCHOLY.

TO THE REV. JAMES BROWN.

September 7, 1758.

*   *   *   *   *   *   *   *   *

My health I cannot complain of, but as to my spirits they are always many degrees below changeable, and I seem to myself to inspire everything around me with *ennui* and dejection ; but some time or other all these things must come to a conclusion, till which day I shall   5 remain very sincerely yours,   T. G.

GRAY'S MOTHER.

TO THE REV. NORTON NICHOLLS.

PEMBROKE HALL, *August 26, 1766.*

DEAR SIR   It is long since that I heard you were gone in hast into Yorkshire on account of your mother's illness ; and the same letter informed me that she was recovered ; otherwise I had then wrote to you, only to beg you would take care of her, and to inform you that I   5 had discovered a thing very little known, which is, that in one's whole life one never can have any more than a single mother.   You may think this is obvious, and (what you call) a trite observation.   You are a green gosling ! I was at the same age (very near) as wise as you, and yet   10 I never discovered this (with full evidence and convic- tion, I mean) till it was too late.   It is thirteen years ago, and seems but yesterday ; and every day I live it sinks deeper into my heart.   Many a corollary could I draw from this axiom for your use (not for my own) but I   15 will leave you the merit of doing it yourself. *   *   *

CONSOLATION.

TO THE REV. WILLIAM MASON.

Sunday, February 15, 1767.

* * * THERE are a few words in your letter that make
me believe you wish I were in town.[1] I know myself how
little one like me is formed to support the spirits of
another, or give him consolation ; one that always sees
5 things in their most gloomy aspect.   However, be assured
I should not have left London while you were in it, if I
could well have afforded to stay there till the beginning
of April, when I am usually there.   This, however, shall
be no hindrance, if you tell me it would signify anything
10 to you that I should come sooner.   Adieu : you (both of
you) have my best and sincerest good wishes. — I am
ever yours,   T. G.

SYMPATHY.

TO THE REV. WILLIAM MASON.

March 28, 1767.

MY DEAR MASON — I break in upon you at a moment
when we least of all are permitted to disturb our friends,
only to say that you are daily and hourly present to my
thoughts.   If the worst be not yet passed, you will neglect
5 and pardon me ; but if the last struggle be over, if the
poor object of your long anxieties be no longer sensible
to your kindness, or to her own sufferings, allow me (at
least in idea, for what could I do were I present more
than this), to sit by you in silence, and pity from my
10 heart, not her who is at rest, but you who lose her.   May
He who made us, the Master of our pleasures and of our
pains, preserve and support you.   Adieu !

I have long understood how little you had to hope.

[1] Mason's wife was fatally ill.

THE SHADOW OF DEATH.

TO THOMAS WHARTON.

May 24, 1771.

*   *   *   *   *   *   *   *   *

My summer was intended to have been passed in Switzerland : but I have dropped the thought of it, and believe my expeditions will terminate in Old Park : for travel I must, or cease to exist. Till this year I hardly knew what (mechanical) low spirits were : but now I 5 even tremble at an East-wind. It is here the height of Summer, but with all the bloom and tender verdure of Spring. * * *   [Gray died July 30.]

HIS POETRY.

THE ODE ON WALPOLE'S CAT.

TO HORACE WALPOLE.

CAMBRIDGE, *March 1, 1747.*

As one ought to be particularly careful to avoid blunders in a compliment of condolence, it would be a sensible satisfaction to me (before I testify my sorrow, and the sincere part I take in your misfortune) to know for certain, who it is I lament. I knew Zara and Selima 5 (Selima was it? or Fatima?), or rather I knew them both together; for I cannot justly say which was which. Then as to your handsome Cat, the name you distinguish her by, I am no less at a loss, as well knowing one's handsome cat is always the cat one likes best; or if one be 10 alive and the other dead, it is usually the latter that is the handsomest. Besides, if the point were never so clear, I hope you do not think me so ill-bred or so imprudent as to forfeit all my interest in the survivor; oh no! I would rather seem to mistake, and imagine to 15

be sure it must be the tabby one that had met with this
sad accident. * * *　Heigh ho! I feel (as you to be sure
have done long since) that I have very little to say, at
least in prose.　Somebody will be the better for it; I do
20 not mean you, but your Cat, feuë Mademoiselle Selime,
whom I am about to immortalise for one week or fortnight, as follows.

[Here follows the Ode.]

There's a poem for you, it is rather too long for an
Epitaph.

————————

THE ELEGY.

TO HORACE WALPOLE.

STOKE, *June 12, 1750.*

DEAR SIR — As I live in a place, where even the
ordinary tattle of the town arrives not till it is stale, and
which produces no events of its own, you will not desire
any excuse from me for writing so seldom, especially as
5 of all people living I know you are the least a friend to
letters spun out of one's own brains, with all the toil and
constraint that accompanies sentimental productions.　I
have been here at Stoke, a few days (where I shall
continue good part of the summer); and having put an
10 end to a thing, whose beginning you have seen long ago,
I immediately send it you.　You will, I hope, look upon
it in the light of a thing with an end to it: a merit that
most of my writings have wanted, and are like to want,
but which this epistle I am determined shall not want,
15 when it tells you that I am ever yours,

T. GRAY.

Not that I have done yet; but who could avoid the
temptation of finishing so roundly and so cleverly, in the
manner of good Queen Anne's days? * * *

THE ELEGY.

TO HORACE WALPOLE.

CAMBRIDGE, *February 11, 1751.*

As you have brought me into a little sort of distress,
you must assist me, I believe, to get out of it as well as I
can.   Yesterday I had the misfortune of receiving a letter
from certain gentlemen (as their bookseller expresses it),
who have taken the Magazine of Magazines into their
hands.   They tell me that an *ingenious* Poem, called
reflections in a Country Church-yard, has been com-
municated to them, which they are printing forthwith ;
that they are informed that the *excellent* author of it is I
by name, and that they beg not only his *indulgence*, but
the *honour* of his correspondence, etc.   As I am not at all
disposed to be either so indulgent, or so correspondent,
as they desire, I have but one bad way left to escape the
honour they would inflict upon me ; and therefore am
obliged to desire you would make Dodsley print it
immediately (which may be done in less than a week's
time) from your copy, but without my name, in what
form is most convenient for him, but on his best paper
and character ; he must correct the press himself, and
print it without any interval between the stanzas, because
the sense is in some places continued beyond them ; and
the title must be, — Elegy, written in a Country Church-
yard.   If he would add a line or two to say it came into
his hands by accident, I should like it better.   If you
behold the Magazine of Magazines in the light that I do,
you will not refuse to give yourself this trouble on my
account, which you have taken of your own accord before
now.   If Dodsley do not do this immediately, he may as
well let it alone.

THE ELEGY.

TO HORACE WALPOLE.

Ash-Wednesday, CAMBRIDGE, *1751.*

MY DEAR SIR — You have indeed conducted with great decency my little *misfortune;* you have taken a paternal care of it, and expressed much more kindness than could have been expressed from so near a relation.
5 But we are all frail ; and I hope to do as much for you another time.

Nurse Dodsley has given it a pinch or two in the cradle, that (I doubt) it will bear the marks of as long as it lives. But no matter : we have ourselves suffered
10 under her hands before now ; and besides, it will only look the more careless and by *accident* as it were. I thank you for your advertisement, which saves my honour, and in a manner *bien flatteuse pour moi,* who should be put to it even to make myself a compliment in
15 good English.

You will take me for a mere poet, and a fetcher and carrier of sing-song, if I tell you that I intend to send you the beginning of a drama, not mine, thank God, as you will believe, when you hear it is finished, but wrote by a
20 person whom I have a very good opinion of. It is (unfortunately) in the manner of the ancient drama, with choruses, which I am to my shame the occasion of ; for, as great part of it was at first written in that form, I would not suffer him to change it to a play fit for the
25 stage, and as he intended, because the lyric parts are the best of it, they must have been lost. The story is Saxon, and the language has a tang of Shakespeare, that suits an old-fashioned fable very well. In short I don't do it merely to amuse you, but for the sake of the author,
30 who wants a judge, and so I would lend him *mine :* yet

not without your leave, lest you should have us up to
dirty our stockings at the bar of your house, for wasting
the time and politics of the *nation.* — Adieu, Sir ! I am
ever yours,

T. GRAY.

THE PROGRESS OF POESY.

TO HORACE WALPOLE.

*   *   *   *   *   *   *   *   *

I DO not wonder at Dodsley. You have talked to him
of six *Odes*, for so you are pleased to call everything I
write, though it be but a receipt to make apple-dumplings.
He has reason to gulp when he finds one of them only a
long story. I don't know but I may send him very soon 5
(by your hands) an ode to his own tooth, a high Pindaric
upon stilts, which one must be a better scholar than he is
to understand a line of, and the very best scholars will
understand but a little matter here and there.

It wants but seventeen lines of having an end, I don't 10
say of being finished. As it is so unfortunate to come
too late for Mr. Bentley, it may appear in the fourth
volume of the *Miscellanies*, provided you don't think it
execrable, and suppress it. Pray when the fine book is
to be printed, let me revise the press, for you know you 15
can't ; and there are a few trifles I could wish altered.

*   *   *   *   *   *   *   *   *

THE "SIX POEMS" OF 1753.

TO ROBERT DODSLEY.

CAMBRIDGE, *February 12, 1753.*

SIR — I am not at all satisfied with the title. To
have it conceived that I publish a collection of *Poems,*

and half a dozen little matters (four of which too have already been printed again and again) thus pompously
5 adorned would make me appear very justly ridiculous. I desire it may be understood (which is the truth), that the verses are only subordinate and explanatory to the Drawings, and suffered by me to come out thus only for that reason : therefore, if you yourself prefixed this title,
10 I desire it may be altered. Or, if Mr. W[alpole] ordered it so, that you would tell him why I wish it were changed in the manner I mentioned to you at first, or to that purpose. For the more I consider it, the less I can bear it, as it now stands. I even think there is an uncommon
15 sort of simplicity that looks like affectation, in putting our plain Christian and surnames without a Mr. before them. But this (if it signifies anything) I easily give up, the other I cannot. You need not apprehend that this change in the title will be any prejudice to the sale of
20 the book. * * * Perhaps you may have burnt my letter, so I will again put down the title — " Designs by Mr. R. Bentley for six poems of Mr. T. Gray." — I am, Sir, your humble servant,

T. G.

THE PINDARIC ODES.

TO RICHARD HURD.

STOKE, *August 25, 1757.*

DEAR SIR — I do not know why you should thank me for what you had a right and title to ; but attribute it to the excess of your politeness, and the more so because almost no one else has made me the same compliment.
5 As your acquaintance in the University (you say) do me the honour to admire, it would be ungenerous in me not to give them notice that they are doing a very unfashion-

able thing, for all people of condition are agreed not to
admire, nor even to understand : one very great man,
writing to an acquaintance of his and mine, says that he 10
had read them seven or eight times, and that now, when
he next sees him, he shall not have above thirty questions to ask. Another, a peer, believes that the last
stanza of the Second Ode relates to King Charles the
First and Oliver Cromwell. Even my friends tell me 15
they do not succeed, and write me moving topics of
consolation on that head ; in short, I have heard of
nobody but a player and a doctor of divinity that profess
their esteem for them. Oh yes ! a lady of quality, a
friend of Mason's, who is a great reader. She knew 20
there was a compliment to Dryden, but never suspected
there was anything said about Shakespeare or Milton,
till it was explained to her ; and wishes that there had
been titles prefixed to tell what they were about.

From this mention of Mason's name you may think, 25
perhaps, we are great correspondents ; no such thing ;
I have not heard from him these two months. I will be
sure to scold in my own name as well as in yours. I
rejoice to hear you are so ripe for the press, and so
voluminous, — not for my own sake only, whom you 30
flatter with the hopes of seeing your labours both public
and private, — but for yours too, for to be employed is to
be happy. This principle of mine, and I am convinced
of its truth, has, as usual, no influence on my practice.
I am alone and *ennuyé* to the last degree, yet do nothing ; 35
indeed I have one excuse ; my health, which you so
kindly enquire after, is not extraordinary, ever since I
came hither. It is no great malady, but several little
ones, that seem brewing no good to me.

It will be a particular pleasure to me to hear whether 40
Content dwells in Leicestershire, and how she entertains

herself there ; only do not be too happy, nor forget entirely the quiet ugliness of Cambridge. I am, dear Sir, your friend and obliged humble servant,

T. GRAY.

THE PINDARIC ODES.

TO THE REV. WILLIAM MASON.

DEAR MASON — You are welcome to the land of the living, to the sunshine of a court, to the dirt of a chaplain's table, to the society of Dr. Squire and Dr. Chapman. Have you set out, as Dr. Cobden ended, with a sermon
5 against adultery ? or do you, with deep mortification and a Christian sense of your own nothingness, read prayers to Princess Emily while she is putting on her dress ? Pray acquaint me with the whole ceremonial, and how your first preachment succeeded ; whether you have
10 heard of anybody that renounced their election, or made restitution to the Exchequer ; whether you saw any woman trample her pompons under foot, or spit upon her handkerchief to wipe off the rouge.

I would not have put another note to save the souls of
15 all the owls in London. It is extremely well as it is — nobody understands me, and I am perfectly satisfied. Even the *Critical Review* (Mr. Franklin, I am told), that is rapt and surprised and shudders at me, yet mistakes the Æolian lyre for the harp of Æolus, which, indeed, as
20 he observes, is a very bad instrument to dance to. If you hear anything (though it is not very likely, for I know my day is over), you will tell me. Lord Lyttleton and Mr. Shenstone admire me, but wish I had been a little clearer. Mr. (Palmyra) Wood owns himself disap-
25 pointed in his expectations. Your enemy, Dr. Brown,

says I am the best thing in the language. Mr. Fox, supposing the Bard sung his song but once over, does not wonder if Edward the First did not understand him. This last criticism is rather unhappy, for though it had been sung a hundred times under his window, it was 30 absolutely impossible King Edward should understand him ; but that is no reason for Mr. Fox, who lives almost 500 years after him. It is very well ; the next thing I print shall be in Welch, — that's all.   *   *   *

HIS OWN AIM IN POETRY.

TO THE REV. WILLIAM MASON.

January 13, 1758.

*   *   *   *   *   *   *   *

EXTREME conciseness of expression, yet pure, perspicuous, and musical, is one of the grand beauties of lyric poetry. This I have always aimed at, and never could attain ; the necessity of rhyming is one great obstacle to it : another and perhaps a stronger is, that way you have 5 chosen of casting down your first ideas carelessly and at large, and then clipping them here and there, and forming them at leisure ; this method, after all possible pains, will leave behind it in some places a laxity, a diffuseness ; the frame of a thought (otherwise well invented, well 10 turned, and well placed) is often weakened by it. Do I talk nonsense, or do you understand me ? I am persuaded what I say is true in my head, whatever it may be in prose, — for I do not pretend to write prose.

*   *   *   *   *   *   *   *   *

HIS STERILITY.

TO HORACE WALPOLE.

PEMBROKE COLLEGE, *February 25, 1768.*

* * * DODSLEY told me in the Spring that the plates
from Mr. Bentley's designs were worn out, and he wanted
to have them copied and reduced to a smaller scale for a
new edition. I dissuaded him from so silly an expense,
5 and desired he would put in no ornaments at all. The
Long Story was to be totally omitted, as its only use (that
of explaining the prints) was gone : but to supply the
place of it in bulk, lest *my works* should be mistaken for
the works of a flea, or a pismire, I promised to send him
10 an equal weight of poetry or prose : so, since my return
hither, I put up about two ounces of stuff, viz. the
"Fatal Sisters," the "Descent of Odin" (of both which
you have copies), a bit of something from the Welch, and
certain little Notes, partly from justice (to acknowledge
15 the debt where I had borrowed anything) partly from ill
temper, just to tell the gentle reader that Edward I. was
not Oliver Cromwell, nor Queen Elizabeth the Witch of
Endor. This is literally all ; and with all this, I shall be
but a shrimp of an author. * * * To what you say
20 to me so civilly, that I ought to write more, I reply in
your own words (like the Pamphleteer, who is going to
confute you out of your own mouth) What has one to do
when *turned of fifty*, but really to think of finishing ?
However, I will be candid (for you seem to be so with
25 me), and avow to you, that till fourscore-and-ten, whenever the humour takes me, I will write, because I like it ;
and because I like myself better when I do so. If I do
not write much, it is because I cannot. * * *

II.

LITERATURE.

SHAKSPERE, FIELDING, AND POETRY.

TO RICHARD WEST.

LONDON, *April, Thursday* [*1742*].

YOU are the first who ever made a Muse of a Cough ;[1] to me it seems a much more easy task to versify in one's sleep (that indeed you were of old famous for), than for want of it. Not the wakeful nightingale (when she had a cough), ever sung so sweetly. I give you thanks for your warble, and wish you could sing yourself to rest. These wicked remains of your illness will sure give way to warm weather and gentle exercise ; which I hope you will not omit as the season advances. Whatever low spirits and indolence, the effect of them, may advise to the contrary, I pray you add five steps to your walk daily for my sake ; by the help of which, in a month's time, I propose to set you on horseback.

I talked of the *Dunciad* as concluding you had seen it ; if you have not, do you choose I should get and send it you ? I have myself, upon your recommendation, been reading *Joseph Andrews*.[2] The incidents are ill laid and without invention ; but the characters have a great deal of nature, which always pleases even in her lowest shapes. Parson Adams is perfectly well ; so is Mrs. Slipslop, and the story of Wilson ; and throughout he shows himself well read in Stage-Coaches, Country Squires, Inns, and Inns of Court. His reflections upon high people and

[1] West had sent Gray a Latin poem on his own sickness.
[2] It had just appeared.

low people, and misses and masters, are very good.
25 However the exaltedness of some minds (or rather as I
shrewdly suspect their insipidity and want of feeling or
observation), may make them insensible to these light
things (I mean such as characterise and paint nature),
yet surely they are as weighty and much more useful than
30 your grave discourses upon the mind, the passions, and
what not. Now as the paradisaical pleasures of the
Mahometans consist in playing upon the flute and lying
with Houris, be mine to read eternal new romances of
Marivaux and Crebillon.

35 You are very good in giving yourself the trouble to
read and find fault with my long harangues. Your
freedom (as you call it), has so little need of apologies,
that I should scarce excuse your treating me any otherwise ; which, whatever compliment it might be to my
40 vanity, would be making a very ill one to my understanding. As to matter of stile, I have this to say: the
language of the age is never the language of poetry;[1]
except among the French, whose verse, where the thought
or image does not support it, differs in nothing from
45 prose. Our poetry, on the contrary, has a language
peculiar to itself ; to which almost everyone, that has
written, has added something by enriching it with foreign
idioms and derivatives: nay sometimes words of their
own composition or invention. Shakespear and Milton
50 have been great creators this way ; and no one more
licentious than Pope or Dryden, who perpetually borrow
expressions from the former. * * * In truth, Shakespear's language is one of his principal beauties ; and he
has no less advantage over your Addisons and Rowes in
55 this, than in those other great excellencies you mention.

[1] Compare this, and what follows, with Wordsworth's celebrated
theory.

Every word in him is a picture.   Pray put me the following lines into the tongue of our modern dramatics :

> " But I, that am not shaped for sportive tricks,
>   Nor made to court an amorous looking-glass :
>   I, that am rudely stampt, and want love's majesty   60
>   To strut before a wanton ambling nymph :
>   I, that am curtail'd of this fair proportion,
>   Cheated of feature by dissembling nature,
>   Deform'd, unfinish'd, sent before my time
>   Into this breathing world, scarce half made up — "   65

And what follows.   To me they appear untranslatable ;
and if this be the case, our language is greatly degener-
ated.   However, the affectation of imitating Shakespear
may doubtless be carried too far ; and is no sort of
excuse for sentiments ill-suited, or speeches ill-timed,   70
which I believe is a little the case with me.   *   *   *

COLLINS AND J. WARTON.

TO THOMAS WHARTON.

*   *   * HAVE you seen the works of two young authors,
a Mr. Warton and a Mr. Collins, both writers of Odes ?
It is odd enough, but each is the half of a considerable
man, and one the counterpart of the other.   The first has
but little invention, very poetical choice of expression,   5
and a good ear.   The second, a fine fancy, modelled
upon the antique, a bad ear, great variety of words, and
images with no choice at all.   They both deserve to last
some years, but will not.[1]   Adieu ! dear S$^{r.}$ — I am very
sincerely yours,
                                            T. C.   10

December 27, [1746].

I was thirty years old yesterday.   What is it o'clock
by you?

[1] Joseph Warton's Odes sold much better than Collins's.

CONTEMPORARY POETS.

TO HORACE WALPOLE.

I AM obliged to you for Mr. Dodsley's book,[1] and
having pretty well looked it over, will (as you desire)
tell you my opinion of it. He might, methinks, have
spared the graces in his frontispiece, if he chose to be
5 economical, and dressed his authors in a little more
decent raiment — not in whited-brown paper, and dis-
torted characters, like an old ballad. I am ashamed to
see myself ; but the company keeps me in countenance :
so to begin with Mr. Tickell. This is not only a state-
10 poem (my ancient aversion), but a state-poem on the
peace of Utrecht. If Mr. Pope had wrote a panegyric
on it, one could hardly have read him with patience : but
this is only a poor short-winded imitator of Addison, who
had himself not above three or four notes in poetry,
15 sweet enough indeed, like those of a German flute, but
such as soon tire and satiate the ear with their frequent
return. Tickell has added to this a great poverty of
sense, and a string of transitions that hardly become a
school-boy. However, I forgive him for the sake of his
20 ballad, which I always thought the prettiest in the world.

All there is of M. Green here, has been printed
before ; there is a profusion of wit everywhere ; reading
would have formed his judgment, and harmonised his
verse, for even his wood-notes often break out into strains
25 of real poetry and music. The "School Mistress"[2] is
excellent in its kind and masterly ; and (I am sorry to
differ from you, but) "London" is to me one of those
few imitations that have all the ease and all the spirit of
an original. The same man's verses[3] on the opening of

[1] Dodsley's *Collection of Poems* (1748).
[2] By W. Shenstone.
[3] Dr. Johnson's.

Garrick's theatre are far from bad. Mr. Dyer (here you 30
will despise me highly) has more of poetry in his imagination than almost any of our number ;[1] but rough and
injudicious. I should range Mr. Bramston only a step
or two above Dr. King, who is as low in my estimation
as in yours. Dr. Evans is a furious madman ; and pre- 35
existence is nonsense in all her altitudes. Mr. Lyttleton
is a gentle elegiac person. Mr. Nugent sure did not
write his own Ode. I like Mr. Whitehead's little poems,
I mean the Ode on a Tent, the Verses to Garrick, and
particularly those to Charles Townsend, better than 40
anything I had seen before of him. * * *

A BALLAD.

TO THE REV. WILLIAM MASON.

CAMBRIDGE, *Saturday, June,* [*1757*].

* * * I WISH you were here, for I am tired of writing
such stuff ; and besides, I have got the old Scotch
ballad[2] on which Douglas was founded ; it is divine, and
as long as from hence to Aston. Have you never seen
it? Aristotle's best rules are observed in it in a manner 5
that shows the author never had heard of Aristotle. It
begins in the fifth act of the play. You may read it
two-thirds through without guessing what it is about ;
and yet, when you come to the end, it is impossible not
to understand the whole story. I send you the two first 10
verses —

> Gil Maurice was an Earle's son,
> His fame it wexed wide.
> It was nae for his grete riches,
> Nae for his mickle pride ; 15

---

[1] Wordsworth thought so too. See his Sonnet *To the Poet, John Dyer*.

[2] Child Maurice. (See Child's *Ballads*, II, 263.)

But it was for a ladie gay
   That lived on Carron's side.
"Where shall I get a bonny boy
   That will win hose and shoon,
20   That will gae to Lord Barnard's ha',
   And bid his ladie come?
Ye maun rin this errand, Willie,
   And ye maun rin with pride;
When other boys gae on their feet,
25   On horseback ye sal ride,"
"Ah na, ah na, my master dear," etc. etc.

*   *   *   *   *   *   *

OSSIAN.

TO HORACE WALPOLE.

[*1760.*]

I AM so charmed with the two specimens of Erse
poetry, that I cannot help giving you the trouble to
enquire a little farther about them, and should wish to
see a few lines of the original, that I may form some
5 slight idea of the language, the measures, and the rhythm.

Is there anything known of the author or authors, and
of what antiquity are they supposed to be? Is there any
more to be had of equal beauty, or at all approaching to
it? I have been often told that the Poem called
"Hardicanute" (which I always admired and still admire)
was the work of somebody that lived a few years ago.
This I do not at all believe, though it has evidently been
retouched in places by some modern hand: but however,
I am authorised by this report to ask, whether the two
15 Poems in question are certainly antique and genuine.
I make this enquiry in quality of an antiquary, and am
not otherwise concerned about it: for, if I were sure that
any one now living in Scotland had written them to
divert himself, and laugh at the credulity of the world, I

would undertake a journey into the Highlands only for 20 the pleasure of seeing him.

OSSIAN.

TO RICHARD STONEHEWER.

LONDON, *June 29, 1760.*

* * * I HAVE received another Scotch packet with a third specimen, inferior in kind (because it is merely description), but yet full of nature and noble wild imagination. Five Bards pass the night at the Castle of a Chief (himself a principal Bard); each goes out in his turn to 5 observe the face of things, and returns with an extempore picture of the changes he has seen ; it is an October night (the harvest-month of the Highlands). This is the whole plan ; yet there is a contrivance, and a preparation of ideas, that you would not expect. The oddest thing 10 is, that every one of them sees Ghosts (more or less). The idea, that struck and surprised me most, is the following. One of them (describing a storm of wind and rain) says

> " Ghosts ride on the tempest to-night :   15
> Sweet is their voice between the gusts of wind;
> *Their songs are of other worlds !*"

Did you never observe (*while rocking winds are piping loud*) that pause, as the gust is recollecting itself, and rising upon the ear in a shrill and plaintive note, like the swell of an Æolian harp ? I do assure you there is 20 nothing in the world so like the voice of a spirit. Thomson had an ear sometimes : he was not deaf to this ; and has described it gloriously, but given it another different turn, and of more horror. I cannot repeat the lines : it is in his " Winter." There is another 25

very fine picture in one of them.   It describes the breaking of the clouds after the storm, before it is settled into
a calm, and when the moon is seen by short intervals.

" The waves are tumbling on the lake,
30   And lash the rocky sides.
The boat is brim-full in the cove,
The oars on the rocking tide.
Sad sits a maid beneath a cliff,
And eyes the rolling stream:
35   Her lover promised to come,
She saw his boat (when it was evening) on the lake;
Are these his groans in the gale ?
Is this his broken boat on the shore ? "

OSSIAN.

TO THOMAS WHARTON.

[Endorsed July, 1760].

* * * IF you have seen Stonehewer he has probably
told you of my old Scotch (or rather Irish) poetry.   I am
gone mad about them.   They are said to be translations
(literal and in prose) from the *Erse* tongue, done by one
5 Macpherson, a young clergyman in the Highlands.   He
means to publish a collection he has of these specimens
of antiquity, if it be antiquity : but what plagues me is, I
cannot come at any certainty on that head.   I was so
struck, so *extasié* with their infinite beauty, that I writ
10 into Scotland to make a thousand enquiries.   The letters
I have in return are ill wrote, ill reasoned, unsatisfactory,
calculated (one would imagine) to deceive one, and yet
not cunning enough to do it cleverly.   In short, the whole
external evidence would make one believe these frag-
15 ments (for so he calls them, though nothing can be more
entire) counterfeit : but the internal is so strong on the
other side, that I am resolved to believe them genuine,

spite of the Devil and the Kirk. It is impossible to convince me, that they were invented by the same man, that writes me these letters. On the other hand it is almost 20 as hard to suppose, if they are original, that he should be able to translate them so admirably. What can one do? since Stonehewer went, I have received another of a very different and inferior kind (being merely descriptive) much more modern than the former (he says) yet very old 25 too; this too in its way is extremely fine. In short this man is the very Daemon of poetry, or he has lighted on a treasure hid for ages. The Welch Poets are also coming to light : I have seen a Discourse in MS. about them (by one Mr. Evans, a clergyman) with specimens of their 30 writings. This is in Latin, and though it don't approach the other, there are fine scraps among it.

You will think I am grown mighty poetical of a sudden; you would think so still more, if you knew, there was a Satire printed against me and Mason jointly, it is called 35 *Two Odes.* [1] the one is inscribed to Obscurity (that is me) the other to Oblivion. It tells me, what I never heard before, for (speaking of himself) the Author says, though he has,

> "Nor the Pride, nor self-Opinion, 40
> That possess the happy Pair,
> Each of Taste the fav'rite Minion,
> Prancing thro' the desert air :
> Yet shall he mount, with classic housings grac'd,
> By help mechanick of equestrian block ; 45
> And all unheedful of the Critic's mock
> Spur his light courser o'er the bounds of Taste."

The writer is a Mr. Colman, who published the *Connoisseur*, nephew to the late Lady Bath, and a friend of Garrick's. I believe his Odes sell no more than mine 50

[1] A Parody on Gray's *Pindaric Odes.*

did, for I saw a heap of them lie in a bookseller's window,
who recommended them to me as a very pretty thing.

If I did not mention *Tristram*[1] to you, it was because
I thought I had done so before. There is much good
55 fun in it, and humour sometimes hit and sometimes
missed. I agree with your opinion of it, and shall see
the two future volumes with pleasure. Have you read
his sermons (with his own comic figure at the head of
them)? they are in the style, I think, most proper for the
60 pulpit, and shew a very strong imagination and a sensible
heart : but you see him often tottering on the verge of
laughter, and ready to throw his periwig in the face of his
audience. * * *

OSSIAN.

TO THE REV. WILLIAM MASON.

PEMBROKE HALL, *August 7, 1760.*

* * * THE Erse Fragments have been published five
weeks ago ·in Scotland, though I had them not (by a
mistake) till last week. As you tell me new things do
not soon reach you at Aston, I enclose what I can ; the
5 rest shall follow when you tell me whether you have not
got it already. I send the two which I had before, for
Mr. Wood, because he has not the affectation of not
admiring. I continue to think them genuine, though my
reasons for believing the contrary are rather stronger
10 than ever : but I will have them antique, for I never
knew a Scotchman of my own time that could read, much
less write, poetry; and such poetry too ! I have one
(from Mr. Macpherson) which he has not printed : it is
mere description, but excellent, too, in its kind. If you
15 are good, and will learn to admire, I will transcribe it.

[1] Sterne's *Tristram Shandy*, published 1759.

Pray send to Sheffield for the last *Monthly Review :* there is a deal of stuff about us and Mr. Colman. It says one of us, at least, has always borne his faculties meekly. I leave you to guess which that is : I think I know. You oaf, you must be meek, must you ? and see what you get 20 by it ! * * *

OSSIAN.

TO DR. CLARKE.

PEMBROKE HALL, *August 12, 1760.*

* * * HAVE you seen the Erse Fragments since they were printed ? I am more puzzled than ever about their antiquity, though I still incline (against everybody's opinion) to believe them old. Those you have already seen are the best ; though there are some others that are 5 excellent too.

OSSIAN.

TO THOMAS WHARTON.

LONDON, *October 21, 1760.*

* * * THERE is a second edition of the Scotch Fragments, yet very few admire them, and almost all take them for fictions. I have a letter from D. Hume, the historian, that asserts them to be genuine, and cites the names of several people (that know both languages) who 5 have heard them current in the mouths of pipers, and other illiterate persons in various and distant parts of the Highlands. There is a subscription for Mr. Macpherson, which will enable him to undertake a mission among the Mountaineers, and pick up all the scattered remnants of 10 old Poetry. He is certainly an admirable judge ; if his *learned* friends do not pervert or overrule his taste. * * *

OSSIAN.

TO THOMAS WHARTON.

PEMBROKE COLLEGE, *January, 1761.*

* * * FOR me, I admire nothing but " Fingal " (I conclude you have read it : if not Stonehewer can lend it
you), yet I remain still in doubt about the authenticity
of those poems, though inclining rather to believe them
5 genuine in spite of the world. Whether they are the
inventions of antiquity, or of a modern Scotchman, either
case is to me alike unaccountable. Je m'y pers. * * *

OSSIAN.

TO THE REV. JAMES BROWN.

February 17, 1763.

* * * NEITHER Count Algarotti, nor Mr. Howe (I
believe) have heard of *Ossian, the Son of Fingal.* If Mr.
Howe were not upon the wing, and on his way home-
wards, I would send it to him in Italy. He would there
5 see, that Imagination dwelt many hundred years ago in
all her pomp on the cold and barren mountains of Scotland. The truth (I believe) is that without any respect
of climates she reigns in all nascent societies of men,
where the necessities of life force every one to think and
10 act much for himself. Adieu !

JEREMY TAYLOR.

TO THE REV. WILLIAM MASON.

LONDON, *January 22, 1761.*

* * * * * * * * *

I HAVE long thought of reading Jeremy Taylor, for I
am persuaded that chopping logic in the pulpit, as our

divines have done ever since the Revolution, is not the thing; but that imagination and warmth of expression are in their place there as much as on the stage, moderated however, and chastised a little by the purity and severity of religion.   *   *   *

CASTLE OF OTRANTO AND ROUSSEAU.

TO HORACE WALPOLE.

Sunday, December 30, 1764.

I HAVE received the *Castle of Otranto*, and return you my thanks for it. It engages our attention here, makes some of us cry a little, and all in general afraid to go to bed o' nights. We take it for a translation, and should believe it to be a true story, if it were not for St. Nicholas.

When your pen was in your hand you might have been a little more communicative, for though disposed enough to believe the opposition rather consumptive, I am entirely ignorant of all the symptoms. Your canonical book I have been reading with great satisfaction. He speaketh as one having authority. If Englishmen have any feeling left, methinks they must feel now; and if the Ministry have any feeling (whom nobody will suspect of insensibility) they must cut off the author's ears, for it is in all the forms a most wicked libel. Is the old man and the lawyer put on, or is it real? or has some real lawyer furnished a good part of the materials, and another person employed them? This I guess; for there is an uncouthness of diction in the beginning which is not supported throughout, though it now and then occurs again, as if the writer was weary of supporting the character he had assumed, when the subject had warmed him, beyond dissimulation.

Rousseau's *Letters* I am reading heavily, heavily ! He
25 justifies himself, till he convinces me that he deserved
to be burnt, at least that his book did. I am not got
through him, and you never will. Voltaire I detest, and
have not seen his book : I shall in good time. You
surprise me, when you talk of going in February. Pray,
30 does all the minority go too ? I hope you have a reason.
Desperare de republica is a deadly sin in politics.

Adieu ! I will not take my leave of you ; for (you
perceive) this letter means to beg another, when you can
spare a little.

DAVID HUME AND SKEPTICISM.

TO JAMES BEATTIE.

PEMBROKE HALL, *July 2, 1770.*

* * * * * * * * *

I HAVE always thought David Hume a pernicious
writer, and believe he has done as much mischief here as
he has in his own country. A turbid and shallow stream
often appears to our apprehensions very deep. A pro-
5 fessed sceptic can be guided by nothing but his present
passions (if he has any) and interests ; and to be masters
of his philosophy we need not his books or advice, for
every child is capable of the same thing, without any
study at all. Is not that *naiveté* and good humour, which
10 his admirers celebrate in him, owing to this, that he has
continued all his days an infant, but one that has
unhappily been taught to read and write ? That childish
nation, the French, have given him vogue and fashion,
and we, as usual, have learned from them to admire him
15 at second hand.

III.

NATURE.

EARLY APPRECIATION.

TO HORACE WALPOLE.

September, 1737.

* * * I ARRIVED safe at my uncle's, who is a great
hunter in imagination ; his dogs take up every chair in
the house, so I am forced to stand at this present writing ;
and though the gout forbids him galloping after them
in the field, yet he continues still to regale his ears and 5
nose with their comfortable noise and stink. He holds
me mighty cheap, I perceive, for walking when I should
ride, and reading when I should hunt. My comfort
amidst all this is, that I have at the distance of half a
mile, through a green lane, a forest (the vulgar call it a 10
common) all my own, at least as good as so, for I spy no
human thing in it but myself. It is a little chaos of
mountains and precipices ; mountains, it is true, that do
not ascend much above the clouds, nor are the declivities
quite so amazing as Dover cliff ; but just such hills as 15
people who love their necks as well as I do may venture
to climb, and crags that give the eye as much pleasure as
if they were more dangerous. Both vale and hill are
covered with most venerable beeches, and other very
reverend vegetables, that, like most other ancient people, 20
are always dreaming out their old stories to the winds,

> And as they bow their hoary tops relate,
> In murm'ring sounds, the dark decrees of fate ;
> While visions, as poetic eyes avow,
> Cling to each leaf, and swarm on every bough. 25

At the foot of one of these squats ME I (il penseroso), and there grow to the trunk for a whole morning. The timorous hare and sportive squirrel gambol around me like Adam in Paradise, before he had an Eve; but I think he
30 did not use to read Virgil, as I commonly do there. * * *

ALPINE SCENERY.

TO MRS. DOROTHY GRAY.

LYONS, *October 13, 1739.*

*   *   *   *   *   *   *   *   *

IT is a fortnight since we set out from hence upon a little excursion to Geneva. We took the longest road, which lies through Savoy, on purpose to see a famous monastery, called the grand Chartreuse, and had no
5 reason to think our time lost. After having travelled seven days very slow (for we did not change horses, it being impossible for a chaise to go post in these roads) we arrived at a little village, among the mountains of Savoy, called Échelles; from thence we proceeded on
10 horses, who are used to the way, to the mountain of the Chartreuse. It is six miles to the top; the road runs winding up it, commonly not six feet broad; on one hand is the rock, with woods of pine-trees hanging overhead; on the other, a monstrous precipice, almost perpendicular,
15 at the bottom of which rolls a torrent, that sometimes tumbling among the fragments of stone that have fallen from on high, and sometimes precipitating itself down vast descents with a noise like thunder, which is still made greater by the echo from the mountains on each
20 side, concurs to form one of the most solemn, the most romantic,[1] and the most astonishing scenes I ever beheld:

[1] This word was not at that time often used in a favourable sense.

add to this the strange views made by the craggs and
cliffs on the other hand ; the cascades that in many places
throw themselves from the very summit down into the
vale, and the river below ; and many other particulars
impossible to describe ; you will conclude we had no 25
occasion to repent our pains. * * *

ALPINE SCENERY.

TO MRS. DOROTHY GRAY.

TURIN, *November 7, 1739.*

I AM this night arrived here, and have just set down to
rest me after eight days' tiresome journey. For the
three first we had the same road we before passed through
to go to Geneva; the fourth we turned out of it, and for
that day and the next travelled rather among than upon 5
the Alps; the way commonly running through a deep
valley by the side of the river Arve, which works itself a
passage, with great difficulty and a mighty noise, among
vast quantities of rocks, that have rolled down from the
mountain-tops. The winter was so far advanced, as in 10
great measure to spoil the beauty of the prospect;
however, there was still somewhat fine remaining amidst
the savageness and horror of the place : the sixth we
began to go up several of these mountains ; and as we
were passing one, met with an odd accident enough : Mr. 15
Walpole had a little fat black spaniel, that he was very
fond of, which he sometimes used to set down, and let it
run by the chaise side. We were at that time in a very
rough road, not two yards broad at most ; on one side
was a great wood of pines, and on the other a vast preci- 20
pice ; it was noonday, and the sun shone bright, when
all of a sudden, from the wood-side (which was as steep

upwards as the other part was downwards), out rushed a
great wolf, came close to the head of the horses, seized
25 the dog by the throat, and rushed up the hill again with
him in his mouth.   This was done in less than a quarter
of a minute ; we all saw it, and yet the servants had not
time to draw their pistols, or do anything to save the dog.
If he had not been there, and the creature had thought
30 fit to lay hold of one of the horses ; chaise, and we, and
all must inevitably have tumbled above fifty fathoms
perpendicular down the precipice.   The seventh we came
to Lanebourg, the last town in Savoy ; it lies at the foot
of the famous Mount Cenis, which is so situated as to
35 allow no room for any way but over the very top of it.
Here the chaise was forced to be pulled to pieces, and
the baggage and that to be carried by mules.   We ourselves were wrapped up in our furs, and seated upon a
sort of matted chair without legs, which is carried upon
40 poles in the manner of a bier, and so begun to ascend by
the help of eight men.   It was six miles to the top, where
a plain opens itself about as many more in breadth,
covered perpetually with very deep snow, and in the
midst of that a great lake of unfathomable depth, from
45 whence a river takes its rise, and tumbles over monstrous
rocks quite down the other side of the mountain.   The
descent is six miles more, but infinitely more steep than
the going up ; and here the men perfectly fly down with
you, stepping from stone to stone with incredible swift-
50 ness in places where none but they could go three paces
without falling.   The immensity of the precipices, the
roaring of the river and torrents that run into it, the huge
craggs covered with ice and snow, and the clouds below
you and about you, are objects it is impossible to con-
55 ceive without seeing them ; and though we had heard
many strange descriptions of the scene, none of them at

all came up to it. We were but five hours in performing
the whole, from which you may judge of the rapidity of
the men's motion. We are now got into Piedmont, and
stopped a little while at La Ferrière, a small village about 60
three-quarters of the way down, but still among the
clouds, where we began to hear a new language spoken
round about us; at last we got quite down, went through
the Pas de Suse, a narrow road among the Alps, defended
by two fortresses, and lay at Bussoleno. Next evening 65
through a fine avenue of nine miles in length, as straight
as a line, we arrived at this city, which, as you know, is
the capital of the Principality, and the residence of the
King of Sardinia. * * * We shall stay here, I believe, a
fortnight, and proceed for Genoa, which is three or four 70
days' journey to go post. — I am, etc.

ALPINE SCENERY.

TO RICHARD WEST.

TURIN, *November 16, 1739.*

* * * I OWN I have not, as yet, anywhere met with
those grand and simple works of Art, that are to amaze
one, and whose sight one is to be the better for : but
those of Nature have astonished me beyond expression.
In our little journey up to the Grande Chartreuse, I do 5
not remember to have gone ten paces without an exclama-
tion, that there was no restraining. Not a precipice, not
a torrent, not a cliff, but is pregnant with religion and
poetry. There are certain scenes that would awe an
atheist into belief, without the help of other argument. 10
One need not have a very fantastic imagination to see
spirits there at noonday; you have Death perpetually
before your eyes, only so far removed, as to compose the

mind without frighting it. I am well persuaded St.
15 Bruno was a man of no common genius, to choose such
a situation for his retirement ; and perhaps should have
been a disciple of his, had I been born in his time. You
may believe Abelard and Heloise were not forgot upon
this occasion. If I do not mistake, I saw you too every
20 now and then at a distance along the trees ; il me semble,
que j'ai vu ce chien de visage là quelque part. You seemed
to call to me from the other side of the precipice, but the
noise of the river below was so great, that I really could
not distinguish what you said ; it seemed to have a cadence
25 like verse. In your next you will be so good to let me
know what it was. The week we have since passed
among the Alps, has not equalled the single day upon
that mountain, because the winter was rather too far
advanced, and the weather a little foggy. However, it
30 did not want its beauties ; the savage rudeness of the
view is inconceivable without seeing it : I reckoned in
one day, thirteen cascades, the least of which was, I dare
say, one hundred feet in height. * * * Mont Cenis,
I confess, carries the permission mountains have of being
35 frightful rather too far ; and its horrors were accompanied
with too much danger to give one time to reflect upon
their beauties. There is a family of the Alpine monsters
I have mentioned, upon its very top, that in the middle
of winter calmly lay in their stock of provisions and firing,
40 and so are buried in their hut for a month or two under
the snow. * * *

MOUNTAINS.

TO THE REV. WILLIAM MASON.

1765.

*　*　*　*　*　*　*　*　*

I am returned from Scotland charmed with my expedition ; it is of the Highlands I speak ; the Lowlands are

worth seeing once, but the mountains are ecstatic, and
ought to be visited in pilgrimage once a year. None but
those monstrous creatures of God know how to join so 5
much beauty with so much horror. A fig for your poets,
painters, gardeners, and clergymen, that have not been
among them; their imagination can be made up of
nothing but bowling-greens, flowering shrubs, horse-
ponds, Fleet ditches, shell grottoes, and Chinese rails. 10
Then I had so beautiful an autumn, Italy could hardly
produce a nobler scene, and this so sweetly contrasted
with that perfection of nastiness, and total want of
accommodation, that Scotland only can supply. Oh, you
would have blessed yourself. I shall certainly go again; 15
what a pity it is I cannot draw, nor describe, nor ride on
horseback.

* * * * * * * * *

JOURNAL IN THE LAKES.[1]

JOURNAL, 30 SEPT. 1769.

WIND at N. W.; clouds and sunshine. A mile and a
half from Brough on a hill lay a great army encamped.
To the left opened a fine valley with green meadows and
hedge rows, a gentleman's house peeping forth from a
grove of old trees. On a nearer approach, appeared 5
myriads of horses and cattle in the road itself and in all
the fields round me, a brisk stream hurrying cross the
way, thousands of clean healthy people in their best
party-coloured apparel, farmers and their families,
esquires and their daughters, hastening up from the dales 10
and down the fells on every side, glittering in the sun

---

[1] This Journal was kept merely for the amusement of Dr. Wharton,
whose illness prevented him from accompanying Gray.

and pressing forward to join the throng: while the dark hills, on many of whose tops the mists were yet hanging, served as a contrast to this gay and moving scene, which continued for near two miles more along the road, and
5 the crowd (coming towards it) reached on as far as Appleby.

On the ascent of the hill above Appleby the thick hanging wood and the long reaches of the Eden (rapid, clear, and full as ever) winding below with views of the
10 castle and town gave much employment to the mirror; [1] but the sun was wanting and the sky overcast. Oats and barley cut everywhere, but not carried in. Passed Kirby-thore, Sir W. Dalston's house at Acorn-Bank, Whinfield Park, Hart-horn Oaks, Countess-Pillar, Broug-
15 ham-Castle, Mr. Brown (one of the Six Clerks) his large new house, crossed the Eden and the Eimot (pronounce Eeman) with its green vale, and at three o'clock dined with Mrs. Buchanan, at *Penrith*, on trout and partridge. In the afternoon walked up the Beacon-hill a mile to the
20 top, saw Whinfield and Lowther Parks, and through an opening in the bosom of that cluster of mountains, which the Doctor [2] well remembers, the lake of Ulz-water, with the craggy tops of a hundred nameless hills. These to W. and S.; to the N. a great extent of black and dreary
25 plains; to E. Crossfell just visible through mists and vapours hovering round it.

October 1. Wind at S. W.: a gray autumnal day, air perfectly calm and gentle. Went to see Ulz-water, five miles distant. Soon left the Keswick road, and turned
30 to the left through shady lanes along the vale of *Eeman*,

---

[1] Mr. Gray carried usually with him on these tours a plano-convex mirror, of about four inches diameter, on a black foib, and bound up like a pocket-book. — *Mason.*

[2] Thomas Wharton.

which runs rapidly on near the way, rippling over the stones. To the right is *Delmaine*, a large fabric of pale red stone, with nine windows in front, and seven on the side built by Mr. Hassle, behind it a fine lawn surrounded by woods and a long rocky eminence rising over them. 5 A clear and brisk rivulet runs by the house to join the Eeman, whose course is in sight and at a small distance. Farther on appears *Hatton St. John*, a castle-like old mansion of Mr. Huddleston. Approached *Dunmallert*, a fine pointed hill, covered with wood planted by old Mr. 10 Hassle, before mentioned, who lives always at home, and delights in planting. Walked over a spungy meadow or two and began to mount this hill through a broad and strait green alley among the trees, and with some toil gained the summit. From hence saw the lake opening 15 directly at my feet majestic in its calmness, clear and smooth as a blue mirror, with winding shores and low points of land covered with green inclosures, white farm houses looking out among the trees, and cattle feeding. The water is almost every where bordered with cultivated 20 lands gently sloping upwards till they reach the feet of the mountains, which rise very rude and awful with their broken tops on either hand: directly in front, at better than three miles distance, *Place Fell*, one of the bravest among them, pushes its bold broad breast into the midst 25 of the lake and forces it to alter its course, forming first a large bay to the left, and then bending to the right.

I descended *Dunmallert* again by a side avenue, that was only not perpendicular, and came to *Barton* bridge over the *Eeman*, then walking through a path in the wood 30 round the bottom of the hill came forth, where the *Eeman* issues out of the lake, and continued my way along its western shore close to the water, and generally on a level with it. Saw a cormorant flying over it and fishing.

The figure of Ulz-water nothing resembles that laid
down in our maps: it is 9 miles long, and (at widest)
under a mile in breadth.   After extending itself three
miles and a half in a line to S. W. it turns at the foot of
5 *Place Fell*, almost due W. and is here not twice the
breadth of the Thames at London.   It is soon again
interrupted by the roots of Helvellyn, a lofty and very
rugged mountain, and spreading again turns off to S. E.
and is lost among the deep recesses of the hills.   To this
10 second turning I pursued my way about 4 miles along its
borders beyond a village scattered among trees, and
called *Water-Mallock*, in a pleasant grave day, perfectly
calm and warm, but without a gleam of sunshine.   Then
the sky seeming to thicken the valley to grow more
15 desolate, and evening drawing on, I returned by the way
I came to *Penrith*.

October 2. Wind at S. E.; sky clearing, *Cross Fell*
misty, but the outline of the other hills very distinct.
Set out at 10 for *Keswick*, by the road we went in 1767.
20 Saw *Greystock* town and castle to the right, which lie
only 3 miles (over the Fells) from Ulz-water.   Passed
through *Penradock* and *Threlcot* at the feet of *Saddleback*,
whose furrowed sides were gilt by noonday sun, while its
brow appeared of a sad purple from the shadow of the
25 clouds, as they sailed slowly by it.   The broad and green
valley of *Gardies* and *Lowside*, with a swift stream glittering among the cottages and meadows lay to the left ; and
the much finer (but narrower) valley of St. *John's* opening
into it.   *Hill-top*, the large, though low, mansion of the
30 Gaskarths, now a farm-house, seated on an eminence
among woods under a steep fell, was what appeared the
most conspicuous, and beside it a great rock like some
ancient tower nodding to its fall.   Passed by the side of
Skiddaw, and its cub called *Latterrig;* and saw from an

eminence, at two miles distance, the vale of Elysium in all its verdure, the sun then playing on the bosom of the lake, and lighting up all the mountains with its lustre.

Dined by 2 o'clock at the Queen's head, and then straggled out alone to the *Parsonage*, fell down on my back across a dirty lane, with my glass open in one hand, but broke only my knuckles, staid nevertheless, and saw the sun set in all its glory.

October 3. Wind at S. E.; a heavenly day. Rose at 7, and walked out under the conduct of my landlord to *Borrodale*. The grass was covered with a hoar frost, which soon melted, and exhaled in a thin blueish smoke. Crossed the meadows obliquely, catching a diversity of views among the hills over the lake and islands, and changing prospect at every ten paces; left *Cockshut* and *Castlehill* (which we formerly mounted) behind me, and drew near the foot of *Walla-crag*, whose bare and rocky brow, cut perpendicularly down above 400 feet, as I guess, awefully overlooks the way; our path here tends to the left, and the ground gently rising, and covered with a glade of scattering trees and bushes on the very margin of the water, opens both ways the most delicious view, that my eyes ever beheld. Behind you are the magnificent heights of *Walla-crag;* opposite lie the thick hanging woods of Lord Egremont, and *Newland* valley, with green and smiling fields embosomed in the dark cliffs; to the left the jaws of *Borrodale*, with that turbulent chaos of mountain behind mountain, rolled in confusion; beneath you, and stretching far away to the right, the shining purity of the *Lake*, just ruffled by the breeze, enough to shew it is alive, reflecting rocks, woods, fields, and inverted tops of mountains, with the white buildings of *Keswick*, *Crosthwait* church, and *Skiddaw* for a back ground at a distance. Oh! Doctor! I never

wished more for you; and pray think, how the glass played its part in such a spot, which is called Carf-close-reeds; I chuse to set down these barbarous names, that any body may enquire on the place, and easily find the
5 particular station, that I mean. This scene continues to *Barrow-gate*, and a little farther, passing a brook called *Barrow-beck*, we entered *Borrodale*. The crags, named *Lodoor-banks*, now begin to impend terribly over your way; and more terribly, when you hear, that three years
10 since an immense mass of rock tumbled at once from the brow, and barred all access to the dale (for this is the only road) till they could work their way through it. Luckily no one was passing at the time of this fall; but down the side of the mountain, and far into the lake lie
15 dispersed the huge fragments of this ruin in all shapes and in all directions. Something farther we turned aside into a coppice, ascending a little in front of *Lodoor* water-fall, the height appears to be about 200 feet, the quantity of water not great, though (these three days excepted) it
20 had rained daily in the hills for near two months before: but then the stream was nobly broken, leaping from rock to rock, and foaming with fury. On one side a towering crag, that spired up to equal, if not overtop, the neighbour-ing cliffs (this lay all in shade and darkness) on the other
25 hand a rounder broader projecting hill shagged with wood and illumined by the sun, which glanced sideways on the upper part of the cataract. The force of the water wearing a deep channel in the ground hurries away to join the lake. We descended again, and passed the
30 stream over a rude bridge. Soon after we came under *Gowder* crag, a hill more formidable to the eye and to the apprehension than that of *Lodoor;* the rocks a-top, deep-cloven perpendicularly by the rains, hanging loose and nodding forwards, seem just starting from their base in

shivers ; the whole way down, and the road on both sides is strewed with piles of the fragments strangely thrown across each other, and of a dreadful bulk. The place reminds one of those passes in the Alps, where the guides tell you to move on with speed, and say nothing, 5 lest the agitation of the air should loosen the snows above, and bring down a mass, that would overwhelm a caravan. I took their counsel here and hastened on in silence.

Non ragionam di lor ; ma guarda, e passa ! 10

The hills here are clothed all up their steep sides with oak, ash, birch, holly, &c. : some of it has been cut 40 years ago, some within these 8 years, yet all is sprung again green, flourishing, and tall for its age, in a place where no soil appears but the staring rock, and where a 15 man could scarce stand upright.

Met a civil young farmer overseeing his reapers (for it is oat-harvest here) who conducted us to a neat white house in the village of Grange, which is built on a rising ground in the midst of a valley. Round it the mountains 20 form an awful amphitheatre, and through it obliquely runs the Derwent clear as glass, and shewing under its bridge every trout that passes. Beside the village rises a round eminence of rock, covered entirely with old trees, and over that more proudly towers Castle-crag, invested 25 also with wood on its sides, and bearing on its naked top some traces of a fort said to be Roman. By the side of this hill, which almost blocks up the way, the valley turns to the left and contracts its dimensions, till there is hardly any road but the rocky bed of the river. The 30 wood of the mountains increases and their summits grow loftier to the eye, and of more fantastic forms : among them appear *Eagle's Cliff*, *Dove's-Nest*, *Whitedale-pike*, &c., celebrated names in the annals of Keswick. The

dale opens about four miles higher till you come to *Sea
Whaite* (where lies the way mounting the hills to the
right, that leads to the *Wadd-mines*) all farther access is
here barred to prying mortals, only there is a little path
5 winding over the Fells, and for some weeks in the year
passable to the Dale's-men ; but the mountains know
well, that these innocent people will not reveal the
mysteries of their ancient kingdom, the reign of Chaos
and Old Night. Only I learned, that this dreadful road,
10 dividing again leads one branch to *Ravenglas*, and the
other to *Hawkshead*.

For me I went no farther than the farmer's (better
than 4 m : from Keswick) at *Grange :* his mother and he
brought us butter, that Siserah would have jumped at,
15 though not in a lordly dish, bowls of milk, thin oaten
cakes, and ale ; and we had carried a cold tongue thither
with us. Our farmer was himself the man, that last year
plundered the eagle's eirie : all the dale are up in arms
on such an occasion, for they lose abundance of lambs
20 yearly, not to mention hares, partridge, grouse, &c. He
was let down from the cliff in ropes to the shelf of rock,
on which the nest was built, the people above shouting
and hollowing to fright the old birds, which flew screaming round, but did not dare to attack him. He brought
25 off the eaglet (for there is rarely more than one) and an
addle egg. The nest was roundish and more than a yard
over, made of twigs twisted together. Seldom a year
passes but they take the brood or eggs, and sometimes
they shoot one, sometimes the other parent, but the
30 survivor has always found a mate (probably in Ireland),
and they breed near the old place. By his description I
learn, that this species is the *Erne* (the Vultur *Albicilla*
of Linnæus in his last edition, but in yours *Falco Albicilla*)
so consult him and Pennant about it.

Walked leisurely home the way we came, but saw a new landscape: the features indeed were the same in part, but many new ones were disclosed by the midday sun, and the tints were entirely changed. Take notice this was the best or perhaps the only day for going up 5 Skiddaw, but I thought it better employed: it was perfectly serene, and hot as Midsummer.

In the evening walked alone down to the Lake by the side of *Crow-Park* after sun-set and saw the solemn colouring of night draw on, the last gleam of sunshine 10 fading away on the hill-tops, the deep serene of the waters, and the long shadows of the mountains thrown across them, till they nearly touched the hithermost shore. At distance heard the murmur of many waterfalls not audible in the day-time. Wished for the Moon, but 15 she was *dark to me and silent, hid in her vacant interlunar cave.*

October 4. Wind E.; clouds and sunshine, and in the course of the day a few drops of rain. Walked to *Crow-Park*, now a rough pasture, once a glade of ancient oaks, 20 whose large roots still remain on the ground, but nothing has sprung from them. If one single tree had remained, this would have been an unparalleled spot; and Smith judged right, when he took his print of the Lake from hence, for it is a gentle eminence, not too high, on the 25 very margin of the water and commanding it from end to end, looking full into the *gorge* of *Borrodale*. I prefer it even to Cockshut-hill, which lies beside it, and to which I walked in the afternoon: It is covered with young trees both sown and planted, oak, spruce, Scotch-fir, &c., all 30 which thrive wonderfully. There is an easy ascent to the top, and the view far preferable to that on Castle-hill (which you remember) because this is lower and nearer to the Lake: for I find all points, that are much

elevated, spoil the beauty of the valley, and make its parts (which are not large) look poor and diminutive. While I was here, a little shower fell, red clouds came marching up the hills from the east, and part
5 of a bright rainbow seemed to rise along the side of Castle-hill.

From hence I got to the *Parsonage* a little before sunset, and saw in my glass a picture, that if I could transmit to you, and fix it in all the softness of its living
10 colours, would fairly sell for a thousand pounds. This is the sweetest scene I can yet discover in point of pastoral beauty. The rest are in a sublimer style.

October 5. Wind N. E. Clouds and sunshine. Walked through the meadows and corn-fields to the Derwent and
15 crossing it went up How-hill. It looks along the Basinth-waite water and sees at the same time the course of the river, and a part of the upper lake with a full view of Skiddaw. Then I took my way through Portingskall village to the *Park*, a hill so called covered entirely with
20 wood: it is all a mass of crumbling slate. Passed round its foot between the trees and the edge of the water, and came to a Peninsula that juts out into the lake, and looks along it both ways. In front rises Walla-crag, and Castle-hill, the town, the road to Penrith, Skiddaw and
25 Saddle-back. Returning met a brisk and cold North Eastern blast, that ruffled all the surface of the lake and made it rise in little waves that broke at the foot of the wood. After dinner walked up the Penrith road two miles or more and turning into a corn-field to the right,
30 called Castle-Rigg, saw a Druid circle of large stones 108 feet in diameter, the biggest not eight feet high, but most of them still erect: They are fifty in number, the valley of *Naddle* appeared in sight, and the fells of St. John's, particularly the summits of *Catchidecam* (called by

Camden, *Casticand*) and *Helvellyn*, said to be as high as *Skiddaw*, and to arise from a much higher base. A shower came on, and I returned.

October 6. Wind E. ; clouds and sun. Went in a chaise eight miles along the west side of Bassinthwaite-water, to *Ouse*-bridge (pronounce *Ews bridge*) the road in some part made, and very good, the rest slippery and dangerous cart-road, or narrow rugged lanes, but no precipices : it runs directly along the foot of Skiddaw. Opposite to Thornthwaite falls, and the brows of *Widhope-brows* (covered to the top with wood) a very beautiful view opens down the lake, which is narrower and longer than that of Keswick, less broken into bays and without islands, at the foot of it a few paces from the brink gently sloping upward stands *Armathwaite* in a thick grove of Scotch firs, commanding a noble view directly up the lake. At a small distance behind the house is a large extent of wood, and still behind this a ridge of cultivated hills, on which (according to the Keswick Proverb) the sun always shines. The inhabitants here on the contrary call the vale of Derwent-water the *Devil's Chamber-Pot*, and pronounce the name of *Skiddaw-Fell* (which termi-nates here) with a sort of terror and aversion. *Armath-waite-house* is a modern fabric, not large, and built of dark red stone, belonging to *Mr. Spedding*, whose grand-father was steward to old Sir James Lowther, and bought this estate of the *Himers*. So you must look for Mr. Michell in some other country. The sky was overcast and the wind cool, so after dining at a public house, which stands here near the bridge (that crosses the Derwent just where it issues from the lake), and saunter-ing a little by the water-side, I came home again. The turnpike is finished from Cockermouth hither (five miles) and is carrying on to Penrith ; several little showers to-day. A man came in, who said there was snow on *Cross-fell* this morning.

Oct. 7. Market day here. Wind, North East. Clouds and sunshine: little showers at intervals all day: yet
5 walked in the morning to Crow-park, and in the evening up Penrith road: the clouds came rolling up the mountains all round very unpromising, yet the moon shone at intervals, it was too damp to go towards the lake. To-morrow mean to bid farewell to Keswick.

10   Botany might be studied here in perfection at another season because of the great variety of soils and elevations all lying within a small compass. I observed nothing but several curious Lichens, and plenty of Gale, or Dutch Myrtle perfuming the borders of the lake. This year the
15 Wadd-mine had been opened (which is done once in five years) it is taken out in lumps sometimes as big as a man's fist, and will undergo no preparation by fire, not being fusible. When it is pure, soft, black, and close grained, it is worth sometimes 30 shillings a pound. The
20 mine lies about a mile up the Fells, near *Sea-waite*, at the head of Borrodale. There are no charr ever taken in these lakes, but plenty in Buttermere-water, which lies a little way north of Borrodale, about Martlemas, which are potted here. They sow chiefly oats and bigg here, which
25 are now cutting and still on the ground. There is some hay not yet got in. The rains have done much hurt ; yet observe, the soil is so thin and light, that no day has passed, in which I could not walk out with ease, and you know, I am no lover of dirt. Their wheat comes from
30 Cockermouth or Penrith. Fell-mutton is now in season for about six weeks ; it grows fat on the mountains, and nearly resembles venison : excellent pike and perch (here called *bass*) trout is out of season: partridge in great plenty.

Receipt to dress Perch (for Mrs. Wharton). "Wash, but neither scale, nor gut them. Broil till they are enough, then pull out the fins, and open them along the back, take out the bone and all the inwards without breaking them: put in a good lump of butter and salt, 5 clap the sides together, till it melts, and serve very hot; it is excellent. The skin must not be eaten."

October 8th. Bid farewell to Keswick and took the Ambleside road in a gloomy morning; wind east and afterwards north east; about two miles from the town 10 mounted an eminence called *Castle Rigg*, and the sun breaking out discovered the most beautiful view I have yet seen of the whole valley behind me, the two lakes, the river, the mountain, all in their glory! had almost a mind to have gone back again. The road in some little 15 patches is not completed, but good country road through sound, but narrow and stony lanes, very safe in broad daylight. This is the case about *Causeway-foot*, and among *Naddle-fells* to *Lanthwaite*. The vale you go in has little breadth the mountains are vast and rocky, the 20 fields little and poor, and the inhabitants are now making hay, and see not the sun by two hours in a day so long as at Keswick. Came to the foot of Helvellyn, along which runs an excellent road, looking down from a little height on Lee's-water, (called also Thirl-meer, or 25 Wiborn-water) and soon descending on its margin. The lake from its depth looks black, (though really as clear as glass) and from the gloom of the vast crags, that scowl over it: it is narrow and about three miles long, resembling a river in its course; little shining torrents hurry 30 down the rocks to join it, with not a bush to overshadow them, or cover their march: all is rock and loose stones up to the very brow, which lies so near your way, that not above half the height of Helvellyn can be seen. (To be continued, but now we have got franks.)

Past by the little chapel of *Wiborn*, out of which the Sunday congregation were then issuing. Past a beck near *Dunmailraise* and entered Westmoreland a second time, now begin to see *Helm-crag* distinguished from its
5 rugged neighbours not so much by its height, as by the strange broken outline of its top, like some gigantic building demolished, and the stones that composed it flung across each other in wild confusion. Just beyond it opens one of the sweetest landscapes that art ever
10 attempted to imitate. The bosom of the mountains spreading here into a broad bason discovers in the midst *Grasmere-water;* its margin is hollowed into small bays with bold eminences : some of them rocks, some of soft turf that half conceal and vary the figure of the little lake
15 they command. From the shore a low promontory pushes itself far into the water, and on it stands a white village with the parish-church rising in the midst of it, hanging enclosures, corn-fields, and meadows green as an emerald, with their trees and hedges, and cattle fill up
20 the whole space from the edge of the water. Just opposite to you is a large farm-house at the bottom of a steep smooth lawn embosomed in old woods, which climb half way up the mountain's side, and discover above them a broken line of crags, that crown the scene. Not
25 a single red tile, no flaming gentleman's house, or garden walls break in upon the repose of this little unsuspected paradise, but all is peace, rusticity, and happy poverty in its neatest, most becoming attire.

The road winds here over *Grasmere-hill*, whose rocks
30 soon conceal the water from your sight, yet it is continued along behind them, and contracting itself to a river communicates with *Ridale-water*, another small lake, but of inferior size and beauty ; it seems shallow too, for large patches of reeds appear pretty far within it. Into this

vale the road descends: on the opposite banks large and ancient woods mount up the hills, and just to the left of our way stands *Ridale-hall*, the family seat of Sir Mic. Fleming, but now a farm-house, a large old fashioned fabric surrounded with wood, and not much too good for 5 its present destination. Sir Michael is now on his travels, and all this timber far and wide belongs to him, I tremble for it when he returns. Near the house rises a huge crag called *Ridale-head*, which is said to command a full view of *Wynander-mere*, and I doubt it not, for 10 within a mile that great lake is visible even from the road. As to going up the crag, one might as well go up Skiddaw.

Came to *Ambleside* eighteen miles from *Keswick*, meaning to lie there, but on looking into the best bed-chamber 15 dark and damp as a cellar, grew delicate gave up *Wynander-mere* in despair, and resolved I would go on to *Kendal* directly, fourteen miles farther; the road in general fine turnpike but some parts (about three miles in all) not made, yet without danger. 20

Unexpectedly was well rewarded for my determination. The afternoon was fine, and the road for full five miles runs along the side of *Wynander-mere*, with delicious views across it, and almost from one end to the other: it is ten miles in length and at most a mile over, resembling 25 the course of some vast and magnificent river, but no flat marshy grounds, no osier beds, or patches of scrubby plantation on its banks: at the head two valleys open the mountains, one, that by which we came down, the other Langsledale in which Wrynose and Hard-knot two great 30 mountains rise above the rest. From thence the fells visibly sink and soften along its sides. Sometimes they run into it, (but with a gentle declivity) in their own dark and natural complexion, oftener they are green and culti-

vated with farms interspersed and round eminences on
the border covered with trees: towards the South it
seems to break into larger bays with several islands and
a wider extent of cultivation: the way rises continually
5 till at a place called *Orresthead* it turns to South East
losing sight of the water.   Passed by *Ing's* chapel and
Stavely, but I can say no farther for the dusk of the
evening coming on I entered *Kendal* almost in the dark,
and could distinguish only a shadow of the castle on a
10 hill, and tenter grounds spread far and wide round the
town, which I mistook for houses.   My inn promised
sadly, having two wooden galleries (like Scotland) in
front of it.   It was indeed an old ill-contrived house, but
kept by civil sensible people, so I stayed two nights with
15 them, and fared and slept very comfortably.

Oct. 9. Wind N. W. clouds and sun air as mild as
summer ; all corn off the ground sky-larks singing aloud
(by the way I saw not one at *Keswick* perhaps because
the place abounds in birds of prey) went up the castle-
20 hill, the town consists chiefly of three nearly parallel
streets almost a mile long, except these all the other houses
seem as if they had been dancing a country-dance and
were out; there they stand back to back, corner to
corner, some up hill some down without intent or mean-
25 ing; along by their side runs a fine brisk stream, over
which are three stone bridges, the buildings (a few comfortable houses excepted) are mean, of stone and covered
with a bad rough cast.   Near the end of the town stands
a handsome house of Col. Wilson's and adjoining to it
30 the church, a very large Gothic fabric with a square
tower, it has no particular ornaments but double aisles
and at the east end four chapels or choirs, one of the
Parrs, another of the Stricklands, the third is the proper
choir of the church, and a fourth of the Bellinghams, a

family now extinct. The remains of the castle are seated on a fine hill on the side of the river opposite to the town, almost the whole enclosure of walls remains with four towers, two square and two round, but their upper part and embattlements are demolished, it is of rough 5 stone and cement; without any ornaments or arms round, enclosing a court of like form and surrounded by a moat, nor ever could have been larger than it is for there are no traces of outworks, there is a good view of the town and river with a fertile open valley through which it winds. 10

After dinner went along the *Milthrop* turnpike four miles to see the falls (or force) of the river Kent: came to *Siserge* (pronounce *Siser*) and turned down a lane to the left, *Siser*, the seat of the Stricklands an old catholic family is an ancient hall-house with a very large tower 15 embattled : the rest of the buildings added to this are of later date, but all is white, and seen to advantage on a back ground of old trees; there is a small park also well wooded, opposite to this turned to the left and soon came to the river: it works its way in a narrow and deep rocky 20 channel overhung with trees. The calmness and brightness of the evening, the roar of the waters, and the thumping of huge hammers at an iron forge not far distant made it a singular walk, but as to the falls (for there are two) they are not four feet high. I went on 25 down to the forge and saw the demons at work by the light of their own fires : the iron is brought in pigs to *Milthrop* by sea from *Scotland*, and is here beat into bars and plates. Two miles farther at *Levens* is the seat of Lord Suffolk, where he sometimes passes the summer; it 30 was a favorite place of his late Countess, but this I did not see.

Oct. 10. Went by *Burton* to *Lancaster*. Wind N. W. Clouds and sun: twenty-two miles: very good country

well inclosed and wooded, with some common interspersed; passed at the foot of *Farlton-Knot* a high fell;
four miles north of *Lancaster*, on a rising ground called
Bolton (pronounce *Bouton*) we had a full view of *Cartmell-*
5 *sands*, with here and there a passenger riding over them,
(it being low water) the points of *Furness* shooting far
into the sea, and lofty mountains partly covered with
clouds extending North of them. *Lancaster* also appeared
very conspicuous and fine, for its most distinguished
10 features, the castle and the church mounted on a green
eminence, were all that could be seen. Woe is me!
when I got thither, it was the second day of their fair;
the inn in the principal street was a great old gloomy
house full of people, but I found tolerable quarters, and
15 even slept two nights in peace.

Ascended the castle-hill in a fine afternoon; it takes
up the higher top of the eminence on which it stands,
and is irregularly round encompassed with a deep moat.
In front towards the town is a magnificent Gothic gate-
20 way, lofty and huge, the over-hanging battlements are
supported by a triple range of corbels, the intervals
pierced through and showing the day from above; on its
top rise light watch-towers of small height, it opens below
with a grand pointed arch; over this is a wrought taber-
25 nacle, doubtless once containing the founder's figure, on
one side a shield of France semy quartered with England,
on the other the same with a label ermine for John of
Gaunt, Duke of Lancaster. This opens to a court
within, which I did not much care to enter being the
30 county gaol and full of prisoners, both criminals and
debtors. From this gate-way the walls continue and join
it to a vast square tower of great height, the lower part
at least of remote antiquity; for it has small round-
headed lights with plain short pillars on each side of

them ; there is a third tower also square and of less
dimensions, this is all the castle : near it and but little
lower stands the church a large and plain Gothic fabric :
the high square tower at the west end has been rebuilt of
late years, but nearly in the same style.   There are no   5
ornaments of arms, &c. any where to be seen, within it is
lightsome and spacious, but not one monument of
antiquity, or piece of painted glass is left : from the
church-yard there is an extensive sea-view (for now the
tide had almost covered the sands, and filled the river),   10
and besides greatest part of *Furness* I could distinguish
Peel-castle on the *Isle of Fowdrey*, which lies off its southern extremity, the town is built on the slope, and at the
foot of the Castle-hill more than twice the bigness of
Auckland, with many neat buildings of white stone, but a   15
little disorderly in their position ad libitum like Kendal.
Many also extend below on the Keys by the river side,
where a number of ships were moored, some of them
three mast vessels, decked out with their colours in
honour of the fair.   Here is a good bridge of four arches   20
over the Lune, which runs when the tide is out in two
streams divided by a bed of gravel, which is not covered
but in spring tides, below the town it widens to near the
breadth of the Thames at London, and meets the sea at
five or six miles distance to the S. W.   25

Oct. 11.   Wind S. W. ; clouds and sun : warm and a
fine dappled sky : crossed the river and walked over a
peninsula three miles to the village of Pooton, which
stands on the beach.   An old fisherman mending his
nets (while I enquired about the danger of passing those   30
sands) told me in his dialect a moving story.   How a
brother of the trade, a cockler (as he styled him) driving
a little cart with two daughters (women grown) in it, and
his wife on horseback following, set out one day to pass

the Seven Mile Sands, as they had frequently been used
to do : for nobody in the village knew them better than
the old man did. When they were about half way over a
thick fog rose, and as they advanced, they found the
5 water much deeper than they expected. The old man
was puzzled, he stopped, and said he would go a little
way to find some mark he was acquainted with. They
staid a little while for him but in vain. They called
aloud, but no reply, at last the young women pressed
10 their mother to think where they were, and go on. She
would not leave the place, she wandered about forlorn
and amazed. She would not quit her horse, and get into
the cart with them. They determined, after much time
wasted to turn back, and give themselves up to the
15 guidance of their horses. The old woman was soon
washed off and perished. The poor girls clung close to
their cart, and the horse, sometimes wading, and sometimes swimming brought them back to land alive, but
senseless with terror and distress and unable for many
20 days to give any account of themselves. The bodies of
their parents were found soon after (next ebb) ; that of
the father a very few paces distant from the spot where
he had left them.

In the afternoon wandered about the town and by the
25 key till it was dark. A little rain fell.

Oct. 12. Wind North-east. Sky gloomy, then gleams
of sunshine. Set out for Settle by a fine turnpike road,
29 miles.

Rich and beautiful enclosed country diversified with
30 frequent villages and churches very uneven ground, and
on the left the river Lune winding in a deep valley, its
hanging banks clothed with fine woods, through which
you catch long reaches of the water, as the road winds
about at a considerable height above it. Passed the

Park (Hon. Mr. Clifford's, a Catholic) in the most picturesque part of the way. The grounds between him and the River are indeed charming: the house is ordinary, and the Park nothing but a rocky fell scattered over with ancient hawthorns. Came to Hornby, a little town on the River Wanning, over which a handsome bridge is now in building. The Castle in a lordly situation attracted me, so I walked up the hill to it. First presents itself a large but ordinary white gentleman's house sashed, behind it rises the ancient keep built by Edward Stanley, Lord Monteagle, in Henry the VIIIth's time. It is now a shell only, though rafters are laid within it as for flooring. I went up a winding stone staircase in one corner to the leads, and at the angle is a single hexagon watch-tower rising some feet higher fitted up in the taste of a modern *Toot*, with sash-windows in gilt frames, and a stucco cupola, and on the top a vast gilt eagle, by Mr. Charteris, the present possessor. But he has not lived here since the year 1745, when the people of Lancaster insulted him, threw stones into his coach and almost made his wife (Lady Catherine Gordon) miscarry. Since that he has built a great ugly house of red stone (thank God it is not in England) near Haddington, which I remember to have passed by. He is the second son of the Earl of Wemyss, and brother to the Lord Elcho; grandson to Colonel Charteris, whose name he bears. From the leads of the tower there is a fine view of the country round and much wood near the Castle. Ingleborough, which I had seen before distinctly at Lancaster, to North east, was now completely wrapt in clouds, all but its summit, which might have been easily mistaken for a long black cloud too, fraught with an approaching storm. Now our road began gradually to mount towards the Appennine, the trees growing less and

thinner of leaves till we came to Ingleton, 18 miles : It is
a pretty village, situated very high and yet in a valley at
the foot of that huge creature of God *Ingleborough*. Two
torrents cross it with great stones rolled along their bed
5 instead of water : over them are two handsome arches
flung.   Here at a little ale-house, where Sir Bellingham
Graham, and Mr. Parker, Lord of the Manor, (one of
them six feet and a half high, and the other as much in
breadth) came to dine.   The nipping air (though the
10 afternoon was growing very bright) now taught us we were
in Craven ; the road was all up and down (though no where
very steep) to the left were mountain-tops, to the right a
wide valley ; (all enclosed ground) and beyond it high
hills again.   In approaching Settle the crags on the left
15 draw nearer to our way ; till we ascended Brunton-brow,
into a cheerful valley, (though thin of trees) to *Giggles-
wick*, a village with a small piece of water by its side
covered over with coots.   Near it a church, which
belongs also to Settle, and half a mile further having
20 passed the Ribble over a bridge arrived at Settle.   It is
a small market-town standing directly under a rocky fell,
There are not a dozen good-looking houses, the rest are
old and low, with little wooden porticoes in front.   My
Inn pleased me much (though small) for the neatness and
25 civility of the good woman that kept it, so I lay there two
nights, and went

Oct. 13, to visit *Gordale-scar*.   Wind N. E. : day gloomy
and cold.   It lay but six miles from Settle, but that way
was directly over a fell, and it might rain, so I went
30 round in a chaise the only way one could get near it in a
carriage, which made it full thirteen miles ; and half of it
such road ! but I got safe over it, so there's an end ;
and came to Mallham (pronounce it Maum) a village in
the bosom of the mountains seated in a wild and dreary

valley: from thence I was to walk a mile over very rough
ground. A torrent rattling along on the left hand. On
the cliffs above hung a few goats; one of them danced
and scratched an ear with its hind foot in a place where
I would not have stood stock-still for all beneath the 5
moon: As I advanced the crags seemed to close in,
but discovered a narrow entrance turning to the left
between them. I followed my guide a few paces, and lo,
the hills opened again into no large space, and then all
further way is barred by a stream, that at the height of 10
above 50 feet gushes from a hole in the rock, and spreading in large sheets over its broken front, dashes from
steep to steep, and then rattles away in a torrent down
the valley. The rock on the left rises perpendicular with
stubbed yew-trees and shrubs, staring from its side to the 15
height of at least 300 feet; but those are not the things :
it is that to the right under which you stand to see the
fall, that forms the principal horror of the place. From
its very base it begins to slope forwards over you in one
block and solid mass without any crevice in its surface 20
and overshadows half the area below with its dreadful
canopy. When I stood at (I believe) full four yards
distance from its foot, the drops which perpetually distil
from its brow, fell on my head, and in one part of the top
more exposed to the weather there are loose stones that 25
hang in the air; and threaten visibly some idle spectator
with instant destruction : It is safer to shelter yourself
close to its bottom, and trust the mercy of that enormous
mass, which nothing but an earthquake can stir: The
gloomy uncomfortable day well suited the savage aspect 30
of the place and made it still more formidable.

I stayed there (not without shuddering) a quarter of an
hour, and thought my trouble richly paid, for the impression will last for life: At the ale-house where I dined in

Maum, Vivares, the landscape painter, had lodged for a week or more; Smith and Bellers had also been there; and two prints of Gordale have been engraved by them: I returned to my comfortable inn: Night fine: but windy
5 and frosty.

Oct. 14. Went to Skipton 16 miles. Wind North East; gloomy. At one o'clock a little sleet falls. From several parts of the road, and in many places about Settle, I saw at once the three famous hills of this country, Ingle-
10 borough, Penigent, and Pendle; the first is esteemed the highest; their features are hard to describe, but I could trace their outline with a pencil. [In the manuscript is inserted a rough outline of the shape of these three mountains, in this place.] Craven after all is an unpleas-
15 ing country, when seen from a height. Its valleys are chiefly wide and either marshy or enclosed pasture with a few trees: Numbers of black cattle are fatted here, both of the Scotch breed and a larger sort of oxen with great horns. There is little cultivated ground except a
20 few oats.

Oct. 15. Wind North East. Gloomy. At noon a few grains of sleet fell, Then bright and clear. Went through Long Preston and Gargrave to Skipton, 16 miles: It is a pretty large market town in a valley with one very
25 broad street gently sloping downwards from the castle which stands at the head of it; this is one of our good Countess's buildings, but on old foundations, it is not very large; but of a handsome antique appearance with round towers, a grand gateway, bridge, and moat, and
30 many old trees about it. In good repair, and kept up as a habitation of the Earl of Thanet; though he rarely comes thither. What with the sleet and a foolish dispute about chaises that delayed me, I did not see the inside of it: But went on 15 miles to *Ottley*. First up Shode-

bank, the steepest hill I ever saw a road carried over in England. For it mounts up in a straight line (without any other repose for the horses than by placing stones every now and then behind the wheels) for a full mile. Then the road goes on a level along the brow of this high 5 hill over Rumbold Moor, till it gently descends into Wharfdale. So they call the Vale of the Wharf: and a beautiful vale it is. Well wooded, well cultivated, well inhabited, but with high crags at distance, that border the green country on either hand, through the midst of 10 it, deep, clear, full to the brink and of no inconsiderable breadth runs in long windings the river; how it comes to pass that it should be so fine and copious a stream here, and at Tadcaster (so much lower) should have nothing but a wide stony channel without water, I cannot tell 15 you; I passed through *Long Addingham*, Ilkeley (pronounce Eccla) distinguished by a lofty brow of loose rocks to the right; Burley, a neat and pretty village among trees; On the opposite side of the river lay *Middleton Lodge*, belonging to a Catholic gentleman of 20 that name. *Weston*, a venerable stone fabric with large offices, of Mr. Vavasor. The meadows in front gently descending to the water, and behind a great and shady wood. Farnley (Mr. Fawkes) a place like the last; but larger and rising higher on the side of the hill. *Ottley* is 25 a large airy town, with clean but low rustic buildings, and a bridge over the Wharf. I went into its spacious Gothic church, which has been new roofed with a flat stucco ceiling. In a corner of it is the monument of Thomas Lord Fairfax and Helen Aske, his Lady, descended from 30 the Cliffords and Latimers, as her epitaph says. The figures not ill cut; particularly his in armour, but bareheaded; lie on the tomb. I take them for the grand parents of the famous Sir Thomas Fairfax.

I have utterly forgot, where my journal left off, but (I think) it was after the account of *Gordale*, near Settle. If so, there was little more worth your notice: the principal things were *Wharfdale* in the way from Skipton
5 to Ottley, and *Kirkstall* Abbey, three miles from Leeds. The first is the valley formed by the River Wharf, well cultivated, well inhabited, well wooded, but with high rocky crags at distance, that border the green country on either hand: Through the midst of it, runs the river in
10 long windings deep, clear, and full to the brink, and of no inconsiderable breadth. How it comes to be so fine and copious a stream here, and at Tadcaster (so much lower) should have nothing but a wide stony channel, with little or no water, I cannot tell you. *Kirkstall* is a
15 noble ruin in the Semi-Saxon style of building, as old as K. Stephen, toward the end of his reign, 1152. The whole church is still standing (the roof excepted) seated in a delicious quiet valley on the banks of the River *Are*, and preserved with religious reverence by the Duke of
20 Montagu. Adjoining to the church between that and the river are variety of chapels, and remnants of the abbey, shattered by the encroachments of the ivy, and surmounted by many a sturdy tree, whose twisted roots break through the fret of the vaulting, and hang stream-
25 ing from the roofs. The gloom of these ancient cells, the shade and verdure of the landscape, the glittering and murmur of the stream, the lofty towers and long perspectives of the church, in the midst of a clear bright day, detained me for many hours and were the truest
30 subjects for my glass I have yet met with any where. As I lay at that smoky ugly busy town of Leeds, I dropt all farther thoughts of my journal, and after passing two days at Mason's (though he was absent), pursued my way by Nottingham, Leicester, Harborough, Kettering,

Thrapston, and Huntingdon, to Cambridge, where I arrived, 22 October; having met with no rain to signify, till this last day of my journey. There's luck for you!

NOTES ON THE POEMS.

——•◦•——

I.

ODE ON THE SPRING.

Gray wrote this Ode at Stoke in June, 1742. He sent it to his school friend, Richard West, not knowing that West's death had already occurred on the first of June. The Ode was first published in 1748, in Dodsley's *Collection of Poems by Several Hands*, with no signature; it next appeared in the folio of 1753, *Designs by Mr. R. Bentley, for Six Poems by Mr. T. Gray*. Gray added the foot-notes in the edition of his *Poems* in 1768. Mason said that Gray originally gave the title of *Noontide* to this Ode; and Mr. Gosse, Gray's *Works*, I, 4, notes that in a copy of the poem, in Gray's handwriting, preserved at Pembroke College, the title is : Noon-tide. An Ode. Mason said that Gray probably meant to write two companion pieces, *Morning* and *Evening*. He suggested that the *Ode on the Pleasure Arising from Vicissitude*, beginning "Now the golden Morn aloft" may have been intended for the *Morning* ode, and the *Elegy* for the *Evening*. These conjectures are ingenious, whether true or not.

1. Hours. The *Horae*, goddesses of the changes of the seasons. Cf. *Comus*, 986 : "The Graces and the rosy-bosomed Hours." Mitford notes that the Hours are joined with Aphrodite in the second Homeric Hymn to Aphrodite (5) and that to Apollo (194–5) and are made part of her train in Hesiod (*Works and Days*, 75).

3. Disclose. Open, expand. Cf.

> "The canker galls the infants of the spring,
>   Too oft before their buttons [*i.e.* buds] be disclosed."
>
> > *Hamlet*, i, 2, 39–40.

5. The Attic Warbler. The Nightingale. This bird is very common in Attica. Philomela, daughter of Pandion, king of Athens, was supposed to have been changed into a nightingale. — Wakefield compares Milton, *Par. Reg.*, iv, 245 :

> " Where the Attic bird
> Trills her thick-warbled notes the summer long";

and Mitford adds Pope, *Essay on Man*, iii, 33 :

> " Is it for thee the linnet pours his throat?"

11. Where'er the oak's, etc. The quiet scenery here described exhibits, perhaps, a touch of Romantic feeling ; but the conventional moralizing at the end of the stanza is thoroughly Augustan.

14. The passage from Shakspere that Gray gives in his note on this line is from *Mid. Night's Dream*, ii, 1, 249–251 :

> "I know a bank where the wild thyme blows,
> Where oxlips and the nodding violet grows,
> Quite over-canopied with luscious woodbine."

21. Care. Gray's fondness for personified abstractions is especially noticeable in his early odes. This custom was very fashionable among his contemporaries. They were all much affected in this respect by Milton's early poems. See *Introduction*, p. xxiv.

27. The note by Gray is from the *Georgics*, iv, 59.

30. *Par. Lost*, vii, 405, 406.

31. To Contemplation's, etc. Cf. Gray's Letter to Walpole (Gray's *Works*, ed. Gosse, II, 222): "I send you a bit of a thing for two reasons ; first, because it is one of your favourites, Mr. M. Green; and next, because I would do justice. The thought on which my second Ode [*Spring*] turns is manifestly stole from hence ; not that I knew it at the time, but having seen this many years before, to be sure it imprinted itself on my memory, and, forgetting the Author, I took it for my own. The subject was the Queen's Hermitage." He then quotes a long passage, of which the verses that follow are the most significant :

> " The thinking sculpture helps to raise
> Deep thoughts, the genii of the place:
> To the mind's ear, and inward sight,
> There silence speaks, and shade gives light:
> While insects from the threshold preach,
> And minds dispos'd to musing teach;
> Proud of strong limbs and painted hues,
> They perish by the slightest bruise;
> Or maladies begun within
> Destroy more slow life's frail machine;
> From maggot-youth, thro' change of state,
> They feel like us the turns of fate:

> Some born to creep have liv'd to fly
> And chang'd earth's cells for dwellings high:
> And some that did their six wings keep,
> Before they died, been forced to creep.
> They politics, like ours, profess;
> The greater prey upon the less.
> Some strain on foot huge loads to bring,
> Some toil incessant on the wing:
> Nor from their vigorous schemes desist
> Till death; and then they are never mist.
> Some frolick, toil, marry, increase,
> Are sick and well, have war and peace;
> And broke with age in half a day,
> Yield to successors, and away."

44. A solitary fly. Mason, writing to Gray, 8 January 1761, said, [I am living] "in that state of life which my old friend Jeremy Taylor so well describes in his sermon aptly entitled the Marriage Ring. 'Celibate life,' says he, 'like the flie in the heart of an apple, dwells in a perpetual sweetness, but sits alone, and is confined, and dies in singularity. But marriage, like the useful bee, builds a house, gathers sweetness from every flower, labours, and unites into societys and republics,' &c. If I survive you, and come to publish your works, I shall quote this passage, from whence you so evidently (without ever seeing it) took that thought, 'Poor moralist, and what art thou,' &c. But the plagiarism had been too glaring had you taken the heart of the apple, in which, however, the great beauty of the thought consists. After all, why will you not read Jeremy Taylor? Take my word and more for it, he is the Shakespeare of divines." It is interesting to learn from Mason's letter that at this time Gray had not read Taylor; his remarks in reply to Mason may be found on page 90 of this volume.

48. Thy youth is flown. Gray had reached the age of twenty-five.

II.

ODE ON A DISTANT PROSPECT OF ETON COLLEGE.

Gray wrote this ode in August, 1742, at Stoke, but it was not printed till 1747. It was the first of his English pieces to appear in print, and was published anonymously at sixpence. In 1748 it appeared, once more anonymously, in Dodsley's *Collection of Poems;*

and in 1753 it came third in the ornate *Six Poems* edition. The motto is from Menander, ap. Stobaeum, *Florileg.* 98, 7. *Fragm. Comic. Graec.* ed. A. Meineke IV, 291, fragm. 263; also *Comic. Attic. fragm.* ed. Th. Kock III, 221, fragm. 811. A similar thought in Philemon. fragm. (Meineke *Frag. Com. Gr.* 100).

1. The view here described is full of the quiet beauty of the English landscape.

1. Antique. By this word Gray means simply "ancient"; we often use it with the connotation "old-fashioned."

4. Her Henry's holy shade. Holinshed's words (*Chronicles*, ed. 1808, III, 324–5) give the pertinent facts : "Of his owne naturall inclination he abhorred all the vices as well of the bodie as of the soule. His patience was such that of all the iniuries to him doone (which were innûmerable) he never asked vengeance, thinking that for such adversitie as chanced to him, his sinnes should be forgotten and forgiven. . . . For these before remembered, and other the like properties of reputed holinesse, which was said to rest in him, it pleased God to worke miracles for him in his life time as men have listed to report. By reason whereof, King Henrie the Seaventh sued to Pope Iulio the Second to have him canonized a saint. But for that the c nonizing of a king seemed to be more costlie than for a bishop, the said king left off his sute in that behalf." Wakefield calls attention to some of Gray's other references to Henry VI. : "And spare the meek Usurper's holy head," *Bard*, v. 90 ; "the murther'd saint," *Ode for Music*, v. 46.

5. And ye, etc. The towers of the castle of Windsor, the present residence of the Queen.

9. Hoary Thames. Rivers are often spoken of as old ; cf. "Old Father Tiber." Cf. also. Pope, "Old father Thames advanced his reverend head," *Windsor Forest*, 330. Cf. also Spenser's famous description of "full-aged" Thame (*F. Q.* iv, 11, 25–26), and Milton's of Camus "reverend sire," *Lycidas*, 103 ff.

12. Fields belov'd in vain. They recall to him the happy days he had spent with his school friend Richard West, who had just died (see p. 127). These fields cannot now give him any pleasure, because they remind him of his loss.

16. Momentary bliss. Forgetting his sorrow for a moment in the joy of happy recollections.

19. Gray's note is from Dryden's verses *Of the Pythagorean Philosophy* (v. 110). *From the Fifteenth Book of Ovid's Metamorphoses.*

25–30. Who foremost, etc. Referring to school sports : swimming, bird-snaring, hoop-rolling, and trap-ball. Bentley's Print is my authority for swimming instead of rowing, and for trap-ball instead of cricket.

32. Murm'ring labours. School-boys mouthing over their books.

39. They hear a voice. The pursuing master.

42. Less pleasing when possest. Mildly pessimistic.

48. The easy night. Gray's ill-health made his nights anything but " easy " in later life.

51. Alas, regardless of their doom. Rather heavy moralizing for a poet of twenty-five.

55. Around 'em. This abbreviation sounds vulgar to the taste of to-day ; but it caused no shock then.

60. Ah, tell them, they are men! A stronger touch of pessimism. Cf. the motto of the poem : " Man, a sufficient occasion for calamity."

61–80. Observe the plentiful abstractions (cf. Introduction, p. xxiv).

79. *Palamon and Arcite*, ii, 1192.

81. Lo! in the vale of years, etc. After the mental sufferings caused by sin and failures, come the bodily ills of old age.

83. Cf. *Progress of Poesy*, 42 ff. **Family** is *familia* in the literal Latin sense.

84. More hideous, etc. Diseases worse than death.

92. Alike. "Alike" goes with "condemned," not with "to groan."

95. Yet ah! why should they know their fate? Wakefield gives the following illustrative passages. — Milton's *Comus*, 359–363:

> " Peace, brother: be not over-exquisite
> To cast the fashion of uncertain evils;
> For, grant they be so, while they rest unknown,
> What need a man forestall his date of grief,
> And run to meet what he would most avoid ? "

and from Terence, *Hecyra*, iii, 1, 6:

> " Nam nos omnes, quibus alicunde aliquis objectus labos,
> Omne quod interea tempus, prius quam id rescitumst, lucrost."

The sentiment is common enough, however, and had found perhaps its most familiar expression only a few years before Gray's lines were written, in Pope's *Essay on Man*, i, 77 ff.:

> " Heaven from all creatures hides the book of Fate," etc.

III.

HYMN TO ADVERSITY.

The summer of 1742 was a prolific season for Gray. The two preceding Odes, the following Sonnet, and the present Hymn were all written then. This poem he wrote at Stoke in August, as we learn from his MS. note. It appeared in print for the first time as No. 5 in the *Six Poems* of 1753; and in 1755 it was printed in Vol. IV of Dodsley's *Collection of Poems.* Gray was never in a hurry to publish.

1. Daughter of Jove. Homer, *Iliad*, xix, 91, makes Atē (Ἄτη) the daughter of Zeus, but Mitford goes too far in suggesting that Atē (Infatuation) "may be called the goddess of Adversity." The alternative suggestion is doubtless right: God sends adversity to men with some wise purpose; *Daughter of Jove* alludes to the Greek motto of the poem, *Agamem.* 167–171, which means "Zeus it is who has led mortals to wisdom by establishing it as a fixed law that knowledge comes by suffering." The readings of this passage from Æschylus vary in details in different editions; misprints are τῶ for τῷ : μαθὰν for μάθαν.

1–8. Mitford points out three passages in this stanza apparently suggested by *Paradise Lost:*

> "The vassals of his anger, when the *scourge*
> Inexorably, and the *torturing hour.*" — ii, 90, 91.

> "In *adamantine chains* and penal fire." — i, 48.

> "Strange horror seize thee, and *pangs unfelt before.*" — ii, 703.

But *adamantine chains* is very common among poets.

7. Purple Tyrants. Wakefield quotes Horace, *Od.* i, 35, 12: "Purpurei metuunt tyranni."

10–12. The common thought that virtue springs from adversity, as vice from luxury — as false as common.

18. Folly's idle brood. Cf. *Il Penseroso*, 1–2.

22. The summer friend. Referring to summer's days of ease. Cf. *Hamlet*, iii, 2, 217 ff. Mitford quotes George Herbert:

> ". . . fall and flow
> Like leaves about me, or like summer friends,
> Flies of estates and sunshine."
>
>   *The Temple*, short poem *The Answer.*

26 ff. Wakefield quotes Milton, *Il Penseroso*, 38–44:

> " With even step, and musing gait,
>   And looks commercing with the skies,
>   Thy rapt soul sitting in thine eyes:
>   There, held in holy passion still,
>   Forget thyself to marble, till
>   With a sad leaden downward cast
>   Thou fix them on the earth as fast."

35. Gorgon terrors. The snaky head of Medusa.

36. Vengeful band. The Furies.

40. Ghastly Poverty. Poverty always seemed terrible to Gray. Cf. *Progress of Poesy*, 43 : " Labour, and Penury, the racks of Pain," and *Ode on a Distant Prospect of Eton College*, 88, where Poverty "fills the band " of disease, and "numbs the soul with icy hand."

41–44. To some people Adversity is not a curse ; it brings only a " sweet melancholy," stimulating reflection.

47. Exact my own defects, etc. Gray was proud, fastidious, and over-sensitive, and he knew it.

IV.

SONNET ON THE DEATH OF RICHARD WEST.

Richard West died on the first of June, 1742, and Gray wrote this Sonnet at Stoke in August of the same year ; but it was not published until 1775, when it appeared in Mason's *Life of Gray*.

This poem has a historical significance, as it was the first English sonnet written in the eighteenth century that has survived. With the exception of Walsh's *Sonnet on Death*, this sonnet of Gray's has the distinction of being the first poem of the kind since the sonnets of Milton — another interesting link between Gray and the great Puritan poet. For an account of the disappearance and revival of the Sonnet-form, see Wm. Lyon Phelps, *Beginnings of the English Romantic Movement* (1893), pp. 44–46. Observe the curious metrical form, ab, ab, ab, ab, cd, cd, cd.

This sonnet is full of Miltonic phrases : Bradshaw notes " smiling morn," *Par. Lost*, v, 168 ; xi, 173–175 ; " amorous descant," *Par. Lost*, iv, 603 ; and Milton uses " attire " for the covering of the fields, *Par. Lost*, vii, 501.

2. Phoebus. Wordsworth was no doubt thinking of this and other classicisms in Gray when he made his unjust attack on this Sonnet. See Wordsworth's *Prose Works*, ed. Grosart, II, 85.

4. Chearful fields, etc. Gray was usually a most sympathetic observer of the changes of nature.

5. Other notes. West had been in the habit of sending his verses to Gray, as fast as he composed them. Gray usually carefully and minutely criticised them, as he did the productions of Mason and Beattie. See D. C. Tovey, *Gray and His Friends* (1890), Section II, and the letters from West to Gray in Gray's *Works*, Vol. II.

7. My lonely anguish. Gray never shared his emotions with any one. In spite of the classicisms, the tone of sincerity in this Sonnet is unmistakable. Gray never loved man or woman as he loved Richard West. Observe his apostrophe to West, under the name Favonius, at the end of Gray's Latin fragment, *De Principiis Cogitandi.*

V.

ODE ON THE DEATH OF A FAVOURITE CAT.

This Ode was written early in the year 1747, and first saw the light in a letter to Horace Walpole, dated 1 March, 1747, in which we learn that the poem was playfully written by Gray to commemorate the untimely drowning of one of his friend's pet cats. (See p. 69.) Walpole seems to have admired the poem fully as much as he had loved its object; and after Gray's death the china bowl in which the cat was drowned was placed on a pedestal at Strawberry Hill, with a quotation from the present poem.

This Ode was first published in Vol. II of Dodsley's *Collection of Poems,* 1748, and that Gray himself liked it may be seen from the fact that it appeared also in the *Six Poems* of 1753, and in Gray's own carefully edited volume of 1768. The Ode is a trifle, but is polished with all of Gray's fastidious workmanship. Gray sent it to his friend Thomas Wharton, with some playful comments, March, 1747 (*Works*, II, 164).

3. That blow. The flowers are painted on the vase in full bloom.

4. Tabby. Skeat gives the meaning of this word as "a kind of waved silk," and adds, "A *tabby* cat is one marked like the silk."

The word comes from the Arabic. A tabby cat would, therefore, strictly mean a cat whose fur is streaked black and gray; but in line 10 Gray seems to imply that the cat in question was a tortoise-shell. Tortoise-shell cats are often called tabby; indeed, the adjective is not infrequently applied to cats in general. Gray uses the word again in his letter to Walpole. (See p. 70.) In Bentley's Print the cat is gray, with pronounced black streaks; not a tortoise-shell.

6. The lake. The poem is consistently mock-heroic throughout.

12. She saw. She gazes with pride on the reflection of her own beauty, like Narcissus.

16. Tyrian hue. Alluding to Tyrian purple.

26. Again she stretch'd. A good picture of the comical lengthening out of a cat's form when her eyes are on the game.

31. Eight times. A cat has nine lives, as everybody knows.

34. No Dolphin came. Alluding to the well-known story of the dolphin's carrying Arion on his back to land. It is possible that the allusion in *Nereid* is to the story of Sabrina in *Comus*.

42. Nor all, that glisters, gold. A very old proverb, of which Mitford quotes many examples. His list could be indefinitely extended.

VI.

THE ALLIANCE OF EDUCATION AND GOVERNMENT.

Gray sent a portion of this poem to his friend, Dr. Wharton, in a letter from Stoke, August, 1748, in which he speaks of it as "a sort of Essay." The poem, with its serious ethical purpose, and with its Heroic Couplet form, is distinctly Augustan, and is included in this edition less on account of its intrinsic interest than because of its significance in Gray's career. The fact that he never finished it gives evidence that he outgrew it; and, indeed, it is wellnigh impossible to imagine the Gray of later years writing a piece like this. His friends, who were greatly pleased with such a didactic poem, besought him again and again to complete it; his answer was, *he could not.*

The Alliance was first published by Mason, in 1775, in his *Memoirs* of Gray. Few notes are necessary, as Mason's commentary is enough to satisfy all ordinary curiosity. For the present text, I have collated Mason, Gosse, and Bradshaw.

The Motto from Theocritus, *Id.* i, 62, 63, may be thus translated: "Come on, my friend ; for your song you shall not hoard up for Hades, which brings forgetfulness."

The last couplet quoted by Mason is really worth all the rest of the poem; Gray had a way of omitting extremely good things, as we know by the stanzas he wrote but would not publish with his *Elegy*.

An interesting subject for study would be a metrical analysis of this poem ; although the measure is the regulation Heroic Couplet, Gray's use of it is more free and less monotonous than was customary at the time. Even on a poor limited instrument, confined to only one key, Gray could produce more music than many a poet could with better materials and with a more tuneful theme.

VII.

ELEGY WRITTEN IN A COUNTRY CHURCH–YARD.

Although nearly all the editors state as a fact that the *Elegy* was begun in 1742, there seems to be no actual basis for this statement. In Mason's *Memoirs* of Gray (1775), p. 157, we find : " I am inclined to believe that the Elegy in a Country Church-yard was begun, if not concluded, at this time also " (August, 1742). But this is all the genuine evidence I have been able to discover. In Wakefield's *Poems of Mr. Gray* (1786), p. xi, we find : " It is highly probable that the Elegy in a Country Church-yard was begun also about this time " (August, 1742). Later editors state positively that it was begun in 1742 (Mitford, Gosse, Bradshaw, Rolfe, etc.). Mason seems to have had evidence for the 1742 date sufficient to satisfy Walpole, though what that evidence was we do not know. Writing to Mason, 1 December 1773 (*Letters*, VI, 22), Walpole says, speaking of the forthcoming *Memoirs* of Gray: "There are . . . errors in point of dates. . . . The 'Churchyard' was, I am persuaded, posterior to West's death [1742] at least three or four years, as you will see by my note. At least I am sure that I had the twelve or more first lines from himself above three years after that period, and it was long before he finished it." Mason evidently made some satisfactory reply, for two weeks later, 14 December 1773 (*Letters*, VI, 31), Walpole writes : " Your account of the 'Elegy' puts an end to my other criticism." Then Mason in 1775 made the statement just quoted above. At any rate, 1742 is the traditional date ; we know that it was finished at Stoke Poges, in June, 1750 (see p. 70). It is not probable that Gray was steadily working at it all these years, even if he did begin it in 1742. For interesting conjectures as to causes that inspired the poem, see Gosse, *Life of Gray*, pp. 66, 96.

Gray was in no more haste to publish the poem than he had apparently been to complete it. After June, 1750, it was circulated in manuscript among his friends, and only an accident hastened its publication. An editor of the *Magazine of Magazines*, a cheap periodical, sent word to Gray that he was about to print it, and naturally the author did not care to have a poem of this nature make its entrance into the world by so obscure a by-path. He therefore had it published (anonymously) on February 16, 1751, by the great London publisher, Dodsley.

The *Elegy* leaped immediately into enormous popularity. Edition followed edition in rapid succession ; it was translated into living and dead languages ; and — a sure evidence of popularity — it was repeatedly parodied.

The facts as to its publication, etc., may be found in Gosse's edition of *Gray's Works*, and in Gosse's *Life of Gray*, although Mr. Gosse curiously contradicts himself on pp. 66 and 96 of the latter book.

1. **The curfew tolls.** The passage from Dante quoted by Gray is *Purgatorio*, canto viii, 5, 6.

The standard *History of England* in Gray's time, that by Thomas Carte, describes the curfew law of William the Conqueror as "an ordinance, that all the common people should put out their fire and candle and go to bed at seven a clock, upon the ringing of a bell, called the *couvre feu bell*, on pain of death ; a regulation, which having been made in an assembly of the estates of *Normandie* at *Caen*, in A.D. 1061, to prevent the debauches, disorders, and other mischiefs frequently committed at night, had been practised with good success in that country." (Book v, vol. I, p. 422, 1747.)

2. **Wind.** Often incorrectly printed and quoted "winds." "Wind" is better for two reasons : it is more melodious, as it avoids the hiss of a double *s* ; it has more poetical connotation, for it suggests a long, slowly-moving line of cattle rather than a closely packed herd.

Cf. Joseph Warton's *Ode to Evening*, which contains a number of passages strikingly similar to the *Elegy*, although — so far as I know — the similarity has not been noticed by editors. Warton's *Odes* were published in 1746. One stanza in particular Gray may have had in mind when he composed the first stanza of his *Elegy:*

> " Hail, meek-eyed maiden, clad in sober grey,
> Whose soft approach the weary woodman loves,
> As, homeward bent to kiss his prattling babes,
> He jocund whistles thro' the twilight groves."

Collins's *Odes* were published the same year as J. Warton's (1746), and the whole atmosphere of Collins's *Ode to Evening* is similar to that of the *Elegy*. Cf. especially stanza 10 :

> " And hamlets brown, and dim-discover'd spires ;
> And hears their simple bell, and marks o'er all
> The dewy fingers draw the gradual dusky veil."

For Gray's remarks on Warton's and Collins's *Odes*, see p. 81. Cf. also Ambrose Philips, *Pastoral* ii, end :

> "And now behold the sun's departing ray
> O'er yonder hill, the sign of ebbing day.
> With songs the jovial hinds return from plow,
> And unyok'd heifers, pacing homeward, low."

5. Now fades, etc. This is a bit of the quiet scenery so dear to the hearts of the early Romanticists ; and in the next stanza we have the inevitable owl in the moonlight. The scenery as well as the meditations of the *Elegy* were by no means original ; they simply established more firmly literary fashions which were already fast becoming popular.

6. And all the air. "Air" is subject, not object, of "holds."

7. Save where the beetle. Cf. *Macbeth*, iii, 2 :

> " The shard-borne beetle with his drowsy hums."

Cf. also J. Warton's *Ode to Evening :*

> "And with hoarse hummings of unnumber'd flies."

Cf. also Collins's *Ode to Evening*, stanza 3 :

> "Or when the beetle winds,
> His small but sullen horn,
> As oft he rises 'midst the twilight path,
> Against the pilgrim borne in needless hum."

Milton's *Lycidas*, 28 :

> "What time the grey-fly winds her sultry horn."

11. Bow'r. In the old sense of chamber. The bower was the sleeping apartment for the lord and lady ; while the hall was the living-room, the dining-room, and, for the retainers, the sleeping-room.

16. Rude. Referring to their rustic simplicity. The poor people were always buried in the church-yard ; the rich inside the church.

20. Lowly bed. This probably refers to the humble couch on which they have spent the night ; but it is meant to suggest the grave as well.

21. For them no more, etc. Wakefield quotes Lucretius, iv, 907 :

> "At jam non domus accipiet te laeta ; neque uxor
> Optima, nec dulces occurrent oscula nati
> Praeripere, et tacita pectus dulcedine tangent."

Wakefield also quotes Thomson, *Winter*, 311, describing the man dying in the snow :

> "In vain for him the officious wife prepares
> The fire fair-blazing and the vestment warm :
> In vain his little children, peeping out
> Into the mingling storm, demand their sire
> With tears of artless innocence. Alas !
> Nor wife, nor children, more shall he behold,
> Nor friends, nor sacred home."

26. Glebe. From Latin *glaeba*, meaning the ground.

29–32. The rimes in this stanza are scarcely exact ; but the last line is one of the most famous in the *Elegy*.

33. The boast of heraldry, etc. Mitford compares West's *Monody on Queen Caroline*, Dodsley's *Collection of Poems*, vol. ii :

> "Ah me ! what boots us all our boasted power,
> Our golden treasure, and our purple state ?
> They cannot ward th' inevitable hour,
> Nor stay the fearful violence of fate."

This Monody directly followed Gray's three odes, *Eton, Spring, Cat*, in Dodsley.

35. Awaits. "*Hour*" is the subject, not the object of "*awaits*." Many editors have printed "*await*," doubtless thinking that "*the boast of heraldry*," etc., was meant to be the subject.

43. Provoke. In the Latin sense, *provocare*. (Rolfe.)

46. Pregnant with celestial fire. Divinely inspired.

50. Rich with the spoils of time. Mitford quotes Sir Thomas Browne, *Religio Medici*, section xiii (verse) :

> " Rich with the spoils of nature."

51. Rage. Often used for *enthusiasm*. (Hales.)

52. Genial. This can hardly be taken in the modern sense ; it may be used in the sense of "natural," "belonging to one's genius," or possibly with the meaning "endowed with genius."

53. Full many a gem, etc. There are a number of passages strikingly similar to this. Mitford suggests the following (I give the references more exactly) from *Comus*, lines 22–23 :

> " That, like to rich and various gems, inlay
> The unadorned bosom of the deep."

From Ambrose Philips, *The Fable of Thule:*

> " Like woodland flowers, which paint the desert glades,
> And waste their sweets in unfrequented shades."

From William Chamberlayne, *Pharonnida* (London, 1659), Book iv, canto 5, p. 94 :

> " Like beauteous flowers which vainly waste the scent
> Of odors in unhanted desarts."

From Bishop Joseph Hall, *Contemplations*, Book vi, Cont. i (*Complete Works*, Oxford, 1863, I, 137): "There is many a rich stone laid up in the bowels of the earth, many a fair pearl laid up in the bosom of the sea, that never was seen nor never shall be."

Wakefield quotes Pope, *Rape of the Lock*, iv, 157, 158 :

> " There kept my charms conceal'd from mortal eye,
> Like roses, that in deserts bloom and die."

A writer in the *Gentleman's Magazine* for January, 1782, calls attention to the following lines from Young, *Love of Fame*, Satire v, *On Women*, lines 229–232 :

> " In distant wilds, by human eyes unseen,
> She rears her flow'rs and spreads her velvet green:
> Pure gurgling rills, the lowly desert trace,
> And waste their music on the savage race."

56. This line almost immediately became proverbial.

57. Some village Hampden, etc. See remark in Introduction, p. xxvi, on this passage. Observe that Gray praises Hampden more

than Cromwell, who was at that time still generally misunderstood.
John Hampden, who lived in the same county that contained this
church-yard, refused in 1636 to pay the ship-money tax levied by
King Charles I.

59. Mute inglorious Milton. The glorious Milton rested for
some time in a cottage in the little village of Chalfont St. Giles,
where he finished *Paradise Lost.* This cottage is a very short
distance from Stoke Poges.

72. Here Gray originally inserted the following four stanzas :

> " The thoughtless world to Majesty may bow,
>   Exalt the brave, and idolize success;
> But more to innocence their safety owe,
>   Than Pow'r, or Genius, e'er conspir'd to bless.

> " And thou, who mindful of th' unhonour'd Dead,
>   Dost in these notes their artless tale relate,
> By night and lonely contemplation led
>   To wander in the gloomy walks of fate:

> " Hark! how the sacred Calm, that breathes around,
>   Bids every fierce tumultuous passion cease;
> In still small accents whispering from the ground,
>   A grateful earnest of eternal peace.

> " No more, with reason and thyself at strife,
>   Give anxious cares and endless wishes room;
> But through the cool sequestered vale of life
>   Pursue the silent tenor of thy doom."

One must agree with Mason who said, " I think the third of these
rejected stanzas equal to any in the whole *Elegy.*"

73. Far from, etc. Cf. the well-known line from Drummond
(ed. Turnbull, p. 38) :

> " Far from the madding worldling's hoarse discords."

73. If there were no comma after "strife," the sense of this
couplet would be precisely the opposite of what Gray intended. No
wonder he was particular about his punctuation.

78. Still = always, as commonly in Shakspere.

81. Th' unlettr'd muse. Epitaphs are famous for ridiculous
errors.

85, 86. This may mean one of two things, (a) " For who, a prey
to dumb Forgetfulness, e'er resigned this pleasing anxious being?"

or (b), "For who e'er resigned this pleasing anxious being to be a prey to dumb Forgetfulness?" Hales has discussed the matter at length.

87. Precincts. This word, and the phrase "pleasing anxious being," sound thoroughly Augustan; no wonder Dr. Johnson thought this stanza especially fine.

89–92. This stanza poetically answers the question put in the preceding one. The last two lines are strongly imaginative. Some editors think they refer to the epitaph cut on the stone, though no such interpretation is really necessary. Could Gray have had in mind Chaucer's line, as Mitford suggests?

> " Yet in oure asshen colde is fyr i-reke."
> *Prologue Reeve's Tale,* 28.

92. Petrarch, Sonnet 170, lines 12, 13, 14.

95. Chance = perchance.

97–100. After this stanza Gray originally inserted the following:

> " Him have we seen the greenwood side along,
>   While o'er the heath we hied our labour done,
>   Oft as the woodlark pip'd her farewell song,
>   With wistful eyes pursue the setting sun."

100. Lawn. This means strictly, "a cleared place in a wood." The word indicates nothing artificial, but is used as in Milton: *Lycidas,* 25, 26:

> " Together both, ere the high lawns appeared
>   Under the opening eyelids of the Morn."

Mitford quotes (incorrectly) *Par. Lost,* v, 428, 429:

> " Though from off the boughs each morn we brush mellifluous dews."

101. Of yonder nodding beech. Cf. Gray's letter to Walpole, Sept., 1737, p. 93, line 18 ff.

105–112. These two stanzas are now inscribed on the large and unsightly memorial to Gray, which stands close by the church-yard in Stoke Park.

115. For thou can'st read. This may mean that the "hoary-headed swain" could *not* read; or it may be a bit of poetical emphasis.

116. After this stanza Gray originally inserted the following beautiful quatrain, which, as Mr. Lowell justly said, cannot be obliterated from the memory of men, even if Gray did run his pen through it :

> " There scatter'd oft, the earliest of the year,
>   By hands unseen are show'rs of violets found ;
> The redbreast loves to build and warble there,
>   And little footsteps lightly print the ground."

118. This line, which soon became proverbial, was certainly not descriptive of Gray after the *Elegy* was published.

119. Fair science, etc. Science is here simply a general term for Knowledge. The line means that Knowledge looked favorably upon him at his birth (a quasi-astrological figure).

127. Petrarch, Sonnet 115, line 12 :

> " Ma freddo foco, e paventosa speme."

VIII.

A LONG STORY.

This poem was written in 1750, and was first published in the ornate *Six Poems* edition of 1753. Gray was unwilling to have it published again, saying that it was of only personal interest (see Gray's *Works*, III, 285). It was therefore omitted in the regular 1768 edition. Gosse and Bradshaw are wrong, however, in saying that this poem was printed only once in Gray's lifetime (see Gosse's *Life of Gray*, p. 103, and Bradshaw's Aldine edition, p. 231), for it was published in a Dublin edition of Gray's poetry in 1768. (See Bibliography.)

The circumstances connected with the birth of this poem are as follows : Lady Cobham, who lived at Stoke Poges, had seen a MS. copy of the *Elegy*, and was very anxious to know who the author was. Learning that it was a Mr. Thomas Gray, and that this quiet gentleman was then (August, 1750) living at his aunt's house at Stoke, she determined to seek his acquaintance. She used as a cat's paw two ladies who were then with her, Lady Schaub and Miss Harriet Speed, and persuaded them to call on Gray's aunt. The two ladies did so ; but unfortunately Mr. Gray was not at home. In a spirit of fun they left a little note for him. Gray returned the call, and became afterward intimately acquainted with Miss Speed. He celebrated the call made on him by playfully writing his *Long Story*, in the month of August, 1750, as we know by his own note to the Pembroke MS. of the poem.

What Miss Speed thought we may see from her letter to Gray (Tovey, *Gray and his Friends*, p. 197):

"Sir,

I am as much at a loss to bestow the Commendation due to your performance as any of our modern Poets would be to imitate them; Everybody that has seen it, is charm'd and Lady Cobham was the first, tho' not the last that regretted the loss of the 400 stanzas [should be 500]; all that I can say is, that your obliging inclination in sending it has fully answered; as it not only gave us amusement the rest of the Evening, but always will, on reading it over. Lady Cobham and the rest of the Company hope to have your's tomorrow at dinner.

"I am your oblig'd & obedient
"HENRIETTA JANE SPEED.
"Sunday."
[prob. Aug. 1750.]

2. An ancient pile. The mansion at Stoke was then occupied by Lady Cobham. It had previously belonged to the Earls of Huntingdon and the Hatton family (but see note on v. 11).

11. My grave Lord-keeper. Cf. Naunton's famous sketch : "Sir *Christopher Hatton* came into the Court as his opposite, Sir *Iohn Perrot*, was wont to say by the Galliard, for he came thither as a Private Gentleman of the Innes of Court in a Mask; and for his activity and person, which was tall and proportionable, taken into favour : he was first made Vice-Chamberlain, and shortly afterward advanced to the place of Lord Chancellor : a Gentleman, that besides the graces of his person, and dancing, had also the adjectaments of a strong and subtill capacity, one that could soon learn the discipline and garb both of the times and Court; the truth is, he had a large proportion of gifts and endowments, but too much of the season of envy ; and he was a meer vegetable of the Court, that sprung up at night, and sunk again at his noon." Sir Robert Naunton, *Fragmenta Regalia*, 1653 (written probably about 1630), ed. Arber, p. 44. Hatton was made Lord Chancellor in 1587.

Gray has perhaps purposely mixed up Hatton's two famous dancing exploits (*a*) that in his youth, by which he danced himself into Queen Elizabeth's favor; (*b*) that which has given rise to the "Lie there, Lord Chancellor" anecdote. The famous incident of Hatton's dancing when Lord Chancellor is derived from a letter from Captain

Francis Allen to Anthony Bacon, 17 August 1589, excerpted by Sir Harris Nicolas, *Life and Times of Hatton*, 1847, p. 478 : " My Lord Chancellor's heir, Sir William Hatton, hath married Judge Gawdy's daughter and heir ; and my Lord Chancellor danced the measures at the solemnity. He left the gown in the chair, saying, ' Lie thou there, Chancellor.' " Hatton was then 49 years old (born 1540). Nicolas shows that Gray was " mistaken in supposing that Sir Christopher Hatton ever owned Stoke Pogeis, or ever resided there. The manor house was re-built, in the reign of Queen Elizabeth, by Henry Earl of Huntingdon ; and Sir Edward Coke, who had married Elizabeth, daughter of Thomas Earl of Exeter, and second wife and widow of Sir William Hatton, the Chancellor's nephew, held it as lessee under the Crown in 1601, in which year he entertained the Queen there ; and about 1621 it was granted to him by King James the First," etc. Nicolas, p. 479. A full account of the vicissitudes of ownership may be found in Lysons, *Magna Britannia*, 1806, I, i, 635 ff.

11. Brawls. " A kind of French dance resembling a cotillon." Murray (who gives abundant illustrative quotations). What the letter says the Lord Chancellor actually did is, — to dance *in the measures*, slow, sedate dances, minuets.

13. His bushy beard. The usual portrait of Hatton represents him with a full but not shaggy beard. The reason for Gray's epithet may be seen from the following interesting passage in Joseph Spence's *Polymetis*, dialogue vi, 2d ed., London, 1755, p. 52 : " It is true we scarce ever see a full beard on any but the lowest sort of people among us; and that has given us a mean idea of the thing itself. Nature perhaps designed it for the ornament of old age; but custom has got the better of her. . . . A full beard still carries that idea of majesty with it, all over the East : which it may, possibly, have had ever since the times of the patriarchal government there. The Grecians had a share of this oriental notion of it. The very name is apt to carry something low and rude along with it among us." The two styles of trimming the beard in vogue in the Elizabethan time were the bodkin cut (the peaked beard which we are apt to regard as peculiarly Elizabethan) and the " bush " (see Lyly's *Endimion*, iii, 3); but it is not likely that Gray had this distinction in mind.

16. Tho' Pope and Spaniard. Referring to the defeat of the Spanish Armada in 1588. *Pope* refers more strictly to the papal opposition to Queen Elizabeth, which found its most decided expression in the bull of Pius V. (1570), which released English Catholics from their allegiance and declared that Elizabeth had no right to her crown.

23. A brace of Warriors. Lady Schaub and Miss Speed. — **Buff.** A leather military coat.

25. The first. Lady Schaub. — **Cap-a-pee.** From head to foot, at all points. Gray means she was dressed in the latest French style.

29. The other Amazon. Miss Harriet Speed, or more properly, Miss Henrietta Jane Speed. Their acquaintance led to an intimate friendship, which friends on both sides thought would result in marriage. At any rate, Miss Speed is the only lady whom Gray ever seems to have addressed or considered romantically. For further details, see Tovey, *Gray and His Friends*, section v.

31. Cobham. Lady Cobham treated Miss Speed as a daughter.

37. Capucine. "A female garment, consisting of a cloak and hood, made in imitation of the dress of Capuchin friars ; whence its name." Johnson.

41. P——t. The Rev. Mr. Purt, Gray's neighbor, who had informed Lady Cobham of the name and whereabouts of Gray. Mr. Purt was offended at his name's being mentioned in this poem.

51. Her high commission. Alluding to Henry IV.'s edict against Welsh bards. Mitford quotes as follows : "And it is enacted, that no master-rimour, minstrel, or other *vagabond*, be in any wise sustained in the land of Wales, to make commoiths, or gatherings upon the people there." Mitford's note is defaced by two bad blunders, which Bradshaw repeats. This is the French text of the ordinance of 1403 from Wotton, *Leges Wallicae*, 1730, p. 548: "Item, Pur eschiever plusours diseasz & meschefs quaunt advenuz devaunt cez heurez en la terre de Gales par plusours Wastours, Rymours, Ministralx & autres Vacabundez, ordenuz est & establez que nullez Wastours, Rymours, Ministralx ne Vacabundez soent ascunement sustenuz en la terre de Galez pur faire commortha ou coillage sur la commune poeple illoeques." Observe that Mitford's "master-rimour" is a mistake, and that "commoiths" should be "commorths." In 1401 Henry IV. had also made a previous ordinance, much to the same effect. Henry IV.'s edicts were practically reenactments of Edward I.'s (see notes on the *Bard*). There were many other and more recent enactments against wandering minstrels.

54. Ventur'd. "Entered" rimes with this word here. This rime represents the common pronunciation of "ventured" at that time.

59. His Mother. Gray's mother and aunt lived together.

64. Tester. A canopy over the bed.

65. Into the drawers, etc. Mitford remarks on the similarity between the style of this part of the *Long Story* and that of Prior's *The Dove*, and quotes the following stanzas (9, 25, 27) from Prior's poem:

> "With one great peal they rap the door,
>   Like footmen on a visiting day.
> Folks at her house at such an hour!
>   Lord! what will all the neighbours say?

> "Her keys he takes, her doors unlocks;
>   Through wardrobe and through closet bounces;
> Peeps into every chest and box,
>   Turns all her furbelows and flounces.

> "I marvel much, she smiling said,
>   Your poultry cannot yet be found;
> Lies he in yonder slipper dead,
>   Or may be, in the tea-pot drowned!"

80. A spell. The little note left by the ladies: "Lady Schaub's compliments to Mr. Gray; she is sorry not to have found him at home, to tell him that Lady Brown is very well."

83. Transparent birdlime. Playfully alluding to his being taken captive by the note.

93–96. A thoroughly Augustan stanza.

99. The lady Janes. The great pictures of the Elizabethan ladies that hung in the room come down from their frames, as their spirits were said to do when the nights were especially dark.

103. Styack. Mrs. Tyacke, the housekeeper. Gray may have purposely changed her name a little, in his playful poem.

116. Squib. James Squibb, who was in Lady Cobham's service as Groom of the Chambers.

128. He ne'er was for a conj'rer taken. To say a person is no conjurer is a mild way of calling him not over-wise. Cf. Gray's letter to Wharton, Jan. 1761 (*Works*, III, 83): "he is a very sober man; good natured, and honest, and no conjurer"; and 18 Sept. 1754 (*Works*, II, 255): "Dr. Akenside (I perceive) is no conjurer in Architecture." In the present passage there is an obvious play on words.

129. Prudes. The spirits of the haughty ladies in the paintings. —**Hagged.** Like a hag. Nothing whatever to do with the word "haggard" (cf. note on *The Bard*, v. 18).

135. The square-hoods, *i.e.*, the ladies mentioned above as prudes. They are of course sticklers for exclusiveness and etiquette.

144. Rubbers. The Lady's games at cards.

IX.

THE PROGRESS OF POESY.

This ode Gray wrote in 1754 at Cambridge. It was printed in 1757, in company with *The Bard*, at Horace Walpole's press at Strawberry-Hill, with the following title: "Odes by Mr. Gray. Printed at Strawberry-Hill. For R. and J. Dodsley in Pall-Mall. MDCCLVII." This thin quarto contained only a very few notes. Walpole, writing to Sir Horace Mann, 4 August 1757, said, "I send you two copies . . . of a very honourable opening of my press— two amazing Odes of Mr. Gray: they are Shakspearian, they are Pindaric, they are sublime! consequently, I fear, a little obscure: the second particularly, by the confinement of the measure, and the nature of prophetic vision, is mysterious. I could not persuade him to add more notes; he says, whatever wants to be explained, don't deserve to be." In the 1768 edition of his poems, Gray added explanatory notes to these odes, and in his sarcastic *Advertisement* (see p. 26) told the public why he did so. Gray's foot-notes must certainly be read, as they are exceedingly important for a correct understanding of his Pindaric Odes.

The selections from Gray's letters which contain the most important references to these Odes are given on pp. 73, 74, 76, and 87.

HISTORICAL SKETCH OF THE ENGLISH PINDARIC ODE.

The popular notion is that the poet Cowley (1618–1667) was the first man to write Pindaric Odes in English. He published his *Pindaric Odes* in 1656. They were not a mere imitation, but an invention. But he was more indebted to earlier work than seems to be generally supposed. Spenser's *Epithalamion* (1595) reminds one instantly of later odes. His stanzas fall into three or four parts, with short lines to break the monotony, but the parts are held together by rime. The grouping of verses is somewhat similar to what we see in the *Pindaric Odes*.

It is sometimes claimed that Ben Jonson wrote the first Pindaric Ode. In his *Underwoods* there is a Pindaric Ode *To the Immortal Memory and Friendship of that Noble Pair, Sir Lucius Cary, and Sir H. Morison.* This is divided as Pindar's odes were divided, into Strophes, Antistrophes, and Epodes. Jonson called his Strophe a "Turn," his Antistrophe a ' Counter-turn," and his Epode the "Stand." Undoubtedly he had classic odes in mind. Thomas Randolph, in his Ode to Ben Jonson, upon the occasion of the failure of *The New Inn*, says : " 'Twere fond to let all other flames expire, To sit by Pindar's fire"; thus recognizing Jonson's Pindaric attempts. Randolph himself wrote poems that look something like Pindaric Odes.

Cowley's Pindarics are by no means a strict imitation of Pindar. They are simply groups of verses of irregular length ending with a long line. At the time (1656) his curious metrical forms surprised everybody. He thought his rhapsodies and variations made his odes Pindaric ; and some of his odes were in reality paraphrases of Pindar. But of course it was his deliberately studied enthusiasm joined with his poor ear for music, that killed his odes.

Congreve wrote true Pindaric Odes, going back more to Ben Jonson's notions, without apparently knowing what Jonson had done. The most famous man to write Pindarics after Cowley and Congreve, was Gray. It is unnecessary to say that the *Progress of Poesy* and the *Bard* are the best Pindaric Odes ever written.

THE METRE.

As Hales pointed out, this Ode is really divided into 3 stanzas, with 41 lines in each stanza. Again, each stanza is divided into 3 parts — strophe, antistrophe, and epode — the turn, counter-turn, and after-song, Greek theatrical names. The three strophes, antistrophes, and epodes are identical in construction ; hence the architecture of the whole poem is curiously symmetrical, though one could easily read it without any perception of this fact.

This was, of course, in imitation of the symmetry of the Greek odes, which particularly appealed to Gray's precise metrical sense.

His own remarks on the metre are interesting. In a letter to Wharton, 9 March 1755 (*Works*, II, 262), he said : " I am not quite of your opinion with regard to Strophe and Antistrophe. Setting aside the differences, methinks it has little or no effect upon the ear, which scarce perceives the regular return of metres at so great a

distance from one another. To make it succeed, I am persuaded
the stanzas must not consist of above nine lines each at the most.
Pindar has several such odes."   Mason adds an interesting note :
"He often made the same remark to me in conversation, which led
me to form the last Ode of *Caractacus* in shorter stanzas : But we
must not imagine that he thought the regular Pindaric method
without its use ; though, as he justly says, when formed in long
stanzas, it does not fully succeed in point of effect on the ear : for
there was nothing which he more disliked than that chain of irregular stanzas which Cowley introduced, and falsely called Pindaric ;
and which from the extreme facility of execution, produced a
number of miserable imitators. . . .   It is also to be remarked, that
Mr. Congreve, who first introduced the regular Pindaric form into
the English language, made use of the short stanzas which Mr.
Gray here recommends."

The Motto. Pindar, *Olymp.* ii, 153, 154. Gray himself translates
this motto in a Letter to the Rev. James Brown, 17 Feb. 1763
(*Works*, III, 148) : "The Odes . . ., as their motto shews, were
meant to be *vocal to the intelligent alone.* How few *they* were in my
own country, Mr. Howe can testify ; and yet my ambition was
terminated by that small circle."   Cf. Letter to Wharton, 7 Sept.
1757 (*Works*, II, 330) : "Miss Sp[eed] seems to understand ; and to
all such, as do not, she says — φωνᾶντα συνετοῖσι — in so many
words. And this is both my motto and comment."

The *Critical Review*, IV, 167, says, "The author might, with
great propriety, have added

$$\text{------ } \grave{\epsilon}\varsigma$$
$$\delta\grave{\epsilon} \ \tau\grave{o} \ \pi\hat{a}\nu \ \grave{\epsilon}\rho\mu\eta\nu\acute{\epsilon}\omega\nu$$
$$\chi\alpha\tau\acute{\iota}\zeta\epsilon\iota.\text{"}$$

It is interesting to see that in the edition of 1768, Gray actually
adopted this suggestion.

1. Gray's note on this line inaccurately quotes *Psalms*, 57, 8 :
"Awake up, my glory ; awake, psaltery and harp."   The word
"lute," which occurs in Gray's quotation, does not occur in Young's
Analytical Concordance.

Æolian lyre. Gray's note on this is said to have been called out
by a blundering critic (*Critical Review*, IV, 167) who mistook the
Æolian lyre for the harp of Æolus, or wind-harp : "The first of
these odes is addressed to the Æolian lyre, which it emulates in the
enchanting softness, ravishing flow, and solemn tones of melody.

. . . A severe critic would . . . censure the sentiment . . . which represents the Loves dancing to the sound of this lyre. Such an instrument as the Æolian harp, which is altogether uncertain and irregular, must be very ill adapted to the dance, which is one continued regular movement." The whole article deserves to be read as an example of the puerilities that then passed for criticism. The same critic suggested that v. 20 ff. meant, strictly speaking, that the *lyre* not the *eagle* was perching on Jove's sceptred hand. That Gray had seen this article is obvious from two places in his letters (*Works*, II, 327): "Even the *Critical Review* (Mr. Franklin, I am told), that is rapt and surprised and shudders at me, yet mistakes the Æolian for the harp of Æolus which indeed, as he observes, is a very bad instrument to dance to." A second is in a letter to Wharton, 7 Sept. 1757 : "The *Critical Review* you have seen or may see. He is in raptures (they say it is Professor Franklin) but mistakes the Æolian lyre for the harp of Æolus and on this mistake founds a compliment and a criticism." (*Works*, II, 331.)

7. Cf. Horace, *Odes*, iii, 29, 32 : perhaps Gray thought this too obvious to mention.

12. Rebellow. Imitated from Latin *reboare :* cf. "reboant silvaeque et longus Olympus," Vergil, *Georg.* iii, 223. Mitford refers to Pope's *Iliad*, "Rocks rebellow to the roar."

14. sweet and solemn-breathing airs. Cf. Milton, *Comus*, 555 : "A soft and solemn-breathing sound."

15. Shell. Alluding to the mythical origin of the lyre ; Hermes made it from a tortoise shell.

17. The Lord of War. Ares, or Mars. He was especially worshiped in Thrace. Cf. Chaucer's splendid description of "the grete temple of Mars in Trace" (*Knight's Tale*, vv. 1114 ff.).

21. Feather'd king. The eagle, sacred to Zeus, and often represented with the thunderbolt in his clutch.

27. Idalia. This was a town in the island of Cyprus, containing a temple where Venus was worshiped. Venus first landed on Cyprus, after she had been born from the foam of the sea ; but the island Cythera, in the Ægean sea, gave the name Cytherea to Venus, as many believed that she had appeared there before landing at Cyprus.

31. This line in rhythm is certainly reminiscent of *L'Allegro*. It is useless to point out all the words that Milton and Gray happened to use in common.

35. Homer, *Odyssey*, Θ, 265.

40. Gray's poetry is seldom so warm as this, though this would be cold for some poets.

41. Gray's note on this line refers to lines that are twice quoted in Athenaeus, viz. *Athen.* xiii, 604 (ed. Kaibel): ὡς καλῶς Φρύνιχος ἐποίησεν εἴπας · λάμπει δ᾽ ἐπὶ πορφυρέαις παρῇσι φῶς ἔρωτος, and again, *Athen.* xiii, 564: Φρύνιχός τε ἐπὶ τοῦ Τρωίλου ἔφη λάμπειν ἐπὶ πορφυραῖς παρῇσι φῶς ἔρωτος. Gray no doubt had the former one in mind. The poet is Phrynichus *tragicus* (there was also a comic poet of the name). It is fragment 2 of Phrynichus in the fourth ed. of Bergk's *Poet. Lyr. Gr.*

43. Here Gray drops back into his old fondness for Abstractions.

46. **Fond.** Foolish.

50. **Birds of boding cry.** The regulation Screech-owl.

52. The quotation from Cowley is given inaccurately in Gray's note; it is from the Pindaric ode *Brutus*, 55–57:

> "One would have thought 't had heard the *Morning crow*
> Or seen her well-appointed *Star*
> Come marching up the *Eastern Hill* afar."

53. **Hyperion.** The Titan, who was the father of the sun, moon, and stars. Here used, as often, for the sun.

Glitt'ring shafts. The rays of the morning sun.

54. Vergil, *Aeneid*, vi, 797. Petrarch, *Canzone* 5, line 48.

57. This line is entirely omitted in Bradshaw's Aldine edition of Gray.

68. **Ilissus.** A river flowing through Athens.

69. **Maeander.** The progress of this river was so winding that it gave its name to our verb, "meander." It was in Phrygia.

70–71. Milton suggests "by slow Meander's margent green" as the residence of the nymph Echo (*Comus*, v. 232).

82. Gray means that poetry flourishes best in eras of national vigor and political independence; when Greece was conquered, the Muses went to Rome; after the downfall of the Roman empire, they went to Albion, *i.e.*, England.

84. **Nature's Darling.** In the two centuries that followed Shakspere, he was often spoken of as the child of Nature — in contrast to his more learned contemporaries, who drew their inspiration from the classics. The well-known passage in *L'Allegro* was chiefly responsible for this.

86. **The mighty Mother.** This may refer either to Nature or to Poetry.

89. Pencil. Paint brush.

95. It is an interesting fact that Gray puts Milton apparently equal to Shakspere, and that in this stanza he distinctly puts Dryden below the Puritan poet. In Gray's earlier years, Dryden was his idol and model ; but at this time, in common with all the other Romanticists, he gave himself up to the worship of Milton. It is interesting, however, to observe that Gray never forgot his debt to Dryden. In a letter to Beattie, 2 Oct. 1765 (*Works*, III, 222) he said : " Remember Dryden, and be blind to all his faults." Cf. Mason's note, from which it appears that Gray told Beattie " that if there was any Excellence in his own numbers he had learned it wholly from that great poet. And pressed him with great earnestness to study him, as his choice of words and versification were singularly happy and harmonious."

98. Lucretius, i, 73, 74.

99. The sentence from Ezekiel, i, 28, reads more exactly : " This was the appearance of the likeness of the glory of the Lord."

102. Homer, *Odyssey*, Θ, 64.

Closed his eyes. Referring to Milton's blindness. If Gray's explanation is not scientific, it is certainly poetical. But Dr. Johnson has succeeded in accounting prosaically for this figure. " His account of Milton's blindness, if we suppose it caused by study in the formation of his poem, a supposition surely allowable, is poetically true, and happily imagined." (*Life of Gray.*) Unhappily for this suggestion, Milton's blindness had no such cause.

106. *Job*, xxxix, 19.

107. Long-resounding pace. The comparison in Pope's famous lines (suggested by Mitford) must occur to every one :

> " Waller was smooth ; but Dryden taught to join
> The varying verse, the full-resounding line,
> The long majestic March, and Energy divine."
> *Im. of Horace*, Book ii, Ep. i, vv. 267–69.

108. Fancy. Imagination. The distinction between *fancy* and *imagination* drawn by Wordsworth in the Preface to his *Lyrical Ballads*, ed. 1815, and now usually observed in criticism was not much heeded in the language of the seventeenth and eighteenth centuries.

110. Cowley, *The Prophet* (v. 20) in *The Mistress*. Incorrectly quoted by Gray :

> " Tears, which shall understand, and speak."

111. Gray's note on this line is interesting, as showing how seriously he took Mason and *Caractacus.* The poet William Mason (1725–1797) was an intimate friend of Gray's, a servile imitator of Milton's and Gray's poetry, and the executor of Gray's literary remains. By far his most enduring contribution to literature is his *Memoirs* of Gray (1775). Mason wrote two tragedies, *Elfrida* (1751), and *Caractacus* (1759). These are on the model of the ancient Greek drama, and though they contain some fine passages, they lack vitality. He stoutly upheld the Unities and insisted on the retention of the Chorus. *Caractacus* is a story of Druid times, in which Druids play an important part ; the scene is laid in Mona. Gray criticised Mason's poems in MS. with great care, and often with merciless severity; but in this instance he seems to have seriously believed that Mason had produced something good. Mason and Gray were often coupled together by contemporary critics, and the alleged obscurity of their odes was freely parodied (see pp. 87 and 89). For Gray's remarks on Mason's Choruses in *Caractacus,* see his *Works,* II, 317, 332 ff., 350 ff. Perhaps the best account of Mason's life and works is given in Hartley Coleridge's *Northern Worthies.*

115. Pindar, *Olymp.,* ii, 159.

120. Orient hues. Mitford compares Spenser :

> "With much more orient hue."
>> *An Hymn in Honour of Beauty,* v. 79.

also Milton :

> "With orient colours waving."
>> *Par. Lost,* i, 546.

We might add also,

> "His orient liquor in a crystal glass."
>> *Comus,* v. 65.

"Orient" in these passages of course means "bright," "lustrous," — perhaps because the most beautiful jewels came from the East. Milton uses "orient" in this sense at least nine times in *Paradise Lost* alone.

121. The last three lines are interesting as a description of Gray's own character and poetical aims. Did he himself feel that he was the only poet since Dryden ?

X.

ODE ON THE PLEASURE ARISING FROM VICISSITUDE.

This poem, in its present unfinished state, was found among Gray's papers after his death. He seems to have composed the fragment during 1754 and 1755. Mason first published it, pp. 236 and 237 of his *Memoirs* of Gray (1775). In the *Appendix* to that work Mason published it again, filling out broken lines and adding stanzas with his own pen. The poem is here printed as Gray left it, without any of Mason's additions, although a few fragmentary words and broken lines remain, which are not included here at all. Mason remarked (*Poems of Mr. Gray*, 1775, p. 82): "I have heard Mr. Gray say, that M. Gresset's 'Epitre a ma Sœur' (see his works in the Amsterdam edition, 1748, p. 180) gave him the first idea of this Ode: and whoever compares it with the French Poem, will find some slight traits of resemblance, but chiefly in our Author's seventh stanza." The idea, however, is so common that the likeness to Gresset does not seem especially remarkable. See below.

In Gray's memorandum book for the year 1754, Mason found the following rough notes, which give the poet's plan for this Ode: "Contrast between the winter past and coming spring. — Joy owing to that vicissitude. — Many who never feel that delight. — Sloth. — Envy. — Ambition. How much happier the rustic who feels it, tho' he knows not how."

3. Vermeil-cheek. Vermilion; a bright red. Cf. Milton, *Comus*, 752.

13. These four lines on the sky-lark will stand comparison with Wordsworth's and Shelley's poems on the same subject.

29. Gray's fondness for abstractions appears again in the fifth and sixth stanzas. The whole poem should be read in connection with the *Ode on the Spring;* see notes on that poem.

49–52. These lines are in Gray's best vein, and exhibit the true Wordsworthian attitude toward nature. It is this stanza which Mason said was most similar to Gresset. It may be interesting to quote some lines from Gresset's *Épître à ma Sœur, sur ma Convalescence, Œuvres*, 1777, I, 136:

> "O jours de la Convalescence!
> Jours d'une pure volupté!
> C'est une nouvelle naissance,
> Un rayon d'immortalité.

Quel feu! tous les plaisirs ont volé dans mon ame;
J'adore avec transport le céleste flambeau;
Tout m'intéresse, tout m'enflâme,
Pour moi l'Univers est nouveau.
Sans doute que le Dieu qui nous rend l'existence,
A l'heureuse Convalescence
Pour de nouveaux plaisirs donne de nouveaux sens;
A ses regards impatiens
Le cahos fuit; tout naît, la lumiére commence;
Tout brille des feux du printems;
Les plus simples objets, le chant d'une Fauvette,
Le matin d'un beau jour, la verdure des bois,
La fraîcheur d'une violette;
Mille spectacles, qu'autrefois
On voyoit avec nonchalance,
Transportent aujourd'hui, présentent des appas
Inconnus à l'indifférence,
Et que la soule ne voit pas."

55. Note the pronunciation, *crystálline*, found also in Milton, *P. L.*, iii, 482; vi, 772; and vii, 271.

XI.

THE BARD.

Gray began to write this ode in 1754, and worked at it, but only occasionally, until 1757, when he finished it. We learn from a letter to Mason, 1757 (*Works*, II, 312), that the following incident inspired Gray to finish the *Bard:* "Mr. Parry has been here and scratched out such ravishing blind harmony, such tunes of a thousand years old, with names enough to choke you, as have set all this learned body a-dancing, and inspired them with due reverence for Odikle, whenever it shall appear. Mr. Parry . . . has put Odikle in motion again." He then encloses the conclusion of the poem. In the same year (1757) it was printed as " Ode II " along with the *Progress of Poesy* on Horace Walpole's press at Strawberry Hill. (See Introductory note to the *Progress of Poesy*.) Gray's own foot-notes, added chiefly in the 1768 edition of his poems, are necessary to a correct understanding of this ode.

In Mason's Notes on the *Bard* (p. 91 of his *Poems of Gray*, 1775), he gives " the original argument of this capital Ode, as its author had set it down on one of the pages of his common-place book." It is as follows : " The army of Edward I. as they march through a deep valley, are suddenly stopped by the appearance of a venerable figure seated on the summit of an inaccessible rock, who, with a voice more than human, reproaches the King with all the misery and desolation which he had brought on his country; foretells the misfortunes of the Norman race, and with prophetic spirit declares, that all his cruelty shall never extinguish the noble ardour of poetic genius in this island; and that men shall never be wanting to cele-brate true virtue and valour in immortal strains, to expose vice and infamous pleasure, and boldly censure tyranny and oppression. His song ended, he precipitates himself from the mountain, and is swallowed up by the river that rolls at its foot."

The popular reception of the *Bard*, as well as of the *Progress of Poesy*, was not altogether gratifying. See *Introduction*, part iv, also pp. 74–77, 87, 89, and *Works*, II, 323, 331.

Advertisement. The tradition that Edward I. (reign 1272–1307) hanged all the bards, Gray may have met with in Carte's *History of England*, Book viii, vol. II, p. 196. This second volume was pub-lished in 1750, and Gray did not begin to write until 1754. Carte says : " The only set of men among the Welsh, that had reason to complain of Edward's severity, were the bards who used to put those of the ancient Britons in mind of the valiant deeds of their ancestors : he ordered them all to be hanged, as inciters of the people to sedition." He refers as his authority to a seventeenth-century work, Sir J. Wynne's *History of the Gwedir Family*. The so-called " tradition," which has not been traced to any earlier source than Wynne, is exploded by Thomas Stephens (*Literature of the Kymry*, 2d ed., 93 ff.), who remarks : " It is probable that the worthy Baronet was led to form this conclusion from knowing that Edward issued an edict against the bards." This edict, however, Stephens shows to have been, like all the later edicts, directed merely against vagrant minstrels and not dissimilar probably to those regu-lations which Ritson gleefully quoted against Bishop Percy as to the English minstrels. No one will wish to contend that a vagrant Welsh harper may not at some time have been hanged ; but there is no evidence for it, still less for a general massacre of bards. Henry IV.'s edict was to all intents and purposes a re-enactment of that of Edward I. (See note to *Long Story*, v. 51.)

2. **Confusion.** Destruction.

4. *King John*, v, i, 72.

8. **Cambria.** An old Latinization of Welsh *Cymru*, the land of the Kymry (or Welsh).

9. Gray's quotation in the note is from Dryden's *Indian Queen*, iii, 1. (Vol. I, p. 196, ed. 1735.)

11. The passage from Higden in Gray's note is *Polychronicon Ranulphi Higden*, ed. Lumby, I, 418.

12. It was in the years 1282–84 that King Edward completely conquered Wales.

15–18. These lines are thoroughly romantic in tone.

18. **Haggard.** Gray writing to Thomas Wharton, 21 August 1755 (*Works*, II, 268), said: "Though *haggard*, which conveys to you the idea of a *Witch*, is indeed only a metaphor taken from an unreclaimed Hawk, which is called a *haggard*, and looks wild and *farouche*, and jealous of its liberty." See also note on "hagged," *Long Story*, 129.

20. *Paradise Lost*, i, 537.

28. **High-born Hoel.** The son of Prince Owain Gwynedd, of North Wales (see Introductory Note to *The Triumphs of Owen*). He was both a warrior and a poet. For a full account of him, with specimens of his poetry in the original and in translation, see Thomas Stephens, *Literature of the Kymry*, 2d ed., 1876, pp. 37 ff. Stephens supposes that he is referred to in the line translated by Gray in *Triumphs of Owen*, v. 20.

29. **Cadwallo** and **Urien** were Welsh poets. Nothing is extant of their works. Evans, *Dissertatio de Bardis*, p. 78.

33. **Modred.** Modred or Mordred is the villain of the Arthur story; but no person of this name is known as a bard. Mitford's conjecture that Gray altered "Myrddin ab Morvryn" for the sake of euphony is not probable.

34. **Plinlimmon.** A Welsh mountain.

35. **They lie.** The dead bards.

40. *Julius Caesar*, ii, 1, 289, 290.

44. **A griesly band.** Possibly Gray may be referring to the *Bard* when he writes to Mason in 1756 (*Works*, II, 284): "I am of your opinion, that the ghosts will spoil the picture, unless they are thrown at a huge distance, and extremely kept down."

48. Gray's note refers to the *Fatal Sisters*.

49. At this point, beginning with the words "Weave the warp," the spirits of the dead bards alluded to in the last stanza join in the

song ; this chorus is continued through line 100, where the spirits vanish and the one Singer continues in solitude. This conception of Gray's is as dramatic as it is poetical.

49. Warp and woof. The warp means the threads extended lengthwise in the loom in weaving, and the woof means the threads that cross the warp.

51. Verge. Literally, the border. The passage means simply : " Let there be plenty of room to get everything in."

54. Severn. The river.

55. Berkley's roofs. Berkeley castle, which stands S.-E. of the town of Berkeley. It is said to have been built soon after the Norman conquest, and is in good condition to-day.

57. Mitford quotes *Henry* VI., pt. III, i, 4, 111:

> " She-wolf of France, but worse than wolves of France."

61. Amazement. Confusion, as commonly in Shakspere.

71. In his note Gray refers to Froissart. Writing to Wharton, 23 Jan. 1760 (*Works*, III, 24), he says : "*Froissard* is a favourite book of mine (though I have not attentively read him, but only dipp'd here and there)," and continues with further remarks about him. — **Fair laughs,** etc. Cf. Henry IV.'s description of the levity of his predecessor, Richard II., in *Henry* IV., pt. I, iii, 2, 60 ff.

91. Above, below. In the loom. The two roses were united by the marriage of Henry VII. (Lancaster) and Elizabeth (York). Cf. *Ode for Music.*

99. Half of thy heart. Eleanor, wife of Edward I., died in 1290. The "heroic proof of her affection " alludes to the story of her husband's wound from a poisoned dagger, which she cured by sucking out the venom.

101. Stay, oh stay ! The bard calls on the vanishing spirits of his brother poets.

102. In the fragment sent to Wharton, 21 August 1755 (*Works*, II, 270), this line stood : " Leave your despairing Caradoc to mourn ! " Afterwards, in a letter to Walpole, 11 July 1757 (*Works*, II, 319), Gray said, " Caradoc I have private reasons against ; and besides it is in reality Carādoc, and will not stand in the verse." Cf. the fragment on Caradoc, p. 53.

109. In his *Remarks on the Poems of Lydgate* (*Works*, I, 389), Gray quotes Lydgate's *Fall of Princes*, viii, 24, as evidence that the " notion [was] then [*i.e.* in the 15th century] current in Britain, that King Arthur was not dead, but translated to Fairy-Land, and should come again to restore the Round Table." In a note he adds : " Peter of Blois, who lived in 1170, says ironically, in his epistles, 57 :

> ' Quibus si credideris,
> Expectare poteris
> Arturum cum Britonibus.' "

These passages are interesting as illustrative of the range and minuteness of Gray's studies in what may be called Romantic material. Records of this pathetic confidence in Arthur's return which made " the credulity of the Britons " a by-word for centuries must have come under Gray's eye in many places : for example, in the *Polychronicon* of Ranulphus de Higden *ad ann.* 1177 (ed. Lumby, VIII, 60), a work which Gray quotes in his note to v. 11 of this very poem.

110. The prophecies of Merlin (Merddin) and Taliesin here referred to have been proved by Thomas Stephens not to be earlier than the 12th century and hence to have nothing to do with those bards, whose date is in the 6th century. See his *Literature of the Kymry,* 2d ed., ch. ii, sect. 4, pp. 198 ff.: " Poems fictitiously ascribed to Merddin, Taliesin, Aneurin," etc.

111 ff. Cf. Sir Richard Baker on the " state " of Queen Elizabeth (*Chronicle of the Kings of England,* ed. of 1684, p. 400) : " Never Prince kept greater State with less stateliness : Her Pensioners and Guard were always the tallest and goodliest Gentlemen and Yeomen of the Kingdom : Her Maids of Honor and other Women about her, the fairest and most beautiful Ladies of the Realm ; and yet her self a *Diana* amongst the Nymphs."

112. Starry fronts. Mitford compares Milton, *The Passion,* stanza iii :

> " His starry front low-roofed beneath the skies."

115. A Form divine. This language toward Elizabeth sounds more like Spenser than Gray.

116. Briton-Line. The Welsh were the original Britons ; so the Bard says that in the person of Elizabeth, — who had Welsh blood in her veins, Henry VII. being the grandson of a Welsh chief, — the Welsh once more will rule England.

121. A few of the poems of Taliesin have been preserved, but most of those attributed to him in Gray's time are not earlier than the 12th century. See note on v. 110. Gray had his doubts as to the authenticity of Taliesin's poems. See his note to the *Observations on the Pseudo-Rhythmus (Works,* I, 365).

126. Spenser, *Fairy Queen*, first stanza of dedication.

128. Buskin'd. The buskin was the poetical name for Tragedy. There is a kind of "Progress of Poesy" in this stanza.

135. Fond. Foolish.

140. The different doom. The different judgment on you, King Edward, the destruction of your house, and on me, my final triumph in the house of Tudor and the Elizabethan poets.

XII.

SKETCH OF HIS OWN CHARACTER.

This was first printed by Mason, in his *Memoirs* of Gray (1775), p. 264. Mason especially approved of the theistic sentiment Gray expressed, printing line 4 in capitals.

3. Could love, and could hate. Although Gray was never demonstrative, his likes and dislikes were remarkably strong.

4. In Swift's great *Argument Against Abolishing Christianity*, we find much the same sarcastic tone taken toward affected atheism.

6. Charles Townshend was Chancellor of the Exchequer (1767). He was as famous for wit and oratory as for political versatility. — **Squire.** Dr. Samuel Squire, Fellow of St. John's College, Cambridge. He was Rector of St. Anne's, Soho, afterwards Dean of Bristol, and then Bishop of St. David's in 1761; he died 7 May 1766. Gray mentions him in a letter to Mason (see p. 76).

XIII.

SONG.

Gray wrote these lines in October, 1761, to an old air, at the request of his friend Miss Speed, the heroine of *A Long Story*. Horace Walpole, writing to the Countess of Aylesbury, 28 November 1761, says, " You will like better to see some words which Mr. Gray has writ, at Miss Speed's request, to an old air of Geminiani : the thought is from the French." Then follows the *Song*. (*Works*, ed. 1798, V, 561.)

1. **Thyrsis.** The conventional name for a pastoral lover.

9. **Gales.** A very favorite word with Gray.

XIV.

THE FATAL SISTERS.

This ode was written in 1761, and first published in the 1768 edition of Gray's poems. It is a free rendering of a Latin translation from the Old Norse. (See *Appendix* to *Introduction*, on *Gray's Knowledge of Norse*.) The chief interest of Gray's version is the fact that it shows his love and eager study of strictly Romantic themes.

Torfæus. For particulars, see *Appendix*.

Bartholinus. Thomas Bartholin, the younger (1659–1690). For particulars as to his book on Northern antiquities, and as to Gray's use of it, see *Appendix*.

The Old Norse words quoted by Gray form a part of the opening sentence of the song :

> " Vítt er orpit fyr val-falli
> rifs reiði-ský."

"The pendent cloud of loom [*i.e.* the fateful web which the valkyrjur are weaving] is stretched out wide before the slaughter."

Gray translated from the Latin version in Bartholin, which is repeated in Torfæus. No doubt he referred to the original, which they also print.

This original is to be found in the Icelandic *Njálssaga.* (the Saga of Njáll or Niel), cap. 157 (*Íslendinga Sögur*, Copenhagen, 1875, III, 898–901). The accompanying prose furnishes an introduction and a conclusion, which are put together by Gray in his *Preface.* The text of the song (without the prose) is edited, with an English prose translation, in Vigfússon and Powell, *Corpus Poeticum Boreale*, Oxford, 1883, I, 281–283. The poem is much older than the Saga which has preserved it, and must, indeed, be nearly contemporary with the event which it celebrates — the Battle of Clontarf, fought April 23 (Good Friday) — not Christmas, as Gray has it, — 1014.[1] It is one of the most powerful of the Old Norse poems The metre

---

[1] See Konrad Maurer, *Bekehrung des norwegischen Stammes*, I, 549 ff.

and style are of course entirely different from the metre and style
of Gray's paraphrase. The Latin version is reprinted, not because
it gives a fair idea of the original, but because it is essential for
comparison with Gray's Ode.

Bartholin, *De Causis contemptae a Danis adhuc Gentilibus Mortis*,
1689, pp. 618–624.

Late diffunditur
ante stragem futuram
sagittarum nubes,
depluit sangvis,
jam hastis applicatur
cineracea
tela virorum,
qvam amicae, texunt
rubro subtegmine,
Randveri mortis.

Texitur haec tela
intestinis humanis,
staminiqve stricte alligantur
capita humana;
sunt sangvine roratae
hastae, pro insilibus:
textoria instrumenta, ferrea:
ac sagittae pro radiis:
densabimus gladiis
hanc victoriae telam.

Prodeunt ad texendum Hilda
et Hiorthrimula,
Sangrida et Svipula,
cum strictis gladiis:
hastile frangetur,
scutum diffindetur,
ensisqve
clypeo illidetur.

Texamus, texamus
telam Darradi.
Hunc (*gladium*) rex juvenis
prius possidebat:
Prodeamus
et cohortes intremus,
ubi nostri amici
armis dimicant.

Texamus, texamus
telam Darradi,
et Regi
deinde adhaereamus:
ibi videbant
sangvine rorata scuta
Gunna et Gondula,
qvae regem tutabantur.

Texamus, texamus
telam Darradi,
ubi arma concrepant
bellacium virorum,
non sinamus eum
vita privari,
habent Valkyriae
caedis potestatem.

Illi populi
terras regent,
qvi deserta promontoria
antea incolebant.
dico potenti regi
mortem imminere,
jam sagittis
occubuit Comes.

Et Hibernis
dolor accidet,
qvi nunqvam
apud viros delebitur.
jam tela texta est,
campus vero (*sangvine*) roratus
terras percurret
conflictus militum.

Nunc horrendum est
circumspicere,

cum sangvinea nubes   bene sit nobis canentibus!
per aëra volitet.   Discat autem ille
tingetur aer   qvi auscultat*
sangvine virorum,   bellica carmina multa,
antequam vaticinia nostra   et viris referat.
omnia corruant.

                      Eqvitemus in eqvis
Bene canimus   qvoniam efferimus
de rege juvene   strictos gladios,
victoriae carmina multa,   ex hoc loco.

Advertisement. The "Friend" Gray mentions was Thomas
Warton (1728–1790). Gray had planned to write a History of
English Poetry, but when he heard that Thomas Warton was
engaged in that work, he gave up the idea, and handed over his
general scheme to Warton, who published years afterward the
History. (1st vol. 1774, 2d vol. 1778, 3d vol. 1781.) Gray's scheme
is contained in his letter to Warton, 15 April 1770 (*Works*, III,
364). Parts of the material that Gray had collected may be found
in his *Works*, vol. I. See also a letter from Horace Walpole to
Montagu, 5 May 1761 (Walpole's *Letters*, ed. Cunningham, III,
399).

Preface. Mason, in his 1775 edition of Gray's *Poems*, p. 100,
quotes Gray's MS. note about the conversion of the people of the
Orkney islands: "The people of the Orkney islands were Christians,
yet did not become so till after A.D. 966, probably it happened in
995; but though they, and the other Gothic nations, no longer
worshiped their old divinities, yet they never doubted of their
existence, or forgot their ancient mythology, as appears from the
history of Olaus Tryggueson."

King Olave Tryggvason is said to have forced Sigurd, Earl of the
Orkneys, to accept baptism in 995, but Konrad Maurer (*Bekehrung
des norwegischen Stammes*, I, 339) suggests that the nearness of
Scotland and Ireland, which were Christian, must have previously
caused the conversion of a large portion of the islanders. The
"history of Olaf Tryggvason" to which Gray refers was accessible
to him in Latin in the works of Torfæus.

Sictryg, better Sigtrygg (Old Norse Sigtryggr). Sigtrygg was
King of Dublin, Brian was King of Ireland. Brian was Sigtrygg's
step-father (this is no doubt what Gray means by *father-in-law*).
Both Brian and Sigtrygg fell in the battle.

1. **The valkyrjur.** The information in Gray's note is derived
from Bartholin, bk. ii, chaps. 11 and 12. The account given of the

Valkyrjur (Old Norse plural; singular *Valkyrja*) and of Valhalla (Old Norse *Vahhǫll*) accurately represents the belief that obtained among the vikings at the time when this poem was composed, but must be regarded as a special Scandinavian development, forming itself gradually among the warrior class in what is known as the "viking age" (A.D. 750–1050 roughly), and not as a general Germanic creed (Gray's "Gothic" in this connection doubtless = Germanic, Teutonic), nor even as a creed ever accepted by the common people in Scandinavia. The student who wishes an accurate idea of these matters should not trust the popular handbooks of mythology, which seldom take into account the results of recent scholarship, and, indeed, show little advance beyond the authorities which were accessible to Gray. He may consult for the whole subject Mogk's article *Deutsche Mythologie* in Paul's *Grundriss der germanischen Philologie*, vol. II, or E. H. Meyer's *Deutsche Mythologie* (Berlin, 1891); for the Valkyrjur, W. Golther's *Der Valkyrjenmythus*, in the *Abhandlungen* of the Bavarian Academy, I. Cl., XVIII, ii, 401 ff.; Schullerus, *Zur Kritik des altnordischen Valhǫllglaubens*, in Paul and Braune's *Beiträge*, XII, 221 ff. "Valkalla" in Gray's note is of course a mere misprint for "Valhalla."

3. *Paradise Regained*, iii, 323, 324. The original has "showers."

4. *Julius Caesar*, ii, 2, 22.

8. **Randver's bane.** Gray here follows Bartholin's Latin, which misrepresents the original. The Icelandic has "the friends of the slayer of Randvérr," *i.e.*, "the friends of Odin," *i.e.*, "the valkyrjur," — a typical skaldic phrase. (So Vigfússon, doubtless correctly.)

16. There is something in the rhythm of this line that recalls the witches in *Macbeth*, iv, 1, 32 : "Make the gruel thick and slab."

17–18. Bartholin's Latin has as the names of the valkyrjur in these two lines *Hilda, Hiorthrimula, Sangrida, Svipula* (in the original : *Hildr, Hjǫrþrimul, Sangríðr, Svipul*), and in v. 31 *Gunna, Gondula* (in the original : *Gunnr, Gǫndul*). Gray found the names *Mista* and *Geira* in Bartholin's translation (p. 554) of a stanza in another poem of the *Poetic Edda* (the *Grímnismál*), where they occur in a long list of names of *valkyrjur*. The Old Norse forms in Bartholin's text are *Mist* and *Geira*. The latter is a false form, the correct reading being probably *Geirǫnul*.

24. **Hauberk.** Well explained in Gray's note to the *Bard*, v. 5.

32. According to Vigfússon the young king is Sigtrygg. Cf. v. 56.

37. The Northmen.

41. **The Earl.** Probably Sigurd, though Vigfússon takes it as referring to the son of King Brian.

56. **Younger King.** See v. 32.

XV.

THE DESCENT OF ODIN.

This Ode was written in 1761, and first published in the 1768 edition of Gray's poems. Like the preceding, it is a free rendering of the Latin. Probably Gray was first inspired to write this by reading Mallet's *Monuments de la mythologie et de la poesie des Celtes, et particulièrement des anciens Scandinaves* (1756). Mallet alluded to this Ode in the first volume of his *Introduction à l'histoire de Dannemarc* (1755), and in the second volume, the title of which is quoted above, Mallet gave a French version in prose, of a portion of this very Ode.

The Icelandic line should read "Upp reis Óðinn aldinn gautr" ("Up rose Odin, the old Creator"). Gray followed Bartholin's text (p. 632).

Bartholin, *De Causis contemptae a Danis adhuc Gentilibus Mortis,* 1689, pp. 632–640.

Surgebat Odinus
virorum summus,
et Sleipnerum
ephippio stravit,
eqvitabat deorsum
Niflhelam versus,
obvium habuit catellum
ab Helae habitaculis venientem.

Huic sangvine aspersa erant
pectus anterius,
rictus mordendi avidus,
et maxillarum infima;
allatrabat ille,
et rictum diduxit
magiae patri,
et diu latrabat.

Eqvitavit Odinus,
terra subtus tremuit,
donec ad altum veniret
Helae habitaculum.
tum eqvitavit Odinus
ad orientale ostii latus,
ubi fatidicae
tumulum esse novit.

Sapienti carmina
mortuos excitantia cecinit,
boream inspexit,
literas (*tumulo*) imposuit,
sermones proferre coepit,
responsa poposcit,
donec invita surgeret
et mortuorum sermonem proferret.

Qvisnam hominum
mihi ignotorum,
mihi facere praesumit
tristem animum?
nive eram
et nimbo aspersa,
pluviaque rorata,
mortua diu jacui.

Viator nominor,
Bellatoris filius sum,
enarra mihi qvae apud Helam ge-
runtur,
ego tibi, qvae in mundo.
Cuinam sedes
auro stratae sunt?
lecti pulchri
auro ornati.

Hic Baldero medo
paratus extat,
purus potus,
scuto superinjecto;
divina vero suboles
dolore afficietur.
invita haec dixi,
jamqve silebo.

Noli fatidica tacere,
te interrogare volo
donec omnia novero.
adhuc scire volo,
qvisnam Baldero
necem inferet,
ac Odini filium
vita privabit?

Hódus excelsum fert
honoratum fratrem (*sc. se ipsum*)
illuc.
is Baldero
necem inferet,
et Odini filium
vita privabit.
invita haec dixi
jamqve tacebo.

Noli tacere fatidica,
adhuc te interrogare volo
donec omnia novero,
adhuc scire volo
qvisnam Hódo
odium rependet?
aut Balderi interfectorem,
occidendo, rogo adaptet.

Rinda filium pariet
in habitaculis occidentalibus,
hic Odini filius,
unam noctem natus, armis utetur;
manum non lavabit,
nec caput pectet,
anteqvam rogo imponat
Balderi inimicum.
invita haec dixi,
jamqve tacebo.

Noli tacere fatidica,
adhuc te interrogare volo,
qvaenam sunt virgines
qvae prae cogitationibus lachryman
tur,
et in coelum jaciunt
cervicum pepla?
hoc solum mihi dicas,
nam prius non dormies.

Non tu viator es,
ut antea credidi;
sed potius Odinus,
virorum summus.
Tu non es fatidica,
nec sapiens foemina,
sed potius trium
gigantum mater.

Eqvita domum Odine,
ac in his gloriare,
nemo tali modo veniet
ad sciscitandum,
vsqve dum Lokus
vinculis solvatur:
et Deorum crepusculum
dissolventes aderint.

The original is known as *Vegtamskviða* (*i.e.,* The Song of Vegtamr[1]) or as *Baldrs Draumar* (*Baldr's Dreams*). It is found in the
collection of Old Norse poetry known as the *Elder* or *Poetic Edda*.
This collection was at one time thought to be the work of Sæmund
the Wise (1056–1133). The *Poetic Edda* was discovered in Iceland
in 1643 and until a comparatively recent time very extravagant
notions of its age (which of course Gray shared) were current
amongst scholars. In anything like their present form none of
these poems antedate the 10th century and some of them are much
later. The present poem is one of the later songs and is perhaps
not much older than the Royal MS. of the *Edda* (end of 13th
century). The Old Norse text may be found in any edition of the
Poetic Edda. Vigfússon's text (*Corpus Poeticum Boreale*, I, 181–183)
is accompanied by an English prose translation.

The first stanza, which Gray has omitted (omitted also in Bartholin), says that "all the gods and goddesses were in council to
learn why Baldr's dreams were so threatening." Baldr, the god of
light, was the favorite son of Odin and beloved of all the gods.
Distressed by fears of Baldr's death, Odin determines to learn the
truth from a seeress, long dead, and for that purpose he visits the
underground realm of Hel, goddess of Hades.

4. Gray's note on Niflheimr comes from Bartholin, pp. 387, 585,
and is based on a passage in the *Prose Edda*. It represents, like the
Valhalla creed, a late stage of Viking belief. The Old Norse form
of the goddess's name is *Hel. Hell* in this note should be understood as = *Hades*, not as = a place of torment.

17. The line is from Milton's *L'Allegro*, 59.

22. **Thrice he traced the runic rhyme.** Runic is a term applied
to alphabets used by the Scandinavians and other Germanic races
before the adoption of the Roman letters. Magic power was often
attributed to runes. In an interpolation in the original (which
stood in Bartholin's text), Odin is apparently represented as "laying
runes" on the tomb (though the word runes is not used), but the
text is quite as vague as Gray's "traced." Bartholin translates
"Literas (tumulo) imposuit," which Gray seems to have taken as
meaning that spells were written on the tomb by Odin. Gray's
information about the magic powers of runes was derived from
Bartholin, pp. 641 ff.

24. **verse that wakes the dead.** "The original word is *Valgalldr*
[read *valgaldr*]; from *Valr*, mortuus, and *Galldr* [read *galdr*],

---

[1] Name assumed by Odin.

incantatio." Gray (as extracted by Mason from the MS.). Gray's note is from Bartholin, p. 640. The etymology is correct.

27 ff. The seeress' unwillingness to be disturbed recalls the words of Samuel when evoked by the Witch of Endor: "Why hast thou disquieted me to bring me up?" 1 *Samuel*, xxviii, 15. The idea is familiar to all nations.

37. A Traveller. In the original, Odin conceals his identity by assuming the name *Vegtamr* (hence the title of the poem *Vegtams-kviða*), which means *Wanderer*.

44. The pure beverage of the bee. Mead, a favorite old Germanic drink made from honey. The heroes drink mead in Valhalla. See Gray's *Preface* to *The Fatal Sisters*, and the note. The periphrasis is Gray's own.

86. Odin recognizes the seeress as the goddess Hel herself. But this interpretation is doubtful. In any case, he taunts her with being an uncanny, diabolic creature: "mother of three giants," as the original has it.

90. In Gray's note *Lok* should be *Loki*. The phrase *Twilight of the Gods* (Götterdämmerung) is an old misunderstanding of the Old Norse *Ragnarøk*, which = merely *The Fates of the Gods*. Gray refers his readers to Mallet as an easily accessible source of information, but he had himself no doubt used Bartholin, pp. 587 ff., where a part of the *Vøluspá* (The Sibyl's Soothsaying), the first poem in the *Poetic Edda* and our chief authority for this belief, is quoted and translated: see especially p. 595.

51. In Mason's *Poems* of Gray (1775), p. 103, he quotes Gray's MS. note: "Women were looked upon by the Gothic nations as having a peculiar insight into futurity; and some there were that made profession of magic arts and divination. These travelled round the country, and were received in every house with great respect and honour. Such a woman bore the name of Volva Seidkona or Spakona. The dress of Thorbiorga, one of these prophetesses, is described at large in Eirik's Rauda Sogu (apud Bartholin, lib. i, cap. iv, p. 688). She had on a blue vest spangled all over with stones, a necklace of glass beads, and a cap made of the skin of a black lamb lined with white cat-skin. She leaned on a staff adorned with brass, with a round head set with stones; and was girt with a Hunlandish belt, at which hung her pouch full of magical instruments. Her buskins were of rough calf-skin, bound on with thongs studded with knobs of brass, and her gloves of white cat-skin, the fur turned inwards, &c. They were also called

Fiolkyngi, or *Fiol-kunnug*, *i.e.*, Multi-scia; and Visinda-kona, *i.e.*, Oraculorum Mulier, *Nornir; i.e.*, Parcæ." This note is almost wholly from Bartholin (see p. xli, above). A few corrections are necessary. Read *vǫlva, seiðkona, spákona, Thorbjǫrg* (for *Thorbiorga*, which is Bartholin's Latinized form), *Eiríks Saga Rauða* (*i.e.*, the Saga of Eric the Red, famous as containing an account of Leif Eiríksson's Vinland voyage). The passage referred to by Gray is one of capital importance. It is in ch. 3, and has been printed, with notes, by Vigfusson and Powell in their *Icelandic Reader* (p. 126). At the end of the note, read *fjǫl-kunnig* for *fiol-kunnug.* *Fjǫlkyngi*, which Gray seems to have got from a false reading in Bartholin's extract from Eric the Red's Saga, is a noun, and means *the prophetic art.* The *Nornir* or *Norns* were really the Norse *Fates.* They are, however, confounded with ordinary seeresses in a story quoted by Bartholin, p. 685 (cf. p. 612).

55. Hoder. Old Norse Hǫðr. The unwitting cause of Baldr's death. The whole story is told in the *Prose Edda* (*Gylfaginning*, ch. 49 ff.), and has been often translated. See Matthew Arnold's *Balder Dead.* Cf. Gayley, *Classic Myths in English Literature*, 1893, pp. 380 ff., where the Edda story is told. For a good brief account of the Eddas, see article *Edda*, in Johnson's Universal Cyclopaedia, revised edition.

XVI.

THE TRIUMPHS OF OWEN.

Gray wrote this ode probably in the year 1764, immediately after the publication of the Rev. Evan Evans's *Specimens of the Antient Welsh Bards* (see *Introduction*, part iv). This was a collection of Welsh poems with English prose translations, followed by a *Dissertatio de Bardis;* Gray turned one of the pieces into rime. The poem was first published in the 1768 edition.

The prose version which Gray versified runs as follows :[1] "A Panegyric upon Owain Gwynedd, Prince of North Wales, by Gwalchmai, the son of Melir, in the Year 1157.

---

[1] A revision of Evans's translation may be found in *The Literary Remains of the Rev. Thomas Price*, 1854, I, 195.

"I will extol the generous hero, descended from the race of Roderic, the bulwark of his country, a prince eminent for his good qualities, the glory of Britain, Owain the brave and expert in arms, a prince that neither hoardeth nor coveteth riches. — Three fleets arrived, vessels of the main, three powerful fleets of the first rate, furiously to attack him on a sudden. One from Iwerddon, the other full of well-armed Lochlynians, making a grand appearance on the floods, the third from the transmarine Normans, which was attended with an immense, though successless toil.

"The Dragon of Mona's sons were so brave in action, that there was a great tumult on their furious attack, and before the prince himself, there was vast confusion, havock, conflict, honourable death, bloody battle, horrible consternation, and upon Tal Moelvre a thousand banners. There was an outrageous carnage, and the rage of spears, and hasty signs of violent indignation. Blood raised the tide of the Menai, and the crimson of human gore stained the brine. There were glittering cuirasses, and the agony of gashing wounds, and the mangled warriors prostrate before the chief, distinguished by his crimson lance. Lloegria was put into confusion, the contest and confusion was great, and the glory of our prince's wide-wasting sword shall be celebrated in an hundred languages to give him his merited praise."

Advertisement. A convenient account of Owain Gwynedd may be found in B. B. Woodward, *History of Wales*, London, 1859, pp. 265–288. He succeeded his father Gruffydd ab Cynan (the last prince of North Wales who bóre the title of king) in 1137, and died in 1169 (or, less probably, 1171). The Battle of Tal y Moelvre, which this poem celebrates, is thought to be identical with "the defeat of the fleet entrusted by Henry II. to Madoc ab Meredydd in 1157." See Thomas Stephens, *Literature of the Kymry*, 2d ed., p. 17.

3. **Roderic's stem.** "Owain Gwynedd . . . was descended in a direct line from Roderic the Great (Rhodri Mawr), prince of all Wales (in the tenth century), who (according to tradition) divided his principality amongst his three sons." Evans's note.

4. **Gwyneth.** North-Wales (Gray). *I.e.*, Gwynedd (Venedotia). Owain took the surname Gwynedd on succeeding to this principality.

10. **Squadrons three.** The fleets from the three countries mentioned below.

11. **Eirin.** Ireland.

13. **On her shadow,** etc. "The Danish fleet (Lochlin) in a long and gay line, sails on its own shadow."

20. Cadwallader (Gray's note). Cf. *Henry* V., v, 1, 28 : " Not for Cadwallader, and all his goats."

20. Mona. Anglesea. Cf. Gray's letter to Mason, 25 July 1756 (*Works*, II, 286): " I can only tell you not to go and take Mona for the Isle of Man ; it is Anglesey, a tract of plain country, very fertile, but picturesque only from the view it has of Caernarvonshire, from which it is separated by the Menai, a narrow arm of the sea."

20. See note on *Bard*, v. 28.

25. Talymalfra. A little bay on the N. E. coast of Anglesea.

26. In Mason's edition of Gray's poems (1775), he added after this line the following four lines, saying they were " from the Author's MS.":

> " Check'd by the torrent-tide of blood
> Backward Meinai rolls his flood ;
> While, heap'd his master's feet around,
> Prostrate Warriors gnaw the ground."

XVII.

THE DEATH OF HOEL.

This and the two following poems were probably written in 1764, and, like the *Triumphs of Owen*, came from Evans's *Specimens*. They were first published by Mason, in 1775.

The *Gododin*, from which these three pieces are extracts, is one of the few genuine relics of ancient (sixth-century) Welsh poetry. The author, Aneurin, was contemporary with Taliesin. Gray translated from the Latin version given by Evans in the *Dissertatio de Bardis* appended to his *Specimens*. The occasion of the original poem is disputed, but the most general opinion seems to be that it celebrates a battle between the Strathclyde Britons and Northumbrian Saxons (see D. W. Nash, *Taliesin*, 1858, p. 65; but cf. Thos. Stephens, *Lit. of the Kymry*, 2d ed., p. 3).

The Latin version is as follows :

Evans, pp. 71, 73.

" Si mihi liceret sententiam[1] de Deirorum populo ferre,
Aeque ac diluvium omnes una strage prostrarem ;

[1] " Fortasse, ' Vindictam in Deirorum populum,' &c."

Amicum enim amisi incautus,
Qui in resistendo firmus erat
Non petiit magnanimus dotem a socero,
Filius CIANI ex strenuo GWYNGWN ortus.

"Viri ibant ad CATTRAETH, et fuere insignes,
Vinum et mulsum ex aureis poculis erat eorum potus.

. . . . . .

Trecenti et sexaginta tres aureis torquibus insigniti erant,
Ex iis autem qui nimio potu madidi ad bellum properabant,
Non evasere nisi tres, qui sibi gladiis viam muniebant,
Sc. bellator de *Aeron* et CONANUS DAEARAWD,
Et egomet ipse (sc. Bardus Aneurinus) sanguine rubens,
Aliter ad hoc carmen compingendum non superstes fuissem."

Evans, p. 73.

"Quando ad bellum properabat CARADOCUS,
Filius apri sylvestris qui truncando mutilavit hostes,
Taurus aciei in pugnae conflictu,
Is lignum (*i. e.* hastam) ex manu contorsit."

Evans, p. 75.

"Debitus est tibi cantus, qui honorem assecutus es maximum,
Qui eras instar ignis, tonitrui et tempestatis,
Viribus eximie, eques bellicose
RHUDD FEDEL, bellum meditaris."

3. Deïra. This included about what is now Yorkshire.

11. Cattraeth's vale. In Yorkshire, near Richmond. *Cattraeth* is not called a vale in the original. Stephens, *Lit. of the Kymry*, 2d ed., p. 3, supposes it to be the Roman town "Cataracton, now called Catterick," in York.

XIX.

CARADOC.

For Gray's remark on the pronunciation of this word, see note on v. 102 of the *Bard*.

XX.

WILLIAM SHAKESPEARE.

These verses were sent in a letter to Mason under date 16 July 1765. They were first published by Mitford in *The Correspondence of Thomas Gray and William Mason*, 1853, pp. 339–40.

1. Mistress Anne. The servant of the Rev. Wm. Mason at York.

3. Proper. Handsome.

5. Much have I borne. Referring to the eighteenth-century Shaksperian critics and commentators.

12. Residence. Mason disliked his compulsory residence at York cathedral.

Marriage. Mason was then engaged, and was married on 25 September.

Sore eyes. Mason was constantly troubled with weak eyes.

17. Better to bottom tarts, etc. Better use the paper on which Shakspere's works are printed for cooking purposes than to let the commentators disfigure him.

21. Clouet. A famous cook. For Gray's studies in gastronomy, see *Works*, III, 81.

XXI.

ODE FOR MUSIC.

This was the last poem Gray wrote. It was published in the year of its composition (1769) as a thin quarto of eight pages, with the following title-page: *Ode Performed in the Senate-House at Cambridge, July 1, 1769, At the Installation of his Grace Augustus-Henry Fitzroy, Duke of Grafton, Chancellor of the University. Set to Music by Dr. Randal, Professor of Music. Cambridge, Printed by J. Archdeacon Printer to the University. M.DCC.LXIX.* The title over the first page of the text is simply *Ode for Music.* It is interesting to notice that Gray's name nowhere appears in the quarto. In this volume this ode is for the first time given exactly as it appeared in the original 1769 edition. The circumstances which called it into being are as follows : The Duke of Grafton had in 1768 made Gray Professor of Modern History and Languages at Cambridge, an honor for which the poet felt genuine gratitude. When the Duke was elected Chancellor of the University, Gray offered to write an

Ode to be sung at the Installation on July 1, 1769. Gray performed this task with reluctance, and evidently felt that the poetry was more artificial than spontaneous. The first stanza, with its personified abstractions, reminds one of his earliest period, and immediately suggests Milton's minor poems.

The poem has really added nothing to Gray's reputation, and the following contemporary criticism seems just: "The Installation Ode of Mr. Gray is a recent instance of flattery bestowed indiscriminately on the great, and will do no credit to that celebrated writer." — Joseph Cockfield to the Rev. Weeden Butler, 27 July 1769, Nichols, *Illustr. of Lit.*, V, 797.

Mason appended notes on the personages mentioned in this Ode. I have made use of these often, but with corrections and additions.

13. Empyrean. "Empyrean," and " empyreal " are favorite words with Milton. The word is from Gk. $\pi\hat{v}\rho =$ fire ; and means the highest heaven, where the ancients supposed the region of pure fire to be.

18. Accomp. This meant that, though the recitative was held, the next nine lines were also accompanied.

25. Newton's self. Sir Isaac Newton (1642–1727). He is said to have resided at Trinity College, Cambridge, for thirty-five years, without a month's interruption.

His state sublime. His chair of state, as often in Shakspere.

27. Ye brown, etc. Mason remarks that "this stanza, being supposed to be sung by Milton, is very judiciously written in the metre" of the great Christmas hymn. The stanza is also full of Miltonic expressions.

39. Edward. Edward III., who in 1340 formally claimed to be king of France ; and quartered the French arms (the fleur de lys) with his own.

41. Sad Chatillon. Aymer de Valence married, as his third wife, Marie de Castillon (Châtillon), daughter of Guy IV., count of St. Pol, 5 July 1321 ; he died suddenly (murder was suspected) near Paris, 23 June 1324. See *Annales Paulini*, in Stubbs, *Chronicles of the Reigns of Edward I. and Edward II.*, I, 292, 307. His widow, who founded Pembroke Hall in 1343, long survived him.

42. Clare. Elizabeth de Burgh, daughter of Gilbert de Clare, Earl of Gloucester, by Joan of Acres, daughter of Edward I. She married John de Burgh, son and heir to the Earl of Ulster. She afterwards married Roger Damory. She rebuilt Clare Hall (which had been founded by Dr. Richard Badew in 1326 under the name of

University Hall), and gave it this name, about 1342. See Dugdale, *Baronage of England*, 1675, I, 209, 217.

43. Anjou's Heroine. Margaret of Anjou, wife of King Henry VI.; she founded Queen's College in 1448 ; though the foundation was not completed until 1465, and then, curiously enough, by Elizabeth, wife of Edward IV., Henry's rival. Gray alludes to Margaret in the *Bard*, v. 89. — **Paler Rose.** Elizabeth Woodville ; she is called the paler rose because her husband, Edward IV., was of the house of York — as distinguished from the red rose, Lancaster.

45. Either Henry. Henry VI. and Henry VIII. Henry VI. founded King's College in 1441, and Henry VIII. was Trinity's greatest benefactor ; Henry VI. is also said to have trebled the revenue of Pembroke Hall.

51. Granta. The river Cam.

54. Fitzroy. The family name of the Duke of Grafton.

66. The Lady Margaret Beaufort, daughter of John, Duke of Somerset, married, 1454, Edmund Tudor, Earl of Richmond. Their son succeeded to the throne as Henry VII. See Doyle, *Official Baronage*, III, 118. "Although *Christ's College* was originally founded in the reign of King Henry VI. by the name of God's House, yet its foundation is usually dated from its second and more ample establishment, by Margaret Countess of Richmond, in 1505." Lysons, *Magna Britannia*, I, 120. "The foundation of *St. John's College* was projected and begun by Margaret Countess of Richmond a short time before her death, which happened in 1509." *Ibid.*, I, 121.

70. A Tudor's fire, etc. "The Countess was a Beaufort, and married to a Tudor; hence the application of this line to the Duke of Grafton, who claims descent from both these families."— *Mason*.

72. The flower unheeded. Cf. *Elegy*, v. 55. Gray means here that the Duke will discover obscure men of genius and make their merits known.

78. Obvious. In the literal Latin sense. Cf. *Par. Lost*, viii, 504 : " Not obvious, not obtrusive."

84. Cecil. William Cecil, Lord Burghley, Queen Elizabeth's famous Lord Treasurer. He was elected Chancellor of the University of Cambridge in 1558. He was not made Lord Burghley until 1571.

89. Thro' the wild waves, etc. Mr. Gosse justly calls this stanza the only absurd thing in Gray's poetry. It might indeed have been written by any Augustan parasite.

NOTES ON THE PROSE.[1]

PAGE 61, l. 23. Gray was probably thinking of *Isaiah*, xxxiv, 13, 14, 15: "It shall be an habitation of dragons, and a court for owls. The wild beasts of the desert shall also meet with the wild beasts of the island, and the satyr shall cry to his fellow; the screech owl also shall rest there, and find for herself a place of rest. There shall the great owl make her nest, and lay, and hatch, and gather under her shadow."

62, 36. **Hyp.** Hypochondria.

64, 17. **Sack and silver.** 'Silver' of course refers to the poet laureate's salary, the 'sack' is the famous yearly butt of Canary wine from the king's cellars which was formerly allowed to this official.

65, 18. **Rowe.** Nicholas Rowe (1673–1718), the dramatist.

65, 19. **Settle.** Elkanah Settle (1648–1723), the dramatist, now remembered only for his literary controversy with Dryden in 1673.

65, 20. **Eusden.** "Appointed poet laureate by Lord Halifax, in 1716." *Mitford.*

65, 22. **Dryden.** It is interesting to observe Gray's strong moral feeling asserting itself; he greatly admired Dryden's poetry.

65, 34. **Dick.** The Rev. Richard Forester. He gave up his fellowship at the end of this month (December, 1757).

65, 35. **Mr. Treasurer.** "Mr. Joseph Gaskarth was the college treasurer, but the subject of his disagreement with Sir M. Lamb does not appear to be known." *Mitford.*

Sir M. Lamb. "Probably Sir Matthew Lamb, of Brocket Hall, Herts, created a Baronet in 1755." *Mitford.*

72, 18. **A drama.** *Elfrida*, by Mason, published 1751.

73, 12. **Mr. Bentley.** Mr. Richard Bentley, son of the great scholar, made the designs for Gray's poems in the sumptuous edition of 1753.

---

1 Some of the important allusions that required only a word of explanation are discussed in foot-notes to the text.

73, 13. **Miscellanies.** Dodsley's *Collection of Poems.* Three volumes were published in 1748, and with the fourth edition of these in 1755 a fourth volume was added. *The Progress of Poesy,* however, was not included.

74, 21. **Designs,** etc. The exact title, as it finally appeared, was slightly different : "Designs by Mr. R. Bentley, for Six Poems by Mr. T. Gray " — " by " substituted for " òf " (before " Mr. T. Gray ").

74, 24. Richard Hurd (1720–1808), the famous Bishop, author of the *Moral and Political Dialogues,* and *Letters on Chivalry and Romance.* For an account of his important influence on English Romanticism, see the editor's *Beginnings of the English Romantic Movement,* pp. 112–115.

75, 18. **A player and a doctor of divinity.** Garrick and Dr. Warburton. Cf. Gray's letter to Wharton, 7 October 1757 (*Works,* II, 341).

75, 29. **So ripe for the press.** Probably alluding to Hurd's *Moral and Political Dialogues,* published shortly after this.

77, 35. These remarks were made in a letter criticising Mason's *Caractacus.*

80, 34. **Marivaux.** Pierre Carlet de Marivaux (1688–1763), dramatist and novelist. He was the author of the famous romance *Marianne* (1731–1742), which has been sometimes called the origin of Richardson's *Pamela.* — **Crebillon.** C. P. Jolyot de Crébillon (1707–1778), called Crébillon the Younger, son of the dramatist Crébillon the Elder (1674–1762). He was a writer of novels, as corrupt as they are brilliant and entertaining. For the influence of Gray's French reading on his style, see *Introduction,* part iii.

80, 51. **Licentious.** Free in coining words.

82, 9. **Tickell.** Thomas Tickell (1686–1740). His poem *On the Prospect of Peace* stood first in Dodsley's *Collection.*

82, 20. Ballad, *Colin and Lucy* (Dodsley, I, 28).

82, 21. **M. Green.** Matthew Green (1696–1737), author of *The Spleen* (1737). For Gray's debt to Green, see p. 128.

83, 3. **Douglas.** The famous drama (1756) by John Home (1722–1808).

83, 30. **Dyer.** He alludes to the nature-poem *Grongar Hill,* and possibly to the *Ruins of Rome* (Dodsley, I, 220, 226), by John Dyer (died 1758).

83, 38. **Whitehead's.** William Whitehead (1715–1785), the Poet-Laureate.

84, 10. **Hardicanute.** Gray was deceived. *Hardicanute* was written in imitation of the old Scottish ballad style by Lady Wardlaw of Pitrevie in Fife (1677–1726-7). It may be found in Percy's *Reliques.*

85, 25. **"Winter."** Probably alluding to lines 175–201 in *Winter*, beginning,

> " Nor less at land the loosen'd tempest reigns."

87, 30. **Mr. Evans.** See note on *The Triumphs of Owen*, and *Introduction*, part iv.

94, 15 ff. Cf. Gray's Latin Alcaics written in the travelers' book at the Grande Chartreuse (*Works*, I, 182).

106, 3. **Wadd-mines.** Plumbago, or black lead.

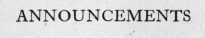

ANNOUNCEMENTS

ATHENÆUM PRESS SERIES

Issued under the general editorship of
Professor GEORGE LYMAN KITTREDGE of Harvard University, and
Professor C. T. WINCHESTER of Wesleyan University

Addison, Joseph : Selections (Wendell and Greenough) . . . $0.80
Burke : Speech on Conciliation with America (Lamont) 50
Burns : Selections (Dow) 70
Carlyle : Heroes, Hero-Worship, and the Heroic in History
    (MacMechan) 80
Carlyle : Sartor Resartus (MacMechan) 80
Collins : Poems of (Bronson) 60
Cowper : Selections (Murray) 60
De Quincey : Selections (Turk) 90
Elizabethan Lyrics (Schelling) 75
Fielding : Selected Essays (Gerould) 60
Gibbon : Memoirs (Emerson) 75
Gray : Selections (Phelps) 60
Herrick : Selections from Poems (Hale) 60
Jeffrey : Selections (Gates) 60
Jonson : Timber ; or Discoveries (Schelling) 80
Keats : Selections (Bates) 60
Landor : Selections (Clymer) 60
Malory : Morte Darthur (Mead) 80
Old English Ballads (Gummere) 80
Pre-Shaksperean Drama, Specimens of (Manly). *In three volumes.*
    Vols. I and II now ready . . . . *each* 1.25
Seventeenth Century Lyrics (Schelling) 75
Shakespeare : Sonnets (Beeching) 60
Shelley : Selections (Alexander) 80
Sheridan : Major Dramas (Nettleton) 90
Sidney : Defense of Poesy (Cook) 65
Steele : Selections (Carpenter) 60
Tennyson : Poems (Van Dyke and Chambers) 90
Wordsworth : Selections (Dowden) 90

GINN AND COMPANY PUBLISHERS

BOOKS ON
ENGLISH LITERATURE

List price

Alexander: Introduction to the Poetry of Robert Browning . . . $1.00
Athenæum Press Series: 26 volumes now ready
Baldwin: Inflections and Syntax of Malory's Morte d'Arthur . . 1.40
Bellamy: Twelve English Poets 75
Bright and Miller: Elements of English Versification 80
Browne: Shakspere's Versification 25
Corson: Primer of English Verse 1.00
Emery: Notes on English Literature 1.00
Garnett: Selections in English Prose from Elizabeth to Victoria 1.50
Gayley: Classic Myths in English Literature 1.50
Gayley and Scott: Literary Criticism 1.25
George: Hudson's Essays on English Studies 75
Gummere: Handbook of Poetics 1.00
Hudson: Classical English Reader 1.00
Hudson: Essays on English, Studies in Shakespeare, etc. . . .25
Hudson: Life, Art, and Characters of Shakespeare. 2 vols.
            retail, cloth, $4.00; half morocco, $8.00
Kent: Shakespeare Notebook 60
Lewis: Beginnings of English Literature 90
Long: English Literature 1.35
Manly: English Poetry 1.50
Manly: English Prose 1.50
Maxcy: Shakespeare's Tragedy of Hamlet 45
Minto: Characteristics of the English Poets 1.50
Minto: Manual of English Prose Literature 1.50
Painter: Elementary Guide to Literary Criticism 90
Parrott and Long: English Poems from Chaucer to Kipling . . .90
Phelps: Beginnings of the English Romantic Movement . . . 1.00
Saintsbury: Loci Critici. Passages Illustrative of Critical Theory
        and Practice from Aristotle Downwards 1.50
Sherman: Analytics of Literature 1.25
Smith: Synopsis of English and American Literature 80
Standard English Classics: 54 volumes now ready
Thayer: Best Elizabethan Plays 1.25
White: Philosophy of English Literature 1.00
Winchester: Five Short Courses of Reading in English Literature .40

GINN AND COMPANY Publishers

THE
NEW HUDSON SHAKESPEARE

Introduction and Notes by HENRY HUDSON. Edited and Revised
by E. CHARLTON BLACK, Professor of English Literature in Boston
University, with the coöperation of ANDREW J. GEORGE, late of the
Department of English in the High School, Newton, Mass., and M.
GRANT DANIELL, late Principal of Chauncy-Hall School, Boston

DR. HUDSON'S great work as a Shakespeare editor and interpreter still remains, in all the elements of æsthetic criticism, the most significant yet produced in America. Since his time, however, there have been interesting and significant developments in the study of Elizabethan literature, language, and prosody; and the careful research of scholars in Europe and America has made available much new and important matter bearing directly upon Shakespeare criticism and comment.

In the New Hudson Shakespeare the results of the latest research and scholarship are incorporated with the introductions, notes, and critical apparatus which have given the old edition its commanding place. The following distinctive features characterize the new edition:

1. A new text, based directly upon that of the First Folio.

2. The modernization of the spelling and punctuation of the text.

3. Two sets of notes at the foot of a page, — one giving textual variants, and the other a brief philological explanation of unusual words and constructions.

4. A brief essay on versification and an analysis of the dramatic construction of each play.

5. An authentic portrait of a facsimile of an important page of a Quarto or a Folio to illustrate each play.

6. The insertion of line numbers and the giving of the names of the characters everywhere in full.

7. A chronological chart.

8. Large, clear type from new plates.

We shall be glad to send to any address a descriptive pamphlet giving sample pages and further information relating to this new edition.

GINN AND COMPANY PUBLISHERS

ENGLISH LITERATURE

ITS HISTORY AND SIGNIFICANCE FOR THE LIFE OF THE ENGLISH–SPEAKING WORLD

By WILLIAM J. LONG

12mo, cloth, vi + 582 pages, illustrated, with frontispiece
in eleven colors, $1.35

A DIRECT, simple, interesting account of the great periods of English literature. The emphasis is always upon men rather than upon classes or periods, and upon literature rather than upon what has been written about it. There is an interesting biography of every great literary man in his own natural and social environment, followed by a study of his best works, and then a clear, concise summary or criticism of his place and influence in the history of literature. The book is delightfully readable, showing admirable judgment in the treatment of the different periods, and all the graces of a finished prose style.

No English text-book in literature, of equal size, can compare with this in wealth and quality of illustrations. The frontispiece — The Canterbury Pilgrims — is a lithograph in eleven colors of a direct copy taken from a manuscript in the British Museum, and is believed to be the finest illustration ever printed in a text-book.

Besides giving the pupil a keen insight into English literature, this book is sure to stimulate him to read more for himself. Bibliographical helps and questions supply every need.

38½

GINN AND COMPANY PUBLISHERS